(seppuku)
suicide: 137, 74*
equality —
name giving: 84, 109, 111-112
"chivalry": 113

challenge:
pride in lineage

THE HEART OF THE WARRIOR
ORIGINS AND RELIGIOUS BACKGROUND
OF THE SAMURAI SYSTEM IN FEUDAL JAPAN

In memory of my mother, Dagmar Blomberg née Tygnaeus,
14 September 1904 – 17 October 1993

The Heart of the Warrior

Origins and Religious Background of the Samurai System in Feudal Japan

Catharina Blomberg

Japan Library

Sandgate, Folkestone, Kent

THE HEART OF THE WARRIOR
Origins and Religious Background
of the Samurai System in Feudal Japan

JAPAN LIBRARY
Knoll House, 35 The Crescent
Sandgate, Folkestone, Kent, CT20 3EE

Japan Library is an imprint of Curzon Press Ltd
St. John's Studios, Church Road, Richmond, Surrey, TW9 2QA

First published 1994
© Catharina Blomberg 1994

British Library Cataloguing in Publication Data

A CIP catalogue record for this book
is available from the British Library

ISBN: 1-873410-06-9 (Case)
ISBN: 1-873410-13-1 (Paper)

Typeset in Bookman Roman 10 on 11½pt by
Motilal Banarsidass Publishers, Delhi.
Printed in England by BPCC Wheatons Ltd., Exeter

Contents

Acknowledgements   *vi*

Introduction   *vii*

CHAPTER 1
The Formation of a Warrior Nobility   1

CHAPTER 2
Bushi Attitudes Towards the Traditional Religions   18

CHAPTER 3
Duty, Privilege and Loyalty: Religious and Practical
Concerns
Part I   : Swords and Sword-fighting Techniques   48
Part II   : *Seppuku, Junshi* and the Taking of Heads   72
Part III : Allegiance, Oaths and *Bushi* Organisations   91

CHAPTER 4
Bushidō: The Concept of Chivalry
Part I   : Early Notions of Chivalry and Its Legal Aspects   105
Part II   : Warrior Ethics East and West   123
Part III : Early Confucian Influence   135
Part IV   : The Tokugawa *Bakufu* and the Codification   149
             of *Bushidō*
Part V   : The Akō Affair   167
Part VI   : The Tokugawa Peace and the Intrusion of the   177
             Western World

CHAPTER 5
Bushi Influence on Culture and the Arts   194

Footnotes   207

Bibliography   216

Index   222

Acknowledgements

A number of institutions have provided me with financial and other assistance during the research for and writing of this book, and I would like to express my profound gratitude to them all.

The Japan Foundation awarded me a twelve-month Fellowship in 1980-1981, enabling me to gather material in Tokyo, Nara and Kyoto and view temples, shrines and museum collections.

The then Japan Institute at Harvard University, now the Reischauer Institute, provided me with an office during Michaelmas Term 1984.

Adolf Lindgrens Stiftelse of Örebro, my native city, honoured me in 1984 with the first of their newly instituted research grants, making it possible for me to spend Michaelmas Term 1985 in Cambridge, working on material in the University Library.

I returned to Cambridge and my research in the University Library for the academic year 1986-1987, when Clare Hall awarded me the Hambro Fellowship, providing me with excellent board and lodging in College.

Finally, I wish to extend my warm thanks once again to the Japan Foundation for a second twelve-month Fellowship in 1991-1992, which will, D.V., eventually result in a book on another aspect of the lives of the *bushi*.

Stockholm, Summer 1993
CATHARINA BLOMBERG

Introduction

'Le guerrier/BUSHI/est pour le Japon ce que le Chevalier
est pour l'Occident, sa religion a, comme la Chevalerie, son
éthique propre qui a ses fidèles et peut avoir ses martyrs.'

'The warrior (bushi) is for Japan what the knight is for the
West. His religion, like Chivalry, has its own ethic, which
has its faithful and may have its martyrs.'

Frédéric Joüon des Longrais, L'Est et l'Ouest, Institutions du Japon et
de l'Occident Comparées, Maison Franco-Japonaise, Tokyo/Institut de
Recherches d'Histoire Etrangère, Paris, 1958, p.146.

The samurai in full and resplendent armour springs
suddenly out of the pages of the early Kamakura period
war chronicles, *Gunki Monogatari*, not unlike Pallas Athene
emerging fully armed from the forehead of her father Zeus.

The real turning-point in the fortunes of the samurai, or
bushi, came with the *Gempei* War, 1180-1185. The outcome of this war determined the political situation in Japan during the following seven centuries. While the victorious Minamoto clan had retained a firm power base in the
Kanto region, the so-called Eastern Provinces, the Taira
clan had become closely allied with the court nobility, or
kuge. Taira Kiyomori, the leader of the clan, not only held
the highest ministerial office, but was also the maternal
grandfather of the young Emperor Antoku. Especially among
the Kanto *bushi* the *rapprochement* between warrior and
court nobilities effected by the Taira was regarded as one
of the principal reasons for the downfall of the clan.

For centuries the warrior nobility had led lives completely different from those of the *kuge*, despite the fact that
many of the leading *bushi* families were descended from

cadet branches of the *kuge*, or even from Imperial princes. For younger sons, even of illustrious families, few opportunities presented themselves for making a career in the capital and obtaining a suitable position at the Imperial court. In the provinces, however, there was scope for considerably improving their economic conditions. There they were able to live off the land, more or less as gentlemen farmers, setting up and maintaining local guard forces. The Imperial rule of the Asuka period had developed out of a system of *primus inter pares*, and even in the Heian period there were occasionally rebellious local chieftains to subdue and attacks by pirates and Ainu to repel. When they returned to the Imperial capital on guard duty, however, the provincial *bushi* were treated with disdain by the *kuge*. For centuries the *bushi* remained in a subordinate position, being regarded as uncouth rustics and denied access to polite society. The Heian court ladies, who created an entire literary genre with their novels and diaries, were members of the *kuge* and displayed a remarkable lack of interest in the provincial guardsmen at the Imperial court, whom they regarded as no more than another category of servants.

With the *Gempei* War and the ascendancy of the warrior nobility the situation changed drastically. The *bushi* were henceforth not only the holders of political power, they also turned into arbiters of fashion and patrons of the arts, becoming the leading force behind cultural and ethical developments. Life at the Imperial court continued along much the same lines as before, although the customary splendour must have seemed a little lacklustre. Kamakura, on the East coast, where the victorious Minamoto Yoritomo established his warrior government, *Bakufu*, was the centre from which new ideas were disseminated. From the outset the *Bakufu* made strenuous efforts to maintain the simple and frugal habits which had characterised the provincial *bushi*, and on which the successful outcome of the *Gempei* War was considered to have been founded. Minamoto Yoritomo was the first to lay down the stern precepts of his so-called House Laws, which later developed into the legal code regulating the practical aspects of the lives of the *bushi*.

Many ethical aspects of *bushi* life and thought are illustrated by the *Gunki Monogatari* (Tales of Warfare) a literary genre which flourished in the early Kamakura period. In works such as the *Hōgen* and *Heike Monogatari* the samurai are presented to the reader as they saw themselves and as they wished to be seen. Heian literary influence is noticeable, although the tables were now turned in that the samurai were the undisputed heroes. The *Gunki Monogatari*, especially the *Heike Monogatari* which is an account of the *Gempei* War, represented the *bushi* as dashing, splendidly attired warriors of prodigious military prowess. These tales became classics of popular entertainment until modern times. They were recited in public by blind ambulant monks, *biwa-hōshi*, who accompanied themselves on the *biwa*, a string instrument resembling a lute. The *Gunki Monogatari* combined epic accounts of battles and the exploits of famous samurai with the unmistakably Buddhist flavour of moral tales designed to illustrate the vanity of human endeavour. The popular conception of what the samurai were like and how they ought to behave was formed at least partly by the *Gunki Monogatari*. Their themes were embroidered upon and embellished over the centuries as the samurai and their warlike feats became part of the traditional folklore.

Apart from frequent mentions of warfare and warriors in the earliest historical chronicles, the *Kojiki* and the *Nihongi*, and occasional references by Heian poets and poetesses, the *Gunki Monogatari* are the first literary sources dealing with warriors in their own right. In contrast to the *Kojiki* and the *Nihongi*, where the mythical and semi-mythical warrior heroes vanquished their foes by treacherous means without the slightest hint of remorse, the *Gunki Monogatari* represented the *bushi* as thinking individuals endowed with human feelings. On the battlefield they were shown to act in an almost ritualistic manner according to certain rules of conduct. At this stage, however, it is apparent that these rules were not yet completely fixed, and many deviations from the norm are recorded. What might, somewhat anachronistically, be called unchivalrous behaviour was sometimes condemned in strong terms, but there are not a few examples in the tales of war of rewards and favours obtained by unfair or treacherous means. The code of behaviour which later became known as *Bushidō* (the Way of the Warrior) was still being formed during the *Gempei War* and its aftermath. The *Gunki Monogatari* show us the ideals which the *bushi* were striving to attain, and demonstrate the ideas they had about themselves and their role in society.

This form of self-presentation, written by *bushi* for a primarily *bushi* audience, is of great importance for our understanding of their mentality. The samurai had their own, rather different, attitude towards the traditional religions, i.e. Shinto, Buddhism and Confucianism. As professional warriors they were obliged to take life, despite the strict injunctions of Shinto and Buddhism against all forms of bloodshed and killing. They were pragmatists, not romantics, and were able to adapt themselves to the world in which they were living by developing their own system of values and ethics, in which loyalty to the feudal lord was one of the dominating principles.

With the establishment of a warrior government at Kamakura there was increased emphasis not only on a frugal and simple lifestyle becoming to a samurai, but also on chivalrous behaviour. Minamoto Yoritomo's efforts at regulating the daily lives of the *bushi* according to a fixed code of conduct may be regarded as an attempt to curb and control potentially dangerous and subversive factors inherent in a warrior society. By means of elaborate arrangements of vassalage the Kamakura *Bakufu* established a feudal system under a Shōgun (Generalissimo) which lasted until 1868. The shōgunal dynasties were however to change many times during the seven centuries of warrior rule, and there were periods when the country was reduced to a state of virtual anarchy. It is interesting, however, that even during the turbulent century known as the *Sengoku jidai* (the Period of the Warring States) the warlords vying for political power still by and large adhered to the old values of the warrior ethic. Despite frequent violations the code of *Bushidō* was generally recognised as the cement which held society together. There was no questioning of its principles, even by the many soldiers of fortune who were able to acquire samurai status during the period of political turmoil.

The peaceful and orderly conditions which prevailed during the two and a half centuries of the Tokugawa *Bakufu* were ensured by means of a new system of legal codes, regulating the lives of the *bushi* in great detail. The term *Bushidō* was coined and the concept of chivalry became codified and was commented on by Confucian and Neo-Confucian scholars, remaining one of the most important topics of learned discussion throughout the reign of the Tokugawa Shōguns. The idealised literary descriptions of samurai deportment and military valour greatly influenced *bushi* and commoners alike. Most of the heroes of the *Gunki Monogatari* were identifiable historical persons, even if some of the remarkable feats ascribed to them owed a great deal to the enthusiasm of the story-tellers, and they and other famous samurai came to serve as models for later generations. Like all warrior castes the samurai took great pride in their superior status, and they were acutely conscious of their privileges, which were jealously guarded. Because of their practically unlimited power over life and death where their inferiors were concerned they were held in great awe by commoners. In popular beliefs they were sometimes linked to various supernatural phenomena, e.g. the *tengu*, mythical beings which inhabited the deep mountain forests and were masters of swordsmanship.

A number of traditional sayings about samurai illustrate their opinion of themselves as well as the way they were regarded by the people. The expression '*Bushi no nasake*', 'the pity of a samurai', denotes clemency on the part of the strong towards the weak. The Confucian teachings which so influenced Japanese society stressed that while a superior had the right to expect subordination from an inferior, this ought to be reciprocated by benevolence on his part. Because of his absolute dominance, however, mercy shown by a samurai was all the more remarkable. The saying '*Bushi ni nigon nashi*', in another version '*Bushi no kotoba ni nigon wa nai*', meaning literally 'A *bushi* has no second word', i.e. that a *bushi* stands by his word and never lies, eloquently illustrated the conception of samurai honour. Similar ideas can be found in many other cultures, and one is reminded of the medieval European knight who would rather forfeit his life than break his word.

The vast superiority of the samurai is expressed with the utmost clarity in the traditional aphorism '*Hana wa sakura ni, hito wa bushi*', 'Among flowers the cherry, among men, the samurai', meaning that as the cherry-blossom is considered foremost among flowers, so the samurai were undisputedly foremost among men. One must not forget, however, that the *bushi* were popularly likened to cherry-blossoms in another respect also, namely that their lives, while glorious, were apt to come to sudden ends. In a violent society which lived by the sword, where private vengeance was the rule, and where matters of honour were settled by means of a duel or suicide, the lives of the *bushi* might seem as evanescent as those of the cherry-blossoms, which one moment are in full bloom and the next scatter their petals in the wind. Even more evocative was the popular parallel between the camellia and the samurai. Camellia blooms do not wither, but drop suddenly like a head cut off with a sword.

Bushidō was a complex code of behaviour consisting of a wealth of religious and ethical elements. It dominated and determined the lives of all members of the warrior nobility, making them an exclusive group in society. For many centuries the rules of *Bushidō* were taught by example, transmitted from parents to children, and its precepts remained one of the privileges of the samurai. To the common people the *bushi*, although superior and remote, appeared as models worthy of emulation, especially where the Confucian virtues of filial piety and loyalty were concerned. Although the *kuge* and Imperial court circles, as well as the high Shinto and Buddhist clergy, retained certain characteristic aspects of their respective cultures, it was *bushi* influence which permeated Japanese society from top to bottom. From costume and manners to the decorative as well as the performing arts they set the standards, creating many of the values which have later come to be regarded as characteristically Japanese.

When warrior rule was brought to a close with the restoration of imperial power under Emperor Meiji in 1868, the ideas of *Bushidō*, far from becoming obsolete, were given an even more widespread diffusion among the people at large. The term *Bushidō* was re-interpreted and its concept altered to fit the atmosphere of nationalism created under the new rule. Despite vulgarisation and abuse, however, the essence of *Bushidō* remained a popular ideal, even if the term itself fell into disrepute after the last war, when it had been used to denote all manner of jingoistic excesses. Its characteristic qualities of loyalty, dedication and perseverance have struck deep roots in the Japanese character, and continue to play a part in modern society.

In Japanese films, and especially in the many television dramas of today, the samurai in all his original glory has been resurrected. He has assumed mythical proportions on a scale which even the authors of the most panegyrical passages in the *Gunki Monogatari* could hardly have imagined. For the majority of contemporary Japanese the samurai has the romantic aura of a heroic figure reflecting a glorious past. *Bushi* ancestry is a matter of pride, although like all private affairs it is usually treated with great discretion. To say of someone displaying calm determination and composure in the face of a crisis that he acts like a samurai is to bestow the highest praise. The Tokugawa *Bakufu* is still close in time, and such a remark is of quite different significance than the European figure of speech which likens a courageous man to a knight *sans peur et sans reproche*. Only in the *kyōgen*, comical interludes between *Nō* plays, do we occasionally find samurai being treated with something approaching levity. The main protagonists of this genre are crafty servants who tend to get the better of their masters and other superiors, and from time to time a pompous samurai is the butt of rather innocuous jokes. The respect for the samurai which seven centuries of warrior rule inculcated in all Japanese has by no means entirely lost its strength, and the equivalent of *Don Quixote* has yet to be written in Japan.

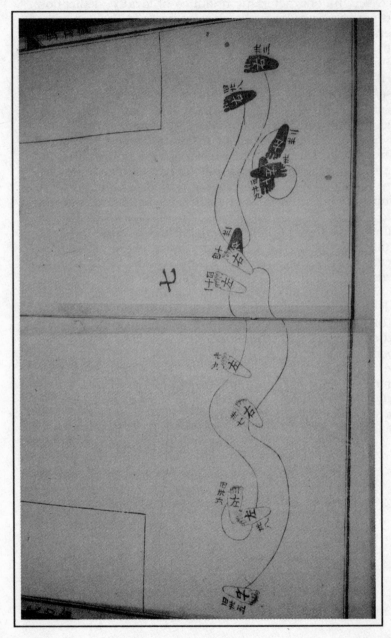

Plan showing the positions of the feet in an encounter between two fencers, from *Bukōron* by Kashiwabuchi Yūgi, 1768. (Nordenskiöld Collection, Royal Library, Stockholm)

1

The Formation of a Warrior Nobility

The earliest representations in Japan of warriors in armour are to be found among the *haniwa*, burned clay figures which were placed on the keyhole-shaped grave mounds of the eponymous Kofun period (250-500 A.D.). The *haniwa* consists of a cylindrical pipe surmounted by a human or animal figure or the depiction of an object. Among the human figures we find farmers carrying tools, women, among them some which are thought to represent shamanesses, and warriors carrying swords, helmeted and clad in body armour. The animals depicted include horses with saddles, bridles, reins and stirrups, as well as dogs and birds. A rectangular object with slightly convex sides is thought to represent a shield. Bronze and iron suits of body armour have been found in a Kofun context, as well as helmets of various designs and iron sword-blades, usually two-edged. The armour consisted of small metal plaques laced together with thongs made of silk or leather according to much the same design as later Japanese armour.

It is important to note here that the large Kofun tombs ascribed to the early semi-mythical Emperors have not been systematically excavated and are unlikely to be exam-

1

ined archaeologically during the reign of the present Imperial family, since any disturbing of the tombs would amount
to *lèse-majesté* and desecration. Many of the tombs were
however raided by grave-robbers in antiquity, and some of
the objects they contained have found their way into mu-
seums via private collections.

Different kinds of weapons have indeed been found also
in earlier contexts. From the Neolithic, i.e. the Jōmon
period (9.000 B.C.-250 B.C.) we have a number of large stone
clubs of distinctly phallic appearance. It seems unlikely
that they could have had any practical use, and they are
usually considered to have been ceremonial objects. Bronze
swords, halberds and spearheads have been found, dating
from the Yayoi period (250 B.C.-250 A.D.), some of them
imported from the mainland, i.e. China or Korea, and some
manufactured locally. Anthropomorphic clay figurines exist from both periods, some archaic and highly stylized in
appearance, and some of them clearly identifiable as female
fertility symbols.

The *haniwa* provide us with quite a few details concerning dress and various utensils. Some are highly stylised,
e.g. the so-called 'funeral attendants', 'dancers' and 'sing-
ers'. The farmers are identified by the implements they
carry, such as sickles or hoes, and there are other figures
holding musical instruments or depicted in attitudes which
seem indicative of prayer or trance. The latter are the so-
called 'shamanesses', who also wear distinctive head-gear.
The warriors are shown in different kinds of attire, some
wearing laced armour and helmets similar to the archaeological finds of the period. A famous example from Gumma
prefecture is clad in a coat with flared skirts and tight
sleeves with wide cuffs, held together with ribbons tied in
bows, and baggy trousers gathered and tied below the
knee. A sword is suspended from a sash around the waist,
and a flat-brimmed hat with a high, rounded crown is worn
with this outfit. Large appendages seem to be suspended
from below the brim of the hat, probably representing plaits
of hair tied up with ribbon.

Another, equally famous, *haniwa* warrior, also from
Gumma prefecture, is shown girded with his sword over a
coat, probably of laced metal plates, and wearing a studded
helmet with cheek-pieces, protective coverings on the lower

arms and hands, including an archer's wrist protector, and the same baggy trousers gathered and tied below the knee as the previous figure. Other warrior *haniwa* carry bows and quivers as well as swords, the details being carefully depicted in spite of the general stylization, especially of the faces of these figures, where the features are simply and effectively indicated by means of holes and slashes.[1]

According to the *Nihongi* (Chronicles of Japan) compiled in 720 A.D. and dealing with the mythological founding of Japan and the country's subsequent history from the age of the gods to the line of human emperors, the *haniwa* were first manufactured in the reign of Emperor Suinin. They were said to have been devised as a humanitarian substitute for the live burial of attendants in the grave-mound of a member of the ruling family. There is however no archaeological evidence of the practice of human sacrifice in connection with burials in Japan, although the custom had certainly existed during the Shang period in China, where the practice of providing the deceased with grave goods such as household utensils persisted until modern times. The recent find of a large number of burnt clay soldiers and horses, somewhat larger than life-size, believed to surround the tomb of the Emperor of Chin, Shi Huang Ti, who died in 251 B.C., provides an interesting Chinese parallel.

The *haniwa* were arranged in rows to form a kind of fence around the grave-mound, and are probably to be interpreted as a symbolic retinue accompanying the deceased, at the same time forming a barrier between the occupant of the tomb and the surrounding world of the living. One of the central ideas in Shinto, a religion which appears to have been fully developed by the late Kofun period, is the clear separation between sacred and profane space and the avoidance of close contact with any form of pollution, especially death.

Our knowledge of the political organisation of the proto-historic period in Japan is far from complete, but it is generally agreed that prior to the Taika Reform of 646 the country was divided into what might be described as petty kingdoms under local chieftains and land-owners, and that the early rulers seem to have occupied the position of *primus inter pares* rather than that of autonomous monarchs. This state of affairs can be deduced from the historical chronicles, the *Kojiki* (Records of Ancient Matters) written by Ō no Yasumaro in 712, and the *Nihongi*, which were commissioned by the ruling dynasty in order to establish and record its divine pedigree once the political power was consolidated. These chronicles frequently mention warfare between different tribes or groups, and both Susanoo no Mikoto, the Shinto storm god, and the semi-divine culture hero Yamato Takeru are depicted as warriors and conquerors of enemy forces. These mythical accounts would seem to record battles and military campaigns, the memories of which were already half lost in a remote past at the time of writing, similar to epic, semi-historical accounts like the Mahābhārata, the Niebelungenlied and Homer's Iliad.

To judge by the very well-equipped warriors immortalised in the *haniwa*, some form of military organisation existed already in the Kofun period. The *haniwa* horses, together with an impressive array of archaeological finds of horse trappings and pieces of harness, indicate the presence of mounted warriors, although it would be rash to conjecture that cavalry was used on a large scale at this early stage. A more realistic picture would seem to be that of mounted chieftains or military leaders commanding troops of foot-soldiers.[2] The earliest organised warriors appear to have been groups of soldiers attached to the local chieftains and landowners as guards against enemy encroachment or invasion of their territories. Whether these warriors were actually conscripts stationed as border guards in what would have been fairly limited areas, or whether they formed a kind of militia whose duty it was to come to the assistance of the chief if called upon to do so, is not clear. Corvée labour was a feature of the later feudal system, and these private warriors may well have been recruited in the same way.

With the unification of the country under the central leadership of an emperor, and the *Taika no kaishin* of 646, which laid the foundation of a political and administrative system modelled on that of the T'ang dynasty in China, the tribal organisation was superseded by a state government which imposed its legislation throughout the country. Before the Taika Reform the Emperor, i.e. the clan chief who towards the end of the Kofun period had managed to gain supremacy over the others, had been regarded as sole owner of the land. This patriarchal rule, which meant that land was distributed as a personal favour by the Emperor, was now altered so that the distribution and administration of land was dealt with by the central government under the Emperor.

Appointments of provincial governors and local officials were made in the capital, which was moved to a new location after the death of each ruler in the early historic period. The first Imperial capital was Asuka, abandoned in 710 for Nara, which was again abandoned for Kyoto in 781, after which time the custom of moving the entire capital ceased, the Imperial court remaining in Kyoto until 1868. The various officials appointed by the government to run the local administration had to reside in the different districts, and this system of dividing the country into a number of provinces continued, with variations as to the number and size of them, until modern times, and still exists.

The old tribal organisation still remained, however, in the form of the *uji*, a term usually translated as 'clan', and which first appears in the *Nihongi*, where it refers to conditions prevailing at the time of the Taika Reform.[3] The *uji* consisted of an extended family, whose members were descended from the same ancestor, venerated as the *ujigami*, tutelary deity, of the *uji*. The head of the family was given the title of *uji no kami*, and his duties included presiding over the cult at the shrine of the *ujigami*. The members of the *uji*, among whom household servants were included, shared a family name, derived from the place where they lived or from the office held by the *uji no kami*. The *uji* were confirmed by the Emperor, according to their influence, by the bestowal of symbolic gifts of weapons on the *uji no kami*. Long swords were given to those of high rank, while the others received short swords, shields or arrows. It also appears that the Emperor could create new *uji*, or rather attribute to an important personage the relationship to a new clan.

Influential *uji* carried an honorary title, *kabane*, the etymology of which is uncertain, and it is not known whether the title originated as a form of recognition of superiority on the part of the members of the *uji*, or whether it designated a special office entrusted to the *uji no kami*. In the seventh century the *kabane* were conferred by the Emperor, and the title was tied to an actual office which became hereditary in the family holding it. This system changed after the Taika Reform, the *kabane* reverting to a purely honorific title, carrying no actual official function with it.

Other elements of the earlier tribal system which continued to exert a certain amount of influence even after the establishment of a central government, were the organisations known as *tomo* and *be*, often translated as 'guilds' and 'corporations'. The *be* were largely hereditary in nature, perhaps the most famous being the *Imbe* or *Imibe*, a corporation of ritual abstainers who lived in a perpetual state of ritual purity in order to safeguard against calamities which might otherwise befall the community, and who were killed for having neglected their duties if disaster did indeed strike. Apart from these very specialised services the *be* were attached to the *uji* in a subordinate position, as agricultural labourers, hunters and fishermen, and as skilled and specialised craftsmen. Among the latter were makers of armour and weapons such as bows and arrows, and some of the *be* seem to have formed part of the active military organization already before the unification of the country in 646.[4] Many of the skilled craftsmen's *be* were later incorporated in the Imperial household and government administration, e.g. Artists (*Ekakibe*), Lacquer Workers (*Nuribe*), Storehouse Attendants (*Kurabe*), et. al., as well as Senior Examiners of Genealogical Disputes (*Ō-Tokibe*), or Prison Wardens (*Mononobe*).

The Taika Edict, as quoted in the *Nihon Shoki* of 720, provided a centralised military organisation. Barriers were established between the provinces, a system which prevailed until the Meiji Restoration 1200 years later. Local guard forces were set up as well as an Imperial Guard in the capital, and levies were imposed for the provision of men, military equipment and post and transport horses according to fixed rates. A certain number of households, usually units of fifty, one hundred or two hundred, had to provide these services. The provincial soldiers were organised into companies of 100 men, ten of which made up a regiment. They were given basic military training, and could be mobilised in an emergency.[5]

The first extant legal code from this period is the so-called *Yōrō* Code (*Yōrō Ryō*) promulgated in 718 as a revised version of the *Taihō* Laws (*Taihō Ritsuryō*) of 701, which in their turn consisted of compilations and revisions of earlier laws.[6] This legal code established rules for military guards in the capital as well as for palace guards and armed escorts for the Emperor. The Ministry of War (*Hyōbu-shō*) was in charge of military matters in the capital and throughout the country, keeping records and registers and being in charge of promotions and the allocation of troops as well as arms and military equipment and fortifications. Under the *Hyōbu-shō* there were five offices.

The first of these was the Remount Office, *Hyōba no Tsukasa*, which provided military mounts, post horses and other horses (and also oxen) for public and private use. As we have seen previously, horses could be requisitioned from their owners for public use. Secondly there was the Arsenal Office, *Tsuwamono-tsukuri no Tsukasa*, which dealt with the manufacture of arms and military equipment, and which had under it a number of artisans' guilds, including smiths and other metal-workers. We may note in this context that there was also a special Smiths' Office, *Kanuchi no Tsukasa* in the Ministry of the Imperial Household, *Kunaishō*, which was probably chiefly engaged in the making of ceremonial and ornamental objects, but which had under it no fewer than twenty smiths and sixteen servants, whereas the *Tsuwamono-tsukuri no Tsukasa* has the same number of artisans not all of them smiths, and twelve servants.

The third office in the *Hyōbu-shō* was the Military Music Office, *Tsuzumi-fue no Tsukasa*, or *Ku-sui no Tsukasa*, literally the 'drum and flute' office. Fourthly there was the Ship Control Office, *Fune no Tsukasa*, again in charge of both public and private vessels, and fifthly there was the Falconry Office, *Takatsukasa*, in charge of hawks and dogs, more suitable for hunting than for actual warfare and an interesting example of the close links between these two disciplines in their early stage of development.

Men from the provinces were sent to the capital to serve as guards, usually for one year, and young men of high-ranking families were selected for service in the palace guard and the Emperor's escort. The *Shoku Nihongi*, completed by 795, records a clear distinction between civilians and military men, however. In the *Engishiki* (Institute of the Engi Era) completed by the early tenth century, it was stated that military officers appearing at the Imperial court were required to wear civilian court dress of the rank corresponding to theirs, but the *Shoku Nihongi* quotes a law which required officers not only to wear civilian dress at court functions, but which forbade them to precede civilians of equal rank.[7]

A system of honorary ranks for the military had been introduced in the *Taihō Ryō* as a means of rewarding valour or special merits. These ranks, called *Kun I*, corresponded to some of the court ranks, *I*, although not the highest ones, and gave the bearer the right to a certain amount of precedence and some privileges, such as the gift of rice-fields. The use of this system was of short duration, however, as it was abolished before the *Jōgan Shiki* (Regulations of the Jōgan Era) were established in 871. The great French scholar of feudal institutions Joüon des Longrais, sees this system of military honours as 'an early precedent for a kind of military élite', and regards the exclusiveness of the aristocracy as the cause of its disappearance.[8]

Protocol at the Imperial court was largely based on that of the Chinese court, from the T'ang dynasty onwards, in the same way that the Taihō Code was strongly influenced by the Chinese legal system, and the inferior ranking of military men seems to reflect the Chinese attitude towards soldiers, who were regarded as members of a necessary and useful profession, but whose rough ways made them strangers and outsiders in court life. The same attitude was to prevail in Japan for most of the Heian period, at least in the rarefied atmosphere of the Imperial court.

When we examine the literature of the times, i.e. the novels and diaries composed by the literary ladies-in-waiting who described daily life in the Imperial palace, the disdain with which soldiers were regarded is very marked indeed. Provincial guardsmen on duty in the capital were mentioned only in passing, and if some comment was made about them at all it was usually to the effect that they were rustic in appearance and manners. In conformity with the peculiarly Japanese notion that anything unfamiliar is to be avoided, the warriors were considered to be beyond the pale. This must be attributed both to the fact that they came from the provinces, i.e. the limits of the civilized world as the Heian courtiers knew it, and to their function, which associated them with bloodshed and death, equally abhorrent to Shinto and Buddhism.

Men of the court nobility, *kuge*, served in the Ministry of War and were given officers' ranks after their *genbuku* (coming of age) ceremonies, but these appointments were largely sinecures, more ceremonial than functional. Like so many other titles of offices long since obsolete, which survived either because they became hereditary or because they were used by the court as a means to show recognition of services rendered, military rank for a court noble became with time a mere courtesy title. Men of the *kuge* were trained from boyhood in horsemanship and the use of arms, although not primarily for military purposes. Hunting was the favourite sport of the aristocracy, as in most other parts of the world, together with archery, the latter being practised on foot as well as on horseback. Although literary ladies such as Sei Shōnagon or Murasaki Shikibu might have mentioned that a certain handsome captain of the guards cut a dashing figure on his fiery mount, or even that he won an archery contest, these were not the qualities which won their hearts, and they never expressed any particular admiration for military prowess or valour *per se*.

Lineage was of paramount importance, not only among the *kuge*, going back to the *uji* of the proto-historic period, and as we have seen the *be* system of labourers and artisans was hereditary. Most of the government offices were indeed also hereditary, in the sense that they were only awarded to members of certain families, and continued to be so long after having become obsolete after reorganisation or the creation of new posts which might be awarded on merit rather than strictly by pedigree. The Chinese system of public examinations for posts in the government administration, a practice which, at least theoretically, meant that these posts were open to all candidates of sufficient ability and intelligence, was never introduced in Japan. It is one of two remarkable lacunae in the monumental list of ideas and concepts borrowed from China, the other, and perhaps still more noteworthy, being the important coda to the Confucian idea of the Mandate of Heaven, namely that

the unjust ruler acts contrary to the will of Heaven and
may therefore be deposed.

The control exerted by the central government in the
capital and the home provinces did not extend completely
to such outlying districts as the Kantō area and the country north of it, where a certain rebellious spirit continued
to manifest itself for a long time to come. Local risings
against taxes or other stringencies imposed by the government were not infrequent. In Kyushu there were troubles
with pirates from the mainland, and in the north intermittent skirmishes with the Ainu, who were steadily forced
northwards until they were confined to Hokkaido, continued until the end of the Heian period. To complement the
military organisation, a kind of police force, the *Kebiishi*
Chō, was established during the reign of Emperor Saga
(786-842, regnavit 809-823). After 839 the *Kebiishi Chō*
had the power to arrest criminals as well as sentence them
and carry out the punishment.

In spite of these measures the central government had
great difficulty in maintaining order in the provinces, and
was forced to rely on the assistance of the local warriors,
some of whom had already by this time, i.e. the late ninth
or early tenth century, gained a certain prominence. As
Joüon des Longrais points out with some emphasis these
provincial warriors cannot be regarded as forming an aristocracy at this point, since such privileges were conferred
solely by the central government, but they did constitute
an élite. Their pedigree again provided the basis for their
position of authority, since they belonged to families which
had held hereditary posts in the provincial government,
sometimes in a military capacity, and their wealth was
usually founded on the ownership of rice fields. There was
however in the ninth and tenth centuries an influx into the
provinces of members of *kuge* families and descendants of
Imperial princes. Polygamy was practised in the Imperial
family, and concubinage was common practice among the
kuge, customs which led to the continual foundation of
cadet branches. Life in the provinces, while less elegant
than in the capital, afforded more scope for the junior
members, and their noble ancestry gave them prestige,
especially in a society where lineage was of such great
importance.[9] The strong emphasis on pedigree meant that

these provincial families intermarried amongst themselves and did not mingle with the local inhabitants. They were frequently called upon by the Imperial government to conduct special military operations, such as the numerous punitive campaigns against pirates and raiders as well as the Ainu, and to quell provincial risings and rebellions. Initially, military authority and titles such as Shōgun (General) and Dai Shōgun (Generalissimo) were conferred by the Imperial court only for the duration of a specific military operation. Although there were examples of several generations of the same family having held the same appointment, for example the Minamoto, it is worth noting here that the office of *Sei-i-tai-Shōgun* (Barbarian-quelling Generalissimo) as was the resounding full title of the later *de facto* ruler of Japan, was always, until the fall of the Tokugawa Bakufu in 1868, formally conferred by the Emperor. Those warriors who were employed in the Imperial Guard or as the private guards of retired emperors or high-ranking *kuge*, i.e. court and government officials, were even less autonomous.

The term *samurai* can be traced back to a verb, *saburahu*, meaning 'to serve' (a master).[10] Haguenauer considers the probability that the notion 'to serve' also implied armed service, and points out that the term *sabura hito,* which occurs in the *Nihon Shoki,* refers to a brother in arms of Yamato Takeru no Mikoto. In the later Heian period the word *samurai* came to have the sole meaning of 'man-at-arms' or 'warrior', and was used virtually interchangeably with the term *bushi,* for which 'military man' is perhaps the most literal translation. This latter term had been used from the early Heian period, especially to denote the warriors of the eastern region, who were known as *Kantō bushi.* After the establishment of the Kamakura *Bakufu* we find the term *buke,* literally 'military house', i.e. clan or family, being used to denote the warrior nobility. This is in analogy with the term *kuge* used for the court nobility. The *bushi* were thus individual warriors in the service of the different *buke.* As Joüon des Longrais indicates, there were few ties between the provincial warriors and those employed in the capital, even between members of the same clan. As late as at the time of the *Hōgen no Ran,* the *Hōgen* Disturbance of 1156, there were members of the Minamoto family fighting on both sides in the conflict, and the same was true in the *Heiji no Ran*, the *Heiji* Disturbance, a few years later in 1160.[11] By this time a number of warrior clans had gained considerable power in the provinces and began to exert political influence in the capital and at the Imperial court. We may note that Jien, the author of the *Gukanshō*, a historical chronicle written in the early Kamakura period, referred to the period after the *Hōgen* Disturbance as *Bushi no yo*, the 'Military Age'. The ultimate struggle for supremacy eventually stood between the two most powerful clans, the Taira, also known as Heike, and the Minamoto, or Genji. With the victory of the latter in the *Gempei* War of 1180-85, the Heian period came to a close and a completely new era began, with a radically changed form of government. In retrospect it is possible to survey the last twenty-five or thirty years of the Heian period and attempt to establish a pattern of cause and effect. Reality in history always consists of a combination of calculation, strategy and material resources, but it also contains an element of chance, of the unforeseen, and, at the last count, of the irrational. The beginning of the end, however, if we permit ourselves to view events schematically, was the ousting of the Fujiwaras and the ascendancy in their place of Taira Kiyomori (1117-1181) and his family.

For centuries members of the *kuge* clan of Fujiwara had held high offices at the Imperial court. Fujiwara ladies held what virtually amounted to a monopoly of becoming chief Imperial consorts, and their fathers in their turn occupied the position as advisers to their grandsons, who in the fullness of time became Emperors in their turn and married Fujiwara ladies. The paramount importance of lineage in Japanese society has already been stressed, and by means of family ties and relationships the Fujiwara managed for centuries to manipulate the strings of power behind the scenes. When the Taira emerged victorious from the *Heiji* Disturbance in 1160, and forcibly took control of the positions and offices hitherto held almost exclusively by Fujiwara nobles, Taira Kiyomori himself holding the office of *Daijō Daijin* which can be translated as 'Chief Minister of State', they also saw to it that their most dangerous adversaries, the Minamoto, were eliminated from the centre of power, i.e. the capital. Those who were not killed were banished to the East, the provinces collectively known as the Kantō region. This move proved to be the undoing of the Taira. The so-called *Gunki Monogatari* (Tales of Warfare) of the period, notably the *Hōgen Monogatari* (Tales of the *Hōgen* Era) and the *Heike Monogatari* (Tales of the *Heike*) provide romanticised versions of the historical events.[12] Especially the *Heike Monogatari*, which was written as a sort of *apologia pro vita sua* for Taira Kiyomori, and which with strong Buddhist overtones emphasised the vanity of human endeavour, stressed the contrast between the two opposing clans. By living in the capital and indeed at the Imperial court, the Taira had adopted the refined ways of the *kuge*, while the *Kantō Bushi* (warriors from the East) remained rustic boors and had not only retained their warlike qualities but actually perfected them. The *Heike Monogatari*, written during the first century of warrior rule, regretted the passing of the old lifestyle, but made it quite clear that in the struggle between the Taira and the Minamoto those who had become weak and lacking in warlike spirit must go, and that victory belonged to the strong. This sentiment may be partly due to literary, and religious, convention, but a sober look at the historical events shows that the fact that the Minamoto were banished indeed provided the opportunity for a gathering of loyal forces in the provinces. In spite of spies and agents sent from the capital it was impossible to control what went on in the wilds of the Kantō region, and the young sons of Minamoto Yoshitomo (1123-1160), Yoritomo (1147-1199) and Yoshitsune (1159-1189) were able to gather support from Minamoto clansmen as well as many other influential families, notably the Hōjō, into which clan Yoritomo married. Life in the provinces also undeniably provided better opportunities for military training and, not least important, a reliable supply of mounts.

The *Heike Monogatari* presents a somewhat idealised and romanticised picture of the hard life in the eastern provinces and the kind of military men this produced, in a dialogue between Taira Koremori and a *Kantō bushi*: 'Commander-in-chief Koremori summoned Sanemori of the Saitō clan. He was from the village of Nagai and knew the east well. Koremori asked him: 'Sanemori, in the eight eastern provinces are there many men who are as mighty archers

as you are?'—'Do you then consider me a mighty archer?'
asked Sanemori with a scornful smile. 'I can only draw an
arrow thirteen handbreadths long. In the eastern provinces
there are any number of warriors who can do so. There is
one famed archer who never draws a shaft less than fifteen
handbreadths long. So mighty is his bow that four or five
ordinary men must pull together to bend it. When he
shoots, his arrow can easily pierce two or three suits of
armour at once. Even a warrior from a small estate has at
least five hundred soldiers. They are bold horsemen who
never fall, nor do they let their horses stumble on the
roughest road. When they fight, they do not care if even
their parents or children are killed; they ride on over their
bodies and continue the battle. The warriors of the western
provinces are quite different. If their parents are killed, they
retire from the battle and perform Buddhist rites to console
the souls of the dead. Only after the mourning is over will
they fight again. If their children are slain, their grief is so
deep that they cease fighting altogether. When their rations
have given out, they plant rice in the fields and go out to
fight only after reaping it. They dislike the heat of summer.
They grumble at the severe cold of winter. This is not the
way of the soldiers of the eastern provinces.'[13]

The most remarkable result of the *Gempei* War was not
so much the appointment of Minamoto Yoritomo to the
office of *Shōgun* in 1192, as the fact that he managed to
unite the different warrior clans, including those who had
fought on the side of the Taira, and make them his vassals
in a new feudal system. By this time the provincial warriors
really did constitute an élite whose power and privileges
made it a nobility. The transition of the samurai from men-
at-arms in imperial and government employ to a ruling
class of feudal lords and vassals took place in the relatively
short time span of about a century, although, as we have
seen, the ground had been prepared well in advance. If we
look at the rise in fortune of the Minamoto clan we shall
find that it provides a good example of the general ascendancy of the *bushi*. The Minamoto were descended from
Emperor Seiwa (regnavit 858-876), one of whose grandsons, Tsunemoto, also known as Rokuson-Ō, (894-961),
had received the family name and moved to the provinces.
Several cadet branches were established over the genera-

tions, but the family maintained close contacts with the Imperial court, and the Minamoto were often in charge of punitive expeditions against seditious elements.

Once of the most successful Minamoto campaigners was Yoshiie, known as *Hachiman Taro* (Eldest Son of Hachiman), the Shinto God of War. This sobriquet derived from the fact that he had celebrated his *genbuku*, (coming of age) ceremony in a shrine dedicated to Hachiman. In the minds of the general public, however, the name was considered to refer to his prodigious feats as a warrior, performed from an early age. Their services to the Imperial court earned the Minamoto high government offices and very considerable holdings of land, and their long and strenuous campaigns, especially in the north against the Ainu, established firm bonds between the leaders of the clan and the warriors in the provinces under their control. The key to power lay in the hands of the provincial warriors by the twelfth century, and here the Minamoto had the edge over their rivals, the Taira, whose power was concentrated in the capital and the neighbouring provinces.

The Minamoto clan had been established in Kamakura for over a century before the *Gempei* War, but it was a stroke of genius on the part of Minamoto Yoritomo to set up his *Bakufu* (literally 'Military Headquarters') there, far removed from the Imperial capital and its atmosphere, rife with intrigue. Yoritomo's new feudal system, with himself as Shōgun at the head, distinguished between two categories of warriors. The *go-kenin* were the direct vassals of the Shōgun, and controlled by the *Samurai Dokoro* (Bureau of Samurai Affairs). Some had been hereditary retainers of the Minamoto for generations, but there were also newly recruited *go-kenin*. The other category consisted of *bushi* who remained vassals of their old clan and did not become attached to the Minamoto. Yoritomo established three boards of government at Kamakura. The centre of administration was the *Kumonjo* (Bureau of Public Documents) which was later renamed *Mandokoro* (Bureau of Government) and which, following the death of Yoritomo, was run for a quarter of a century by his formidable widow, Hōjō Masako, and the shrewd statesman Ōe Hiromoto. The *Samurai Dokoro* was in charge of official appointments, and the early Kamakura *Bakufu* made a point of selecting the holders of official posts according to merit. Where the common people was concerned the provincial governors retained their judicial functions, but for the *bushi* a special court, the *Monjushō* (Place of Enquiry and Comment) was established in order to deal with matters of common and criminal law.

The establishment of the new seat of government in Kamakura had the advantage of removing it from potential political intrigue. In order to keep the Imperial court under surveillance, however, it was necessary to set up a branch of the Kamakura *Bakufu* in Kyoto, the so-called *Rokuhara*, named after the district where the Shōgun's representative, a member of the Hōjō clan, took up residence. The *Rokuhara* office also acted as an intermediary to the Emperor concerning the conferment of ranks and titles. Throughout the feudal period the Emperor, divested though he was of political power, retained his function as *fons honoris*, although he acted on the suggestion of the *Bakufu* and was unable to confer rank or titles on personal favourites. During the seven centuries of warrior rule there was never any suggestion of abolishing the old Heian system of court rank and official titles, the latter by this time mere sinecures.

The new legal code of the Kamakura *Bakufu* was not promulgated until 1232, after the death of Minamoto Yoritomo and his two sons Yoriie and Sanetomo who succeeded him in the office of Shōgun. By this time the Minamoto line was extinct, and the real power was in the hands of a member of the Hōjō clan, who would act as *Shikken* (Power Holder), during the minority of the Shōgun who was his own son or grandson. This state of affairs thus resembled the practice of *Insei* at the Heian Imperial court, where the retired Emperor, *In*, held the real power during the infancy of his successor on the throne.

The Kamakura legal code, known as the *Go-seibai Shikimoku* (Customs of Civil and Criminal Legislation) of 1232 is a brief document, later divided into 51 articles dealing with the essentials of common and criminal law.[14] It certainly goes back to and include the rules and regulations established by Minamoto Yoritomo for his vassals. These remained the basis for later legal codes such as the *Kemmu Shikimoku* (Legal Code of the Kemmu Period) of the Ashikaga *Bakufu*, promulgated in 1336, and the *Buke Sho-Hatto* (Laws of the Military Houses) promulgated by Tokugawa Ieyasu in 1615 through his son and successor, and augmented and renewed by every successive Tokugawa Shōgun until the Meiji Restoration in 1868. The promulgation of a legal code, theoretically regulating the affairs of the samurai, but in practice having general application, put the final seal of confirmation on the power of the warrior clans. From the establishment of the Kamakura *Bakufu* governmental and political power was in the hands of the samurai, and with it came increasing religious and cultural influence.

2

Bushi Attitudes Towards the Traditional Religions

From the time of the Taika Reform the two dominant religions were Shinto and Buddhism. Without embarking upon a discussion concerning the origins of the Japanese people one may however regard Shinto as an indigenous religion. Its mythology deals with the creation and development of Japan, while the rest of the world receives minimal attention. There is no doctrine or dogma, and no sacred text apart from the *Norito*, prayers used in purification and harvest ceremonies or as supplications for rain or healing from sickness. Shinto is basically an agricultural religion, inextricably linked to the cycle of planting and harvesting the staple crop, rice. It is certainly not pantheistic, as is sometimes erroneously stated, although the deities, *kami*, are legion in number and often connected with climatic or natural features.

The chief tenets of Shinto concern the avoidance of pollution, particularly in the form of contact with illness or death, and purification by means of cold, running water plays an important part. There is little actual cult in Shinto, the *kami* being always present, and apart from local or national festivals (*matsuri*) and ceremonies such as the presentation in shrines of newborn infants, weddings and funerals, people are free to offer a prayer to the *kami* of any shrine they are passing, sometimes without actually knowing to which particular *kami* that shrine is dedicated. Apart from this basic or popular form of Shinto there are various ceremonies concerning the Emperor or performed by him, as well as a complex of esoteric practices, including divination.

Buddhism was brought to Japan in the sixth century A.D. from China, via Korea. Like Christianity a millennium later it first became popular with the nobility and later spread to the common people. The great champion of Buddhism in Japan was Prince Shōtoku, usually known as *Shōtoku Taishi*, (574-622) who is credited with having made the new religion accepted by the Imperial court. The arrival of Buddhism resulted in intensified contact between China and Japan. Chinese monks were invited to teach the scriptures, and Japanese monks were sent to China to be trained in temples and monasteries under famous masters.

A number of different Buddhist schools were introduced in Japan during the Heian period, all of them belonging to the *Mahayana* tradition. Some became extinct at a fairly early stage, but among those which remain in force to this day we may mention the *Kegon, Tendai, Shingon* and *Jōdō* schools. The *Jōdō* school and its off-shoot the *Jōdō Shinshū*, usually translated as the 'Pure Land' schools, had a particularly popular appeal, as they both teach salvation through the simple means of adoring the Buddha of the Western Paradise, *Amida* (Sanskrit: *Amitābha*). Reading of the scriptures was not necessary, the prayer *Namu Amida Butsu* (Hail to Amida Buddha) being sufficient, and the deep piety which the *Jōdō* schools inspired attracted not only the masses but also large numbers of the nobility.

A third and very important factor in the spiritual and moral life of Japan was Confucianism. This religion, which may also be regarded as a philosophy of ethics, was introduced even earlier than Buddhism, by merchants travelling between China and Japan from the fourth century onwards. It did not take root firmly until the consolidation of the country according to the Chinese model of government was completed and the Chinese script came to be officially used. Like Buddhism, Confucianism can only be understood in depth through its scriptures. The Confucian classical literature became the standard school textbooks for every educated man—and woman, a number of the more erudite Heian court ladies mention having learned the Classics with their brothers in the schoolroom—and remained on the curriculum until modern times, just as it did in China.[15]

Confucianism primarily provides a moral code and a model for correct behaviour, based on a strictly hierarchical system where each individual should know his place and aspire to do his best in the position which fate has allotted to him. The Five Relations, between lord and vassal, father and son, husband and wife, older brother and younger brother, and friend and friend, formed the backbone of Japanese society. The relationship was one of mutual interdependence, and although hierarchical in nature it meant that the superior ought to assist his inferior with help and advice as well as expect obedience and service from him. The two parties were also considered to be responsible for each other's actions to a remarkable degree, something which we will find reflected in the legal codes. Where the ruler is concerned Confucianism in China has always emphasised the paramount importance of the Mandate of Heaven, but, as already noted, this aspect was not stressed in Japan. Although the Emperor in Japan was not held personally responsible for natural calamities and catastrophes, the *Kojiki* and *Nihongi* however contain many references to the Emperor performing expiatory ceremonies, e.g. during plagues or droughts. In spite of the basically shintoistic nature of these ceremonies the existence of underlying Confucian ideas should not be disregarded.

It was in the atmosphere of interaction, opposition and contrast between these three religions that the warrior nobility crystallized into a distinct and powerful group in society. Conscious of their privileges from the beginning of their ascendancy the samurai became increasingly exclusive. There was a great deal of general change in social status during the Middle Ages, and especially during the turbulent period of intermittent civil war known as the *Sengoku jidai* from the early fifteenth century until the unification of the country under Oda Nobunaga, Toyotomi Hideyoshi and Tokugawa Ieyasu. *Bushi* rose in the ranks to become feudal lords while *daimyo* and ancient *buke* families became extinct or sank into obscurity. Some old families managed to survive their eclipse, while not all of the families newly risen to prominence were able to last beyond the third generation.

In the very period of transition from the Heian government to the Kamakura *Bakufu* another school of Buddhism was introduced. This was the Chinese *Ch'an* school of meditation, which became known in Japan as *Zen*. The first Zen sect to be introduced was the pragmatic and dynamic *Rinzai Zen*, in 1191, followed in 1205 by the more contemplative *Sōtō Zen*. Zen Buddhism seems to have held an immediate appeal for the *bushi*, and gained many adherents from their ranks. Both *Rinzai* and *Sōtō Zen* aim for sudden enlightenment, *satori*, a state of mind which requires assiduous application through meditation under the guidance of a Zen master. Zen teaching, albeit scriptureless, is intellectually demanding, especially *Rinzai Zen* which employs the *koan* technique of posing paradoxical questions. This is a psychological method of forcing the disciple's thinking into new and unbeaten tracks in order to obtain the sought-after flash of sudden insight. Although intellectual in nature, Zen Buddhism has a directness in its approach to daily life which must have appealed to the *bushi*, who, as men of action, were not inclined to withdraw from the world until their later years. It would however be a mistake to regard Zen as the only Buddhist school which interested the *bushi*. The Amidist *Jōdō* schools remained popular in all social strata, there were many adherents of both *Tendai* and *Shingon*, and *Kannon* (Sanskrit: *Avalokiteśvara*), the Bodhisattva of Mercy, held a great appeal also for the *bushi*.

The samurai attitude to religion and ethics was characterised by a number of distinctive traits which set the warrior apart from the rest of society. The most central point was the fact that as a professional warrior, trained to fight and kill, the samurai acted contrary to the tenets of both Buddhism and Shinto. The former religion categorically forbids all taking of life, animal as well as human. Indeed, until the Meiji Restoration no meat was eaten, with the exception of venison, which keen samurai huntsmen would sometimes partake of. As we shall see below, the *bushi* were fully aware of their contravention of the rules of Buddhism and resorted to different methods of atonement for the sins they committed as active warriors.

Since the chief concern of Shinto is purity, the most serious forms of defilement are death, blood and illness. The samurai came into contact with all of these while exercising their duties, and were thus in conflict with this religion also. The principles of Confucianism presented yet another source of potential problems. The question whether one's own father or one's feudal lord ought to take precedence was the subject of heated discussions among the Confucian scholars, *jusha*, although in the case of children the matter was clear, and a *bushi* would willingly sacrifice his own child in order to save the life of the child of his lord. These questions will be dealt with more fully below in the discussion of *Bushidō* and the significance of this somewhat elusive concept.

Before considering those features of samurai religion and ethics which were exclusive to the *bushi*, it is necessary to observe their attitude towards the traditional religions. What must above all be remembered is that although there have certainly been skirmishes between the priesthood of both religions from time to time, there has never been any serious conflict between Shinto and Buddhism. At an early stage a kind of amalgamation, the so-called *Ryōbu-Shinto*, was effected and laid the foundation for what might best be described as 'peaceful co-existence'. Over the centuries the two religions have varied considerably in power and influence. The last centuries of the Heian period saw the growth of a Buddhist *ecclesia militans*, in the fourteenth century there was a Shinto revival, and the sixteenth century witnessed the violent curbing of the power of the once again militant Buddhist establishments, especially those of Mount Hiei. In the early Tokugawa period a strengthening of Buddhism took place when it was made into a state religion in order to eradicate the last vestiges of Christianity, which was by then proscribed, half a century after its introduction.

Few Japanese seem to have felt that one religion by necessity excluded the other, the general attitude being rather that the two complement each other. Shinto is the religion of Japan, tied with indissoluble bonds to the country itself and its people, and appealing to the collective as a unifying bond between the *kami*, the land and the race. Buddhism, on the other hand, constitutes an individual faith, a conscious effort towards ultimate salvation from the trammels of this world and the relentless cycle of rebirths. Generalisations such as these, however, must not conceal the fact that both religions are multi-dimensional, and that there exists an esoteric side to Shinto, as well as an entire spectrum of Buddhist schools, from the esoteric to the salvationist.

Among the Shinto deities especially revered by the *bushi* the chief position was occupied by the God of War, Hachiman. The character of this *kami*, who was euhemeristically identified with the legendary Emperor Ōjin, but who at an early stage came to be considered as a bodhisattva, is extremely complex. The cult of Hachiman seems to have had its original centre at Usa, in present-day Ōita-ken in Kyushu, where one of the major Hachiman shrines remains to this day. The *Usa Hachiman-jingū* has traditionally been famous for its oracle, which played a decisive part in the history of Japan when it foiled the plot of the Buddhist monk Dōkyō, *éminence grise*—and probably lover—of the Empress Shōtoku (718-770, regnavit 765-769; had also reigned 749-758 as Empress Kōken), to usurp the throne. A female *kami*, Hime-gami, is enshrined with Hachiman, occupying a somewhat inferior position and sometimes being considered as his consort. There is some evidence that the cult of Hime-gami may have preceded that of Hachiman, who is not mentioned either in the *Kojiki* or the *Nihongi*. Some contemporary Shinto scholars are of the opinion that Hime-gami was originally a priestess who functioned as an oracle.[16]

Hachiman has been worshipped from the Heian period as the apotheosis of the Emperor Ōjin, son of the legendary Empress Jingū-Kōgō, and grandson, through his father Emperor Chūai, of Yamato-take or Yamato Takeru, as he is also known, one of the Japanese culture heroes. All these personages are more than semi-mythological, and the accounts of their exploits in the *Kojiki* and the *Nihongi* are full of portents and miracles. Thus Jingū-Kōgō is supposed to have set out on an expedition to conquer Silla, one of the Korean kingdoms, while pregnant with the future Ōjin

Tennō, having tied a stone to her abdomen to postpone the child's birth. Emperor Ōjin, according to the *Kojiki* and the *Nihongi*, in fact also appears as a great culture hero who is said to have improved both the material and cultural standard of his subjects. He was not however remarkable for his martial spirit, and no military feats are credited to him. Another reading of the characters employed to write the name of Hachiman is *Yahata* or *Yawata* meaning 'Eight Banners'. There is a legend that eight flags fell from the sky at the shrine of Usa, which should probably be taken as an attempt at an etymological explanation. The *shintai*, a term often translated as 'god-body', i.e. the material manifestation of a *kami*'s spirit, of Hachiman is the *hossu*, a fly-whisk made of horse-hair. In ancient Central Asia one of the insignia of a ruler was a fly-whisk made of a yak's tail, and this object found its way into Buddhist ceremonies as a symbol of supreme mastery of esoteric knowledge. This would seem to indicate a possible Central Asian origin of Hachiman, and it has been suggested that the *kami* may have been an amalgamation of an ancient Japanese god of war and a Chinese protective deity.[17]

Another remarkable feature of Hachiman is the fact that he came to be considered as a bodhisattva already from the time of the introduction of Buddhism into Japan. He was known as *Hachiman Dai Bosatsu* (The Great Bodhisattva Hachiman) or even *Shō Hachiman Dai Bosatsu* (The True Great Bodhisattva Hachiman) by the early Heian period. According to one tradition, which would seem to be a later explanation of a by then established fact, the Buddhist connection goes back to the sixth century, i.e. the very time when Buddhism was first introduced in Japan. Hachiman is said to have possessed a certain Ōga Hige, in the reign of Emperor Bidatsu (572-585), and to have made the following utterance, using Ōga as his mouthpiece: 'I am the Emperor Honda (another name for Emperor Ōjin) Hirohata ('Broad Banners') no Hachiman-maro. My name is *Gokoku reigen iriki jintsu daijizai-ō Bosatsu* (The Bodhisattva Great Independent King of State-protecting, miraculous, majestic, divine power).[18] This title was however not officially bestowed on the deity until 781, in the reign of Emperor Kōnin. According to the *Jinnō Shōtōki* of Kitabatake Chikafusa (1293-1354), Ōjin referred to himself as *Homuda-*

no-Yahata-maru (Homuda of the Eight Banners).[19] Already
Emperor Shōmu (701-756, regnavit 724-748), at whose
behest the *Daibutsu* (Great Buddha) of the Tōdaiji temple
at Nara was erected, sent offerings to the Hachiman shrine
at Usa, consisting (on different occasions) of *gohei*, the
Shinto wand with paper streamers, and of Buddhist sutras
written in gold characters. His daughter, Empress Kōken,
presided over an elaborate ceremony in 749, when
Hachiman, represented by a Buddhist nun said to have
become possessed by him, visited Nara in order to worship
Roshana Buddha (Sanskrit: *Locanā*, a manifestation of
Vairocana) at the Tōdaiji. On this occasion a shrine, the
Tamuke-yama Hachimangū, just east of the Tōdaiji, was
dedicated to Usa Hachiman.

When the Minamoto clan was established in the tenth
century it adopted Hachiman as its tutelary deity. The
ancestor of the Seiwa Genji, as the Minamoto were also
called, Emperor Seiwa (regnavit 858-876), had shown a
special interest in Hachiman, founding a shrine dedicated
to him at Iwashimizu in 859. This shrine, the *Iwashimizu
Hachiman Daibosatsu-gū*, quickly gained in importance.
At a ceremony held in 861 for the Buddha of the Tōdaiji
temple under the auspices of Emperor Seiwa, Hachiman
Daibosatsu was referred to as chief among the gods of the
empire. Before abdicating in 876 Emperor Seiwa gave orders for an annual gift of 32 *koku* (the standard measure
of rice, one *koku* being 180 litres) of rice to the Iwashimizu
Hachiman-gū, described as 'the state-protecting Buddhist
temple'.[20] The Minamoto, as provincial warriors, were no
doubt originally attracted to Hachiman for his warlike qualities, and as the clan increased in martial valour and political power the cult of Hachiman spread. We have already
noted that Minamoto Yoshiie (1041-1108) was generally
believed to have been endowed with the sobriquet *Hachiman
Taro* (Eldest son of Hachiman) in recognition of his extraordinary feats of martial prowess. His father, Minamoto
Yoriyoshi (995-1082), had founded the *Wakamiya
Hachiman-gū*, dedicated to Iwashimizu Hachiman, at
Kamakura in 1063 in the Kantō region where the Minamoto
clan were to establish their stronghold. Minamoto Yoritomo
appears to have been a devoted worshipper of Hachiman,
to whom he prayed for victory in the *Gempei* War. The

Heike Monogatari describes how he gave thanks to the tutelary deity of his clan after a battle in which the Heike troops had been routed by Yoritomo's warriors: 'Yoritomo alighted from his horse, took off his helmet, washed his hands and rinsed his mouth. Kneeling and facing the capital, he bowed his head down to the ground and said: 'I, Yoritomo, have not won by my own strength. It is the Great Bodhisattva Hachiman who has given me this victory'.[21] With the establishment of the Kamakura *Bakufu*, the *Tsurugaoka Hachiman-gū*, named after the hill to which Yoritomo had moved it, came to be regarded not only as the tutelary shrine of the Minamoto clan, but of the military government and the realm. The tomb of Minamoto Yoritomo is situated in the hills to the east of the shrine, and his son Sanetomo, the third and last Minamoto Shōgun, was assassinated at the foot of the flight of steps leading up to the main building. White was the colour of the Minamoto clan, used for their banners in the *Gempei* War, in contrast to the Taira, whose colour was red. Today white pigeons are to be found in large numbers in the compound of the *Tsurugaoka Hachiman-gū* at Kamakura. The eight flags connected with the Usa Hachiman shrine are sometimes described as white, although in some accounts there are said to have been four white and four red banners. Minamoto Yoritomo's wife, Hōjō Masako, had two ponds constructed at the *Tsurugaoka Hachiman-gū*, one with white lotus blossoms and one with red. There is however also a legend which states that Nitta Yoshisada washed his bloodstained sword in the pond with red blossoms when making his victorious entry in Kamakura in 1333, thus giving the flowers their red colour. This theme is familiar from European folklore and can be found already in the Pyramus and Thisbe episode in Ovid's *Metamorphoses*.

Hachiman remained a focal point of military power throughout the centuries, and many of the most influential *buke* families had their own private shrines dedicated to him. It was customary to pray to Hachiman for victory before a battle, especially during the turbulent period of the *Sengoku jidai*, and in the written oaths of the *bushi* the name of Hachiman is always present and usually first on the list. At the time of the two Mongol invasions, which took place in 1274 and 1281, and which were unsuccessful due to the destruction of the enemy fleet by typhoons, Hachiman was considered to have played a decisive part in protecting the Empire. The Emperors Go Uda (regnavit 1274-87; *Insei* 1287-1324) and Kameyama prayed at the Iwashimizu shrine for protection of the country and defeat of the invaders. The *Usa Hachiman-gū*, situated near the site of the actual invasions, was awarded grants of stewardships, *jitō*, by the Kamakura *Bakufu* in recognition of the intervention of a 'divine wind', *kamikaze*. When claiming the reward the shrine officials quoted witnesses who had seen the flags of the shrine pointing in the direction of the enemy ships, a sign that Hachiman was taking active part in the battle. A shogunal edict from 1284 is quoted by the historian Hori Kyotsu: 'Chief Priest, Usa Shrine, 1284/ 2/28. Enclosed is the patent signifying the donation of the stewardship of Muratsuno Beppu in the province of Hyūga. We had offered a stewardship in the first year of Kenji (1275) for the purpose of repulsing enemies, as a result of which all enemy ships were wrecked or sunk in the fourth year of Kōan (1281). Now, because it is rumoured that enemies may come to attack us again, we would like to make a donation similar to the one given before. We request that you say your prayers with the utmost sincerity. On the order of the Shōgun, (signed) Governor of Suruga Province (Hōjō Naritoki), Governor of Sagami Province (Hōjō Tokimune).'[22]

The cult of Hachiman being firmly associated with not only military valour but also political power, it is hardly surprising to find that Toyotomi Hideyoshi took a special interest in this deity. He made plans to have himself posthumously enshrined as *Shin Hachiman* (The New Hachiman) but the project was abandoned after his death and the subsequent fall of the house of Toyotomi, which only lasted for two generations.

Susanoo, impetuous younger brother of Amaterasu and God of the Storm, plays an important part in the *Kojiki* and the *Nihongi*. His character is complex, combining traits of a culture hero with those of a 'trickster', an ambivalent deity, part benevolent and part malicious. Amaterasu, being the chief *kami* of the Shinto pantheon as well as the ancestress and special protectress of the Imperial house, has little popular appeal and could in that respect be called a *dea otiosa*. Members of the Imperial family address prayers to her, but not the general public, which might venerate Amaterasu but would not ask her to intervene on their behalf in practical matters. The same seems to apply also to Susanoo. His belligerent character ought to have made him popular with the *bushi*, but there is little evidence that he occupied any special position in the pantheon of Shinto and Buddhist deities to which the samurai addressed their prayers. The connection of Susanoo with swords, in particular the Imperial sword forming part of the national regalia of Japan, will be discussed below, in the context of swords and their symbolical as well as practical importance to the samurai.

Several Buddhas and bodhisattvas held special significance for the *bushi*, and there is a host of minor Buddhist deities with warlike connotations. *Amida* Buddha (Sanskrit: *Amitābha*) of the Western Paradise (Sanskrit: *Sukhāvatī*), revered by the two *Jōdō* schools, has the strongest popular appeal of the many incarnations of the Buddha. All that is needed to obtain salvation is sincere devotion, and this kind of pietistic religion tends to find adherents among all classes of society. The cult of *Amida* began in the Nara period, together with another salvationist school, the cult of *Miroku* (Sanskrit: *Maitreya*) the Buddha of the Future. From the early Heian period the cult of Amida had eclipsed that of *Miroku*, and the chief text of amidistic Buddhism, the *Hokkekyō* (Sanskrit: *Saddharmapundarika Sutra*), usually translated as the 'Lotus Sutra', remains the most popular Buddhist text to this day. Hachiman has been considered as a manifestation (*suijaku*) of *Amida*, in analogy with the idea of Amaterasu as a manifestation of *Birushana* (Sanskrit: *Vairocana*) Buddha. The latter is the main object of worship in the Tōdaiji temple at Nara, popularly referred to as the *Daibutsu* (the Great Buddha) as it is represented by a gigantic bronze sculpture, 16 metres in height, originally erected by Emperor Shōmu. The other *Daibutsu* in Japan is the bronze sculpture, 12 metres high, in Kamakura which represents *Amida* Buddha and was erected in the early Kamakura period. Toyotomi Hideyoshi had another, and still larger, figure of *Amida* erected in Kyoto, but this wooden structure was destroyed by fire, and is no longer extant. It is interesting to note that in this case the connection between Hachiman and Amida was again brought up, since, as we have seen above, Hideyoshi expressed his intention of being himself enshrined in the *Amida-ga-mine* as an incarnation of Hachiman.

Among the bodhisattvas which held a special appeal for the *bushi*, *Kannon* was certainly the most popular. This interesting bodhisattva, (Sanskrit: *Avalokiteśvara*) is markedly androgynous in character, and especially later sculptures in China and Japan are distinctly feminine in form. *Kannon*, the Bodhisattva of Mercy, enjoyed great popularity in the Heian period as a benevolent and gentle intermediary, always ready to hear the prayers of a supplicant. The merciful character of *Kannon* seems to have appealed to the samurai, and the *Azuma Kagami*, chronicling the events which brought about the founding of the Kamakura *Bakufu*, records that Minamoto Yoritomo was a devout Buddhist who carried a rosary at all times. He kept a small figure of Kannon, which had been given to him by a Buddhist nun when he was a child, tied up in his top-knot.

The *Azuma Kagami* however goes on to say that at the time when his fate appeared to be uncertain Minamoto Yoritomo removed the figurine from his hair for fear of exposing himself to ridicule if he were killed and the Kannon should be found when his head was presented for inspection. This statement seems to show that such religious devotion as that displayed by Yoritomo would have been subject to derision and considered exaggerated and slightly effeminate in a *bushi*.

Kannon appears in a number of stories concerning the forging of sword blades. There are many legends connected with exceptionally good blades, or those which have belonged to famous men and with which special feats of swordsmanship have been performed. In not a few of these legends Kannon plays a prominent part, suddenly appearing in the smithy and helping the swordsmith in his difficult task by working the bellows. This was an important part of the procedure, as an even temperature was crucial for producing a blade of good quality. The connection of Kannon with the sword, chief weapon of the *bushi*, is interesting. It demonstrates the spiritual significance of the sword, which was seen not merely as an inanimate object but as part of its owner's personality. *Monju* (Sanskrit:

Manjuśrī) is the Bodhisattva of Wisdom, armed with a sword in order to repel enemies of the faith. His warlike aspect as a protector of the faith appealed particularly to the *bushi*, who themselves occupied positions as defenders of the lives and fiefs of their feudal lords. In seventeenth-century treatises on *Bushidō* and swordsmanship we find that the sword of the samurai is sometimes identified with Monju's sword of *prajña* (knowledge) an idea which is further discussed below, in the section dealing with the sword.

There is furthermore an entire pantheon of minor Buddhist deities depicted in armour and carrying swords or spears. Foremost among these are the *Myō-ō*, or *Go Dai Myō-ō*, the 'Five Great *Vidyā-rājas*', who are the terrible aspects of the Buddhas of the five quarters. These are, giving their names in Sanskrit, *Mahāvairocana* for the Centre, *Akṣobya* for the East, *Ratnasambhava* for the South, *Amitābha* for the West, and *Amoghasiddhi* for the North. Their respective *Myō-ō* are *Fudō Myō-ō*, *Gōsanze Myō-ō*, *Gundari Myō-ō*, *Dai-Itoku Myō-ō*, and *Kongō Yasha Myō-ō*. According to some sources their respective elements are Earth, Ether, Fire, Wind and Water, and their colours Yellow, Blue, Red, White and Black, but these attributions vary somewhat already in the writings of the Indian commentators, and different Buddhist schools in Japan have their own traditions. Their general aspects and attributes remain the same, however, four of the five carrying swords or *vajra*, thunderbolts, in their hands. The *Myō-ō*, belonging to the tantric, or esoteric, form of Buddhism, are especially revered by the Shingon school. The five *Myō-ō* or *Vidyā-rājas* are also known under their Sanskrit names of *Açala*, *Trilokya-vijaya*, *Kundali*, *Yamāntaka*, and *Vajra-yakśa*.

Fudō, usually depicted with a bright red face, large, staring eyes, hair standing on end, and surrounded by a halo of flames, was extremely popular with the *bushi*. He carries an upright sword in his right hand, and a wheel of the law or doctrine (Sanskrit: *Dhārmaçakra*) in his left. *Fudō* is sometimes depicted as holding a rope in his left hand, probably as a result of a confusion of him with Monju, who holds a rope to bind the enemies of the faith vanquished by his sword. All the other *Myō-ō* have six

(*Kongo Yasha* and *Dai Itoku*) or eight (*Gundari* and *Gōsanze*) arms and legs. Blue or yellow-faced *Fudō* also occur occasionally, but the *Aka Fudō* or 'Red *Fudō*' is by far the most common. *Gōsanze* has four heads, and *Dai Itoku* six, the others have one each, and all have a terrifying aspect, being sometimes depicted as having long, fang-like teeth. They can furthermore be interpreted as personifications of tantric formulae, originally magic utterings by the five Buddhas whom they represent.[23] Fudō was considered to have the power to avert danger and appease evil intentions. Images of Fudō were painted as votive offerings or prayers for peace in troubled times.

The gate through which one enters a Buddhist temple usually contains two sculptures which flank the entrance. These are the *Niō-ō* (Sanskrit: *Deva rājas*), usually identified as Indra and Brahma and thus of Hindu origin. They are fearsome in aspect with large, staring eyes protruding from their sockets and mouths open in mute howls of rage, and are armed with clubs or swords. Their function is to frighten away evil influences and other enemies of the faith. Other guardians of Buddhist temples are the *Shitennō*, the 'Four Heavenly Kings'. They are the rulers of the four quarters, and are also depicted carrying arms. The most important of them, who has a cult of his own, is *Bishamon* (Sanskrit: *Vaiśravana*) also known as *Tamon*, who is the ruler of the North. He is usually shown wearing armour and carrying a spear and sometimes a miniature pagoda as well. He is regarded as a god of war and was considered a patron deity of warriors, and parents hoping for martial valour in their offspring would consecrate them to Bishamon. Images of Bishamon were carried as amulets by warriors. Already Shōtoku Taishi is said in the *Nihon Shoki* to have carried a small wooden figurine of Bishamon, which he had carved himself, tied up in his hair. He also built the Shitennōji near Osaka, a temple dedicated to the Four Heavenly Kings. Bishamon was however also identified with *Kuvera* (Sanskrit: *Kubera*), a god of riches and one of the Seven Gods of Luck.[24]

Yet another warlike figure must be mentioned, namely the bodhisattva *Jizō* (Sanskrit: *Kśitigarbha*) protector of dead children, especially those who have died in infancy. He is usually depicted as a shaven-headed monk with staff and rosary. Sometimes, however, he is shown as a warrior monk (*sōhei*) on horseback. In the Shingon school of esoteric Buddhism the war god was represented as a mounted warrior known as *Shōgun Jizō*, and this deity was also identified with Hachiman.

Shugendō, a syncretistic sect which incorporates esoteric practices from both Buddhism and Shinto as well as elements from folk religion and Chinese Taoism, has certain warlike features which connect it with the samurai. Its adherents, known as *yamabushi* (those who sleep in the mountains) or *shugenja* (those who practise austerities) lived in wild mountain areas, some of their most famous centres being the peaks of Ōmine, Kumano and Kimpusen. The origins of this sect are obscure, as the supposed founder En no Gyōja, who is said to have lived in the seventh century, is of doubtful historicity, but it certainly existed in the late Heian period. The *yamabushi* wore one or two swords, as well as other distinctive accessories such as the tiny hat tied on the forehead (*tokin*) and the conch trumpet (*hora-gai*). Their general aspect was rather fierce, and the mere fact that they resided in the mountains, considered in Shinto beliefs as the abode of the spirits of the dead, must have set them apart from other people and contributed to their aura of fearsomeness. They practised exorcism and divination, and were sometimes married to female mediums (*miko*). The *yamabushi* worshipped a large pantheon of Buddhist and Shinto deities, among them Fudō Myō-ō, Kannon and Inari, the Shinto deity of rice, and hence wealth, who is represented in his shrines by effigies of bushy-tailed foxes.

Fire ceremonies, *goma*, were practised by the *yamabushi*, among them the famous *hi-watari* (fire-crossing) in which the participants, laymen as well as the priests themselves, crossed a bed of live coals.[25] There was also the *yudate* (boiling water feat) in which the officiating priest sprayed himself with boiling water from a large cauldron without harm to himself or the bystanders. Another remarkable feat was the *katana-watari* (sword-climbing ceremony) in which a priest with bare feet ascended a ladder, the rungs of which consisted of sword blades fixed with the cutting edge upwards. Laymen also took active part in this ceremony as described by Percival Lowell, who witnessed a performance of what was also called the *tsurugi-watari*, translated by Lowell as 'Climbing the Ladder of Sword-blades', in the early 1890s.

The ceremony took place at a Hachiman shrine, where a wooden structure had been erected for the purpose. This consisted of a platform, raised on four poles about four metres above the ground, on which stood a small shrine. Two ladders led to the platform, one ordinary and the other the ceremonial one, the rungs of which consisted of twelve sword-blades of ordinary sharpness, lent by their owners who lived in the vicinity. After purification rites consisting of prayers (*mudras*) i.e. magical gestures, and the twanging of bowstrings to frighten off evil spirits, one of the priests shot arrows into the air in the direction of the four quarters while standing on the edges of two swords set in a stand below the platform.

After further purification the priests began ascending the ladder of sword-blades, pausing to pray at the shrine on the platform and then descending by means of the ordinary ladder at the back. The climbers usually set their feet down along the length of the sword-blades, although some of them stepped across the edge of the blade as if ascending an ordinary ladder. One of the priests cut his hand slightly on one of the blades, which was declared impure by the priests. It was later discovered that this blade had not been properly purified after having been previously used for killing a dog. When all the priests of the shrine had made the climb, some of them several times, a layman successfully made the ascent but managed to gash his foot when passing the ladder of swords as he was returning to his seat. The blood flowed from his wound, and after this incident the ceremony was closed.[26]

Lowell's explanations of how the feat was performed included, apart from a categoric statement that the Japanese have thicker skin on the soles of their feet than Westerners, the technical information that a stationary blade has considerably less cutting power than a moving one. This may well be the case, but the alleged 'pachydermatous' state of Japanese feet seems more doubtful, and the fact remains that the *katana-watari*, which today seems to be extinct, was a remarkable feat, especially since the performers do not appear to have been in a state of trance.

The *hi-watari* and *katana-watari* ceremonies are clearly shamanistic in origin and are undertaken by the faithful as rites of transcendence from the material world into the spiritual one. Fire and water are the two chief elements of purification. The *yamabushi* conform to Shinto practice by purifying themselves by means of cold water ablutions. Part of their customary austerities consists of prolonged immersion, such as standing naked for hours under a waterfall during the cold season. The *hi-watari* can be seen as a spiritual cleansing, the burning away of mental impurities, and a symbolic journey. In *Shugendō* the ritual fire is associated with Fudō Myō-ō, who, as we have seen, is usually depicted surrounded by flames. In the *katana-watari* ceremony the *yamabushi* climbing the ladder of twelve sword-blades ascends symbolically into the other world. The ceremonial climbing of ladders or trees symbolising the world pillar which separates earth and the heavens, seven, nine or twelve in number, is found in the Altaic and circumpolar religions, as well as in many others, and the person who accomplishes the feat is regarded as a mediator between men and deities.

The *yamabushi*, when not practising austerities in the mountains, spent much time wandering about the country. Exorcism as a means of curing illness was their chief occupation, and they also collected subscriptions for their shrines. They were allowed to cross barriers freely, and play a prominent part in the famous legend of the flight of Minamoto Yoshitsune after his fall from grace. According to the story the entire party of men loyal to Yoshitsune disguised themselves as itinerant *yamabushi*, with Yoshitsune dressed as a menial and his famous companion, the Herculean warrior-monk Benkei, as their leader. In this way they managed to cross a heavily guarded barrier where the garrison was on the look-out for the fugitives.[27]

In Shinto, and also in Japanese folk religion, mountains were shunned as the abode of the dead, and only those whose livelihood depended on them, i.e. wood-cutters, hunters and charcoal-burners, entered the mountains voluntarily. Indeed, these categories of people became themselves if not avoided, at least regarded with a certain amount of awe as living near the fringe of society and developed their own traditions. The thick mountain forests were also considered to house a number of supernatural beings, among them the *tengu*.

These creatures, which might perhaps be called 'goblins', are extraordinarily complex, showing many variations and displaying traits from Indian and Chinese mythology.[28] Leaving a detailed analysis of the varying forms of *tengu* aside, we will concentrate here on the two general types of *tengu* such as they were depicted in art, notably the Tokugawa period wood-cut prints and *netsuke*. The creature is described either as a bird, the *karasu* (crow) *tengu*, or as a half human, half bird-like *konoha* (long-nose) *tengu*. The former, which has the keen eyes and strong beak of a bird of prey, will sometimes assume the form and costume of a *yamabushi*, usually retaining the bird-like eyes and the beak. The latter has human form, except for a pair of wings and a very long, pointed nose. In character the *tengu* are ambivalent, being malevolent and dangerous as well as benevolent.

The folklore of rural Japan abounds with beliefs concerning the supernatural power of the *tengu*. People who lost their way in the forest were considered to have been abducted by the *tengu*, who were also thought to punish those who disturbed the peace of the forest or damaged the trees with sudden thunderstorms. They were thus regarded as guardians or protective spirits of the forest, and offerings were made to them in order to ensure success in any undertakings in their domain. Certain mountains were regarded as especially popular among the *tengu*, e.g. Mount Hiei north of Kyoto, but they seem to have been associated generally with mountainous regions all over Japan.

The *tengu* of the different mountains were considered to belong to separate clans, each with its chieftain, and the chief *tengu* of Mount Kurama, Sōjōbō, was regarded as the chieftain of them all. He was also called *Daitengu* (Great *tengu*) or *Tengu Sama* (Lord *Tengu*) and is usually depicted as a *konoha tengu* dressed as a *yamabushi*, while his retainers have the form of *karasu tengu*. In folk beliefs the *tengu* were thought to assemble at night, again in the shape of *yamabushi*, in order to sing and dance, and there are a number of folk tales which tell of people who came across a party of *tengu* making merry, and the outcome of such an encounter. As in European folk tales there was often a granting of wishes, and a good man would benefit from this, whereas a bad man would come to grief, as in the famous story of the good man who had a wen on his neck removed by the *tengu*, and his bad neighbour who had a wen added to the one already disfiguring him.

Most famous of the talents of the *tengu*, however, was their unsurpassed skill as swordsmen. Apart from their skills in fencing the *tengu* were also reputed to be able to bite through sword-blades and bend them with ease. No human could win a duel against a *tengu*, except Minamoto Yoshitsune, the hero of legendary martial prowess, who is said to have been taught swordsmanship by the *tengu*. Yoshitsune, half brother of Yoritomo and the son of Minamoto Yoshitomo by his concubine Tokiwa Gōzen, a famous beauty whose children were spared by Taira Kiyomori, was sent into exile as an infant and forced to enter a monastery. During his novitiate he is said to have gone out secretly at night, making his way to the forest. There the ruler of all the *tengu*, Sōjōbō himself, is supposed to have taught him the martial arts, particularly fencing.

When he had mastered these skills the young Yoshitsune is said to have gone to Kyoto, where a warrior monk named Benkei, a giant of a man, used to stand on a bridge every night, challenging passers-by to a fight. According to the legend he had vowed to collect a thousand swords, and as he defeated all his opponents and took their swords his collection was nearing completion. When Benkei was lying in wait for his one thousandth sword one night he encountered Minamoto Yoshitsune. In the tale Benkei presented a terrifying figure, gigantic in stature and wearing a black suit of armour. Yoshitsune was dressed in Court costume, and came along walking nonchalantly on the railing of the bridge playing a flute. When challenged by Benkei, however, he jumped down from the railing, drew his sword and disarmed Benkei with a stunning display of the most advanced kind of swordsmanship. From this time Benkei was the devoted companion of Yoshitsune, fighting by his side throughout the *Gempei* War, accompanying him in his exile, and finally dying by his side.

Another famous swordsman, Miyamoto Musashi (1584-1645), inventor of the *nitō ryū* school of two-sworded fencing, philosopher and ink painter, of whose genius for fencing the legends are legion, is reputed once to have defeated a *tengu* in a duel, a story which clearly demonstrates that he was considered to be quite extraordinarily skilful. That the belief in *tengu* had permeated all strata of society is clearly illustrated by a shōgunal edict posted by the funerary shrines of Tokugawa Ieyasu and his successors at Nikko in 1860. Announcing that the present Shōgun, Tokugawa Iemochi, the next-to-last person to hold this office, intended to pay a visit to the shrines of his ancestors the following spring, the edict addressed directly the *tengu* and *oni* (demons) of the Nikko area, requesting them to move elsewhere until after the shōgunal visit. It was dated July 1860, and signed by the Daimyo of Dewa, Mizuno.

The belief in and fear of vengeful spirits and the ghosts of the dead has been a prominent feature of Japanese folk religion since the earliest times, and continues even today. The *bushi*, who as professional warriors came to have more contact with violent death than most commoners or *kuge*, shared these beliefs. Their frequent contact, especially in times of war, with pollution in the form of blood and death made them ritually unclean from the point of view of Shinto. Although they were also contravening the Buddhist injunction against the taking of life, they could however carry amulets and pictures of saints or bodhisattvas, such as the Kannon figurine worn by Minamoto Yoritomo in his topknot, and address prayers to them.

The Heian period appears to have been particularly plagued by fears of ghosts and spirits, to whose wrath or vengefulness calamities such as natural disasters or epidemics, as well as personal misfortune or illness, were ascribed. A typical example was that of the eminent statesman Sugawara Michizane (845-903), who was wrongfully accused, removed from office and ignominiously exiled. After his death while in disgrace, a series of misfortunes occurred in Kyoto, including the conflagration of the Imperial Palace, and it was only after Michizane's posthumous pardon and promotion in rank which ended with his elevation to a Shinto *kami* under the name of Tenjin that the calamities ceased. Tenjin is revered as the patron deity of letters and learning. A peculiar feature of this belief in vengeful spirits is the *iki-ryō* or 'living spirit'. Thus the spirit of a person who is still alive may, often without the knowledge of the person himself, torment another person against whom the 'owner' of the *iki-ryō* may bear a conscious or sub-conscious grudge. The occurrence of this phenomenon appears to be more common in women, with jealousy as the prime cause, but it does affect both sexes. Heian literature contains a wealth of instances of the malignant influence of ghosts and spirits and gives many examples of possession. The latter phenomenon was attributed to the pernicious influence of evil spirits in the form of foxes or badgers, or to the restless and unhappy ghosts of dead ancestors or others with whom the victim of illness or misfortune had some karmic link. The Buddhist idea of karmic retribution has remained an important factor in Japanese life, and persons who had committed some offence against the law of Buddha in a previous existence could expect that this deed would result in calamity or misfortune being visited upon their descendants or themselves in another incarnation. In a climate of inexorable cause and effect, *inga*, religious observances were followed scrupulously, including *kata-imi* (forbidden directions) and *kata-tagae* (forbidden days). *Kata-imi* meant that a certain direction was unlucky on a certain day, and there are many mentions in Heian literature of people either being unable to visit each other because the direction in which they would have had to travel was temporarily out of bounds, or being forced to make long detours so as to arrive from an auspicious direction. *Kata-tagae* meant that certain people, even in key government positions, might find themselves unable to take part in an important function or ceremony due to the fact that the particular day chosen was considered inauspicious and indeed dangerous for them. These beliefs were held by the *kuge* as well as the *buke*, and the deaths of both Taira Kiyomori and Minamoto Yoritomo were surrounded by portents. The *Heike Monogatari* tells of the dream of Taira Kiyomori's wife, in which she saw the attendants of Emma-Ō, the King of Hell, arriving with a cart in which they were to take away her husband after his death. In her dream she asked the reason for this, and received the answer that since her husband had destroyed a statue of the Buddha he had been condemned to the hell without end. In his final illness the body of Taira Kiyomori is said to have become so hot that water poured on him turned into steam, and his horrible end was seen as a punishment for his treatment of Buddhist institutions, and also as proof that his fight against the Minamoto had been unjust.

A major earthquake in Kyoto in 1185 was considered to have been caused by the vengeful spirits of fallen Heike warriors, and Minamoto Yoritomo attempted to appease them by having sutras read in their memory. One of the innumerable legends concerning Minamoto Yoshitsune tells of how the ghosts of Heike warriors who had been drowned in the naval battle of Dan-no-Ura in 1185 rose from the sea, threatening him and his party during a sea voyage, and how these spirits were only subdued through the intervention of Benkei, the warrior-monk, who knew the correct incantations with which to render these ghosts powerless.

Most famous of all the stories concerning the Heike warriors is the popular tale of the *biwa-hōshi* whose ears were wrenched off by a ghost. The *biwa-hōshi* were blind monks who travelled the country, reciting ballads about wars and famous battles to the accompaniment of a *biwa* (Chin. *pi-pa*, a stringed instrument resembling a lute). The epic ballad of the fall of the Heike continued to be popular until modern times. According to the story a young and skilful *biwa-hōshi* found himself approached by a *bushi* with a request to give a recital for a company of people. The performances took place at night, and the blind man was led to the venue by the *bushi* whose hand was covered by a mailed glove. The abbot of the temple where the *biwa-hōshi* was staying suspected foul play, followed him one night, and came upon the blind monk sitting alone among the tombs of fallen Heike warriors, singing his ballad. In order to protect him from further visitations by the ghost the abbot painted the *biwa-hōshi*'s body from head to toe with sacred scripture from the sutras. This rendered the monk invisible to the ghost, but the abbot had forgotten to paint his ears, and since they were the only part of him that the ghost could see when he came to fetch him for his appointment he took hold of them and tore them off.

Minamoto Yoritomo is said to have lived in great fear of vengeful spirits, especially those of the Taira. As we have seen, he tried to pacify the spirits of his fallen enemies by arranging readings of the sutras, and he also refrained from persecuting surviving members of the Taira clan after his victory at Dan-no-Ura. His death in 1199 was caused by a fall from his horse on the way to an inauguration ceremony for a bridge over the Sagami River. The ghosts of his half-brother Yoshitsune, his cousin Yukiie, and of Emperor Antoku, Taira Kiyomori's grandson who drowned at Dan-no-Ura at the age of six, were said to have appeared to him, causing his horse to shy. All ghosts were potentially dangerous, but those who had died as a result of treason or injustice were especially intent on seeking revenge, and thus particularly to be feared, as were the ghosts of those who had not had a proper burial with the customary funeral rites.

The idea that the ghost of a warrior was in possession of especially powerful properties was due to several factors. Most important of these was the position of the *bushi* with regard to Shinto and Buddhism. He read the sutras and said the prayers, visited the temples and shrines, and observed the religious festivals like everyone else, but his profession made it necessary for him to disregard the central tenets of both religions. By taking life the *bushi* placed himself mentally and physically apart from the rest of society. According to Buddhist tenets he was a sinner who would be reborn as an *asura*, an infernal spirit, in one of the many hells. Being associated with death, sickness and blood he had also infringed the most important Shinto injunctions against pollution and was ritually unclean. The *bushi* lived a violent life, since as a warrior he must at all times be prepared to kill and ready to die, by his own hand or on the battlefield. His mind was constantly occupied with matters of life and death, and when he died a violent death his concentrated will-power might continue to wreak havoc after death and direct its spirit of vengeance against former enemies. Groups of vengeful spirits would naturally be more dangerous than an individual, hence the dread in which the spirits of those Heike warriors who had drowned at Dan-no-Ura, and whose bodies had never been recovered, were held. An individual could, however, also deliberately set about becoming a demon, in order to take his revenge for unjust treatment. In the *Hōgen Monogatari* we learn how the deposed and exiled Emperor Sutoku, incensed by the refusal to admit some copies of the sutras, written in his own hand, to a temple in the capital, sank the volumes in the sea after having written a curse in one of them with his own blood and then endeavoured to become a demon. He let his hair and nails grow without trimming them for nine years, while concentrating his mind on evil thoughts until he died in 1164, having 'taken on of his own accord the appearance of a *tengu* while he was still living'.[29] Sutoku's acts and behaviour were thought to have brought about a series of catastrophes which affected the Imperial house and those associated with it.

With the exception of Toyotomi Hideyoshi's Korean campaign, the Japanese did not engage in warfare on foreign soil until modern times. In 1869, the year after the Meiji Restoration, the Shōkon-sha, or 'spirit-invoking', shrine was founded in Tokyo for those who had fallen on the Imperial side. The name of this shrine was later changed to Yasukuni Jinja (Pacification of the Nation) and from the Sino-Japanese War of 1895-96 the spirits of Japanese soldiers fallen in battle have been venerated there. Today they number about half a million. Those enshrined in the Yasukuni Jinja are venerated for their loyalty to their country, and the shrine enjoys great popularity.

More recently it has become the centre of political controversy after several visits by Prime Ministers, Cabinet members and high government officials. The shrine was a focal point of nationalistic and militaristic ideas in the prewar years and during the Second World War. When state control over religious establishments ceased with the postwar constitution, the shrine became dependent on private support for its subsistence, and it is the fact that the Prime Minister has taken to visiting the Yasukuni Jinja on 15 August, the anniversary of Japan's surrender in 1945, in a semi-official capacity that has worried those who are opposed to a revival of nationalistic policies. There is an influential lobby in the Diet whose aim it is to have 15 August officially declared a day of national remembrance of the war dead.

We have seen that the *bushi* were set apart from the rest of society by their customs as well as by their position as holders of the political power. Their customs and ideas will be discussed in the following chapters, but something

should also be said concerning their position in society.
From 1192, when Minamoto Yoritomo was appointed
Shōgun, the *buke* were the undisputed rulers of Japan for
very nearly seven centuries. Apart from the so-called *Kemmu*
Episode (1333-35) when the Emperor Go-Daigō tried to
wrest the political initiative from the by then largely inef-
fectual Hōjō *shikken*, there were no serious attempts to
restore Imperial power until 1868. Go-Daigō was aided by
Ashikaga Takauji, who had been sent by the Kamakura
Bakufu to oppose him, but who, temporarily, went over to
the Imperial side. In the end the *buke* triumphed, as
Ashikaga Takauji proclaimed himself Shōgun and moved
him *Bakufu* to Kyoto. For a time this move seemed to
strengthen the political power of the *bushi*, but with the
unification of the country after the civil wars of the *Sengoku
jidai* Tokugawa Ieyasu displayed the same astute grasp of
political reality as that which had characterised Minamoto
Yoritomo and moved his *Bakufu* to a place in the Kantō
region, far away from the palace intrigues of Kyoto, this
time to Edo.

The Emperor and the *kuge* continued to function much
as they had in the Heian period concerning matters of the
Imperial Court. Government appointments were formally
signed by the Emperor, and Court ceremonies were
performed as they had been since time immemorial. It
should be remembered that most of the important *buke*
families were descended from the younger sons of emperors
or from *kuge* families, and that they were fully conscious
of their ancestry. Lineage, as we have already seen, was of
the utmost importance in Japan, and the main obstacle
preventing Toyotomi Hideyoshi from being formally
appointed to the office of Shōgun was his plebeian birth.
When Minamoto Yoritomo's second son, Sanetomo, was
assassinated in 1219 and the line became extinct, the new
Shōgun was an infant, Kujō Yoritsune (1218-56), whose
father was a Fujiwara and whose mother was the daughter
of Minamoto Yoritomo and Hōjō Masako. He was appointed
at the instigation of his maternal grandmother, the real
powerholder from Yotitomo's death in 1199 until her own
death in 1225. This was the first time a *kuge* held a *buke*
office. Although the two kinds of nobility each preserved
their individual identity and took fierce pride in it, they

were in fact interrelated to a large extent. Over the centuries, as *buke* families rose to prominence or sank into obscurity, and as some were created from humble origins and others became extinct through the fortunes of war or some misdemeanour, we find that the older *buke* families regarded the newly created ones with scorn, and that the term *niwaka daimyo* (sudden lord) was used rather as the terms *homo novus* or *parvenu* were employed respectively in Classical Rome and in France during *l'ancien régime*.

One of the chief characteristics of the lives of the provincial warriors as they gained political power in the late Heian period had been their simple and frugal habits, far removed from the exquisite, not to say precious, refinement and luxury of the Imperial Court. In the *Gunki Monogatari* the blunt speech and rustic manners of the *bushi* were contrasted with great effect against the circumspect behaviour of the *kuge*, whose second nature was innuendo. The distinctions made by the *buke* between themselves and the *kuge* were almost as clear as those between the *buke* and commoners. The samurai had made a virtue out of necessity, leading simple and frugal lives and devoting much time to horsemanship and the use of arms. Like the patricians of ancient Rome they despised those who led soft lives and viewed them with distrust. They regarded themselves as the true exponents of old values, and endeavoured to maintain their lifestyle after the establishment of the Kamakura *Bakufu*. The *Gunki Monogatari* of the early Kamakura period, e.g. the *Hōgen* and *Heike Monogatari*, frequently refer to customs and practices as 'old' or typical of 'the old days', and there was already at this stage a certain amount of harking back to the good old times.

The *Go-seibai Shikimoku*, promulgated in 1232 by the Hōjō after the death of Minamoto Yoritomo, his two sons and his widow, Masako, contains a number of restrictions imposed on the individual lives of the *buke*. The Hōjō legal code called for the utmost restraint where abuse and private quarrels were concerned, well knowing that in the case of *bushi* these might easily lead to feuds and vendettas involving a great deal of bloodshed. There was a certain proviso for unpremeditated killings, especially under the influence of alcohol, but the punishment for premeditated murder was death, banishment, or confiscation of the fief, depending on the circumstances. Kamakura vassals were not allowed to apply directly to the Imperial Court for offices, but were required to have a written recommendation from the *Bakufu*. The only exception from this rule was the office *Kebiishi*, which can be translated as Metropolitan Police Megistrate, which could be invested directly by the Emperor. We may note that fiefs awarded by the *Bakufu* in recognition of merit or valour were regarded as permanent loans rather than the personal property of the vassal, and that they could under no circumstances be bought or sold. Exceptions could only be made concerning privately owned and inherited farming estates in times of financial hardship.

These laws certainly go back to the rules established by Minamoto Yoritomo for his retainers. Throughout the centuries of warrior rule we find the *bushi* being constantly reminded to lead frugal and righteous lives, eschewing ostentation and extravagance. Strict injunctions against wanton spending were repeated in every successive legal code, and the law prescribed the amount of money which could be spent on a gift, depending on the respective rank of donor and recipient as well as on the occasion. These sumptuary laws came to regulate the lives of the *bushi* in every detail, not least where their outward appearance was concerned. The materials used for everyday clothing, as well as those suitable for ceremonial wear, were subject to strict regulations according to the rank of the wearer, and this attention to minute and seemingly trivial detail went so far as to prescribe the colours and patterns permitted for the garments. The size of the retinue allowed to accompany a *daimyo* when travelling, the number of mounted men and the number of foot-soldiers (*ashigaru*), all was determined by law as well as by custom. When the fifth Hōjō *shikken*, Tokiyori (1227-63, regnavit 1246-56) once visited the Tsurugaoka Hachiman Shrine at Kamakura, he sent a message notifying Ashikaga Yoshiuji that he wanted to call on him. In true *bushi* fashion Ashikaga Yoshiuji, who held high rank, offered his guest only three small dishes of dried *awabi* (abalone), shrimps, and *senbei* (dry rice cakes), washed down with three cups of *sake*.

The *kuge* continued to lead their lives in attendance on

the Emperor and his consorts and other members of the
Imperial family much in the same way as before where
ceremonies and dress were concerned, albeit in the shadow
of the *Bakufu.* They had their own strict rules of deportment and the old hierarchy of rank to observe. The *kuge*
were not allowed to mix freely with their inferiors. They
were expressly, and repeatedly, forbidden to move about
the streets at random, whether during the day or night, to
take part privately in sports or games except during public
festivals, and to associate with the *bushi.* The gulf between
kuge and *buke* was emphasised also in the matter of
clothing, certain colours, styles and materials being re-
served for the exclusive use of the Emperor, princes of the
blood, and ministers and court officials of the highest
ranks. Various shades of red, yellow, grey, green and blue,
and more or less elaborate patterns woven into the silk or
sometimes embroidered upon it indicated the wearer's rank.
There were concessions and special privileges for certain
families, and the pervasive note sustained throughout the
Kuge Sho-Hatto, as the legal code regulating the court
nobility became known under Tokugawa rule, is a strong
echo from the Heian court.

In an additional clause from 1714 the *kuge* are advised
that garments, decorations and buildings used in *genbuku*
(coming of age) and wedding celebrations must be kept
within the prescribed limits to avoid ostentation. At times,
especially during the turbulent years of the later Ashikaga
Bakufu and the *Sengoku jidai,* the Imperial court was
reduced to a state of penury. More than one Emperor is
reputed to have sold specimens of his calligraphy in order
to raise cash for his subsistence, and imperial ceremonies,
even funerals, had to be postponed, sometimes for years,
until the necessary funds could be collected.

Although politically powerless the Emperor was treated
with great reverence by the *buke,* including the *Shōgun.*
We have already seen that the Emperor retained the formal
position of head of state by conferring rank and government appointments on those suggested by the *Shōgun,*
and that the office of *Shōgun* itself was made valid only by
the signature of the Emperor. In the *Heike Monogatari* we
are told how Minamoto Yoritomo received the edict from
the *In,* retired, Emperor Go-Shirakawa (1127-92, regnavit

1155-58) pardoning him from the exile into which he had
been sent after the execution of his father in 1159. This
edict had been obtained through the *bona officia* of the
monk Mongaku, formerly a *bushi*, Watanabe Moritō. When
Mongaku appeared in Kamakura announcing that he was
bringing the imperial pardon, Minamoto Yoritomo received
it with great reverence. 'When Yoritomo heard the words
"emperor's edict", he was filled with awe. He washed his
hands, rinsed his mouth, put on a new lacquered bonnet
and a white robe, and bowed three times before the edict.
Then he opened it. (. . .) It is said that Yoritomo put this
edict into a brocade bag and hung it around his neck. He
wore it at all times, even at the battle of Ishibashi-yama.'[30]

Not only did Minamoto Yoritomo put on court dress and
hat, the 'lacquered bonnet' being an *eboshi*, the stiff gauze
hat worn by the *kuge*, in order to receive the imperial edict
with due ceremony, but he also performed the ritual ablutions necessary for approaching a Shinto shrine, actions
which clearly demonstrate the degree of reverence in which
the Emperor was held. In this particular case the Emperor
had retired from office, but continued to rule from behind
the scenes as *In-sei*, and the edict was of the utmost
importance to Minamoto Yoritomo. This imperial pardon
from his exile was in fact the formal sanction he needed in
order to begin the Genji insurrection against the Heike.

While *buke* and *kuge* maintained a largely peaceful co-
existence, usually respecting each other's position, absolute obedience was demanded of the common people. There
were three classes of commoners, peasants, artisans, and
merchants, the latter occupying the bottom rung of the
hierarchical ladder. The feudal system meant that the peasants were virtually stationary, tied to the soil they worked
and the village in which their *uji-gami* was enshrined.
According to the principles of Confucianism the common
people should be treated with benevolence and justice,
while reciprocating with work, dutifully carried out, and
respect. This ideal was not always attainable, and there
were many instances throughout Japanese feudal history
of *daimyo* or their officials treating the peasants of the fief
harshly and indeed cruelly, as well as of peasant risings
and rebellions, *ikki*.

Blind obedience was expected from commoners, who

should dismount when they met a *bushi*, mounted or on foot, on the road, and bow deeply keeping their eyes fixed on the ground. When the train of a travelling *daimyo* passed, other wayfarers as well as the inhabitants of villages through which the *daimyo* and his retinue passed, had to prostrate themselves by the roadside. The *buke* had the power of life and death over the common people, and the right to cut down on the spot anyone who behaved insolently or insultingly. Although they were rare, instances of *tsuji-giri*, 'crossroads cutting', did occur from time to time. This meant that a samurai would wait at a crossroads and cut down the first commoner who happened to come along, in order to test a new blade. Swords were, however, normally tested on the corpses of executed criminals. The practice of *tsuji-giri* seems to have been somewhat more prevalent in the Tokugawa period, especially in the large cities where there was a rowdy element made up of *rōnin*, *otokodate*, and young men of uncertain origin who carried swords and formed part of a criminal underworld. The two former categories, *rōnin* and *otokodate*, will be dealt with in more detail in the following chapter.

To sum up the relations between the different social strata we may quote the famous monk Myōe (1173-1232), who adhered principally to the Kegon and Shingon schools of Buddhism. He was born into a *buke* family, entered a monastery at the age of eight having been orphaned, and took holy orders at the age of sixteen. In 1221 he became political adviser to Hōjō Yasutoki, the first Hōjō *shikken*. In his *Toga-no-o Myōe shōnin Yuikun*, 'Teachings of the Master Myōe of Toga-no-o', he outlined the basis of society quite firmly: 'The monks should behave as it suits monks, and laymen as laymen, and in the same way the Emperor should behave as is fitting for an Emperor, and the vassals as befits vassals. All evils arrive from the infringement of this rule.'[31]

3

Duty, Privilege & Loyalty: Religious & Practical Concerns

PART I: SWORDS AND SWORD-FIGHTING TECHNIQUES

The two swords, one long, *katana*, and one short, *wakizashi*, worn at all times by all adult *bushi* males, came to be regarded as the most important mark of their nobility. It was not until the end of the sixteenth century, however, that the carrying of swords was confined by law to the samurai. The 'sword hunt', *katanagari*, carried out in 1588 on the order of Toyotomi Hideyoshi, was an effective and drastic measure designed to put an end to the state of near anarchy which had reigned during the period of civil war, *Sengoku jidai*. From the Onin War of 1467-77 in the later part of the Ashikaga Bakufu until the decisive battle of Sekigahara in 1600, there was virtually continuous warfare between rival *daimyo* vying for power.

These turbulent times caused serious changes in the fortunes of many *buke* families, and a few commoners were able to become accepted among the ranks of the *bushi*. Most important of these was Toyotomi Hideyoshi (1537-1598), the son of a peasant, who began his career as sandal-bearer to a samurai and was noticed for his intelligence and ability by Oda Nobunaga (1534-1582) one of the greatest warlords of the period. Having already risen to the rank of general, and in command of his own army, Toyotomi Hideyoshi was able to take control of most of the country when Oda Nobunaga was assassinated by Akechi Mitsuhide.

In order to disarm the militant Buddhist clergy which had proved a difficult adversary to Oda Nobunaga ever since he started his campaign by burning down the Enryakuji on Mount Hiei in 1571, and also to put an end to the frequent peasant revolts, *ikki*, which were a feature of the fifteenth and sixteenth centuries, Toyotomi Hideyoshi organised his *katanagari*. District officials were ordered to confiscate all swords belonging to people below the rank of *bushi*, the reason given for this operation being that the blades were to be used for the construction of a temple in Kyoto, the Amida-ga-mine, where Toyotomi Hideyoshi was himself going to be enshrined as Shin Hachiman, the new Hachiman. The gigantic statue of the Buddha planned for this temple was even larger than the *Daibutsu* of the Tōdaiji at Nara. It was far from its completion by the time of Toyotomi Hideyoshi's death, having been severely damaged by the great Kansai earthquake of 1596, and the project was completed by Toyotomi Hideyori. By disarming all commoners and prohibiting them from changing their occupation or, in the case of peasants, to move from their land, Toyotomi Hideyoshi, himself a *parvenu*, laid the foundations for the rigid social system which was to provide the framework for the Tokugawa *Bakufu*. Thus it can be said that Toyotomi Hideyoshi did more to safeguard the privileges of the *bushi* than most people born into the nobility.

In the Heian period the two chief weapons of the *bushi* were the bow and sword. The Japanese longbow is a formidable weapon, with a range of about 60 metres. A variety of arrows were used for different purposes, including those with forked arrowheads for cutting through rope or bamboo poles, half-moon shaped arrowheads for cutting the throat of an enemy, incendiary arrows, and the *kaburaya* (turnip arrows) with bulbous, perforated heads which made a humming noise when fired and which were used to frighten and confuse the enemy. The bow was used both by mounted archers and those on foot, and it continued to be used in battle until the beginning of the Tokugawa *Bakufu*. Halberds with slightly curved blades, *naginata*, were also used, and *bushi* women were taught to use a halberd for purposes of self-defence. Archery contests were popular among the *bushi*, and the bow was also used for hunting, a favourite form of recreation which at the same time provided training in marksmanship as well as horsemanship.

Something ought to be said about firearms in this context. They were first introduced by the Portuguese who landed at Tanegashima in 1542. A successful demonstration of a matchlock gun convinced the Japanese of the usefulness of this new weapon, and after some experimenting they themselves began manufacturing guns, known as *Tanegashima* after the place where they were made, or *teppō* (iron tube). Firearms were certainly used in the battles of the later part of the sixteenth century, but they never superseded the traditional weapons.

There has been much speculation among Western and Japanese scholars why firearms were abandoned in the early Tokugawa period, so soon after their discovery by the Japanese. The reasons for this must have been manifold, but the decisive factor was undoubtedly political. The Tokugawa *Bakufu*, having at long last managed to bring about the unification of the country under one ruler, was extremely careful to eliminate all possible risk of armed risings or conspiracies which might threaten its supremacy. After Toyotomi Hideyoshi's *katanagari* the common people was disarmed, and the last thing the *Bakufu* wanted was to see the peasants wielding weapons again. The Shimabara Rebellion of 1637, largely consisting of disgruntled Christian peasants, was the last in the long line of *ikki* to pose any serious threat to the *Bakufu*, and the quelling of it in blood also meant that Christianity was eradicated in Japan.[32] The *e-fumi* (picture-trampling) ceremony, conducted annually until the nineteenth century, in which the entire population was assembled by village or city ward and made to tread on bronze plaques bearing pictures of the crucified

Christ or the Virgin and Child, ensured that there could be no recurrence of Christianity.

Western influences, which had enjoyed a certain vogue among the *buke*, were thus actively discouraged by the *Bakufu*, and strict laws were enforced in order to prevent the provincial *daimyo* from regaining political strength or independence. No new fortresses were to be constructed, and the existing ones could be maintained but not enlarged or otherwise improved upon. The *daimyo* were subject to the *sankin-kōtai*, a hostage system whereby their families, or at least their sons and heirs, had to be left in the capital when they themselves visited their fiefs.

That the sword, or rather the pair of swords, known as *dai-shō*, took pride of place among the weapons of the *bushi*, and was indeed regarded as more than a weapon of attack and defense, is shown by the wealth of ideas and practices surrounding it. In outward appearance it changed little from the Heian period. Early bronze and iron swords found in a Kofun context or belonging to the Asuka/Nara period were straight and often two-edged. With the development of a cavalry in the Heian period the blade became single-edged and was given a slight curve. The curve adds force to a blow delivered by a mounted swordsman, and the Japanese sword was used primarily for cutting, seldom for stabbing, the opponent.

Later works dealing with swordsmanship, such as the *Honchō Gunkikō* (General History of Military Discipline) by Arai Hakuseki (1657-1725), one of the great Neo-Confucian scholars and statesmen of the Tokugawa *Bakufu* and political adviser to the sixth and seventh Tokugawa Shōguns, Ienobu (regnavit 1707-12) and Ietsugu (regnavit 1712-16), give detailed plans of the different types of cuts to be inflicted on the opponent's body, horizontal and diagonal, from the head downwards, but do not illustrate any place suitable for piercing.[33] The *Gunki Monogatari* occasionally mention the stabbing of an enemy through a chink in his armour, often at the throat, an area difficult to protect.

The technique used in forging the sword was an interesting and highly developed one, which produced steel blades of exceptionally high quality. The best Japanese sword blades were certainly equal to the most famous blades known to the West in the Middle Ages, those from Toledo and Damascus. The Japanese swordsmith repeatedly hammered out and folded the piece of iron which was to become the blade, thus producing an astronomical number of microscopic layers. The result of this technique was a springy and resilient steel blade which, if tempered correctly, did not easily break, chip or crack. The right temperature, both for heating the iron to be worked and for tempering the steel, was essential, and the smith depended on an able assistant to work the bellows. The smith himself determined the right temperature of the water used for tempering and closely guarded this crucial secret of his trade. The famous fourteenth-century swordsmith Masamune is said to have cut off the hand of his apprentice when he caught him surreptitiously dipping it into the tempering-vat.

The forging of the blade, an intricate process which demanded great technical skill and craftsmanship, was surrounded by many religious ceremonies. The smith had to prepare himself through fasting, sometimes for seven days, sexual abstinence, and prayer. He purified himself and the smithy according to Shinto rites, and closed off the smithy with a *shimenawa*, the straw rope which marks a sacred area. The smith wore court robes or the robes of a Shinto priest during the process of forging. These elaborate preparations clearly demonstrate the religious significance accorded to the sword. In order to produce a true and reliable blade the smith had to be pure in mind and body, and should invoke divine assistance.

It is interesting to note that the status of the swordsmith was considerably higher than that of other artisans, including ordinary blacksmiths. In the *Nihongi* there is an account of the making of one thousand swords by an imperial prince, Inishiki no Mikoto, during the reign of Emperor Suinin. According to another version, the prince summoned a swordsmith who made the blades, or assisted the prince in forging them, and in recognition of this feat the prince was granted a number of guilds, *be*. These included the makers of shields, bows, arrows and jewels, as well as the keepers of a store-house for the swords and the members of the sword-wearers' *be*.[34] The reference here is thus to the administrative organisation which preceded the Taika Reform. There are also accounts of Emperors forging swords with their own hands, one of the very few forms of menial work ever mentioned in connection with a sovereign, apart from the ritual planting and harvesting of rice. The latter is practised to this day by the ruling Emperor, in a small rice-paddy within the compound of the Imperial Palace in Tokyo and goes back to early ideas, probably influenced by Chinese beliefs, of the microcosm as a reflection of the macrocosm. By tending his own little rice-field the Emperor symbolically cares for those of the entire country, ensuring a bountiful harvest through his virtue and charisma as a ruler, a phenomenon which is well known in many cultures the world over. The retired Emperor Go-Toba (1180-1239, regnavit 1184-1198) is said to have ordered a smithy to be erected in his place of exile. There he himself forged sword blades, known as *Gosho-kaji* (Palace blacksmith) with the assistance of twelve swordsmiths. His blades were engraved with a chrysanthemum, the imperial emblem.

Having purified himself before embarking on his work, sometimes even having gone on a pilgrimage before commencing work on a particularly important blade, the smith continued his purification throughout the process of forging by means of daily ablutions in cold water. This is the customary way of achieving physical and mental purity in Shinto, and it is done either by pouring over the body a fixed number of buckets of cold water daily, or by standing under a waterfall for the duration of a number of prayers. The purification rite takes place out of doors, regardless of the weather or the season of the year. Women, who might be ritually impure through menstruation, were never allowed within the precincts of the smithy, and as we have seen the smith was to have no contact with women for the duration of the process of forging the blade. This could be a lengthy process. Minamoto Mitsunaka (912-997) one of Minamoto Yoritomo's forefathers, commissioned a master swordsmith to make him two swords, a process which required sixty days of tempering and produced two famous blades, known as *Hizamaru* and *Higekiri*, 'Knee-cutter' and 'Beard-cutter', which became Minamoto family heirlooms.

In his prayers the swordsmith invoked the aid of Shinto as well as Buddhist deities. Inari, the Shinto deity of rice, and hence also of wealth, whose messenger is the white fox, was regarded as a special patron of swordsmiths. Nine

Shinto deities are worshipped in the main Inari shrine at Fushimi, outside Kyoto. Male and female, they represent different aspects of rice fields, harvest and food, and include Ō-kuni-nushi-no-kami (Great land-possessor deity), who is also worshipped at Izumo. This deity is also known under a number of other names which allude to his warlike qualities, such as Utsushi-kuni-tama-no-kami (Living-land-spirit-deity), i.e. the leader of the heroes of the nation, Yachi-hōkō-no-kami (Eight-thousand-spears-deity), and Ashihara-shikō-ō-no-kami (Reed-plain-prince-male-deity). These qualities made him a popular deity among military men, and it is easy to see why Inari, through this association with bravery in war and heroic exploits, became a patron of swordsmiths. A festival known as *Fuijo-matsuri* (Bellows festival), or *Hi-taki-sai* (Fire-lighting festival), was celebrated at the Fushimi Inari Shrine, and said to be in remembrance of the swordsmith Kojaku Munechika, who had fetched clay to be used in the process of tempering the cutting edge of the blade on the mountain, Inari Yama, on which the Fushimi Inari is constructed, and prayed there. With the aid of the deity, who worked the bellows, he is said to have forged an exceptional blade, the legendary *Ko-kitsune* (little Fox) for Emperor Ichijō (regnavit 987-1011).

There are many similar stories of divine assistance to the smith, and visions of Kannon seem to have been especially prevalent. The sword of Minamoto Yoshitsune is said to have been forged by a smith who uttered the name of Amida Buddha with every stroke of the hammer. The connection of Buddhist deities with the sword goes back to the many Buddhist ideas of the sword as a weapon against all forms of evil influences. As mentioned above, all Buddhist temples were guarded by sword-wielding, fierce-looking deities, the Niō-ō or 'Heavenly Kings', who were ready to repel all enemies of the faith. Fudō Myō-ō, the terrible aspect of Mahāvairoçana Buddha, also carries a sword with which to quell demons and evil influences.

We have also noted another aspect, namely the Sword of *Prajña*, 'Wisdom', 'Knowledge' or 'Insight', which is carried by Monju (Sanskrit: Manjuśrī). The ideas and intellectual speculation which the concept of the Sword of *Prajña* give rise to in the minds of certain eminent swordsmen will be discussed below, in connection with different sword-fighting techniques, esoteric as well as practical.

The profession of swordsmith was hereditary, as most Japanese crafts, and if there was no son who was considered skilful enough to take over after his father an heir would be adopted, a common Japanese practice. Not a few of the famous swordsmiths were of *bushi* stock, as were those who cleaned and polished sword blades professionally.The latter were often experts, who examined blades and established their authenticity and provenance. In the Tokugawa period the Honami family had a virtual monopoly on the examination and judging of swords, and the head of the family was considered to be the leading authority of his time.

Swordsmiths usually signed their works on the tang of the blade, so that the signature was only visible when the sword was dismounted. It was not uncommon to rework blades later, for example shortening the blade or altering the curve of the tip. In this case the smith doing the alterations might efface the original inscription, or add his own signature to it. Proud owners of blades by famous master swordsmiths sometimes had the name of the smith inlaid in gold on the blade itself, below the hilt, so that it was visible also when the blade was mounted. A change of mounting was not infrequent, and in that case the tang often had to be pierced in a different place to accommodate the pin which fixed the tang in the hilt.

The names of deities were frequently inscribed on the blade, just below the hilt where the inscription would be visible, and images of Fudō or of a dragon were also common motifs. The inscriptions were mostly in the form of *bonji*, or cyphers, modified Sanskrit characters which represented the names of Buddhist deities. Buddhas mentioned were Dainichi (Sanskrit: Vairoçana), Ashuku (Sanskrit: Akśobhya), Yakushi and Shaka (Sanskrit: Śākyamuni) four of the five *Nyōrai* or Buddhas of healing of the Shingon school, and Amida (Sanskrit: Amitābha), the lord of the Western Paradise. The bodhisattvas whose *bonji* were recorded included several of the different forms of Kannon (Sanskrit: Avalokiteśvara), Jizō (Sanskrit: Kśithigarbha), Monju (Sanskrit: Manjuśrī), Fugen (Sanskrit: Samantha-bhadra), Miroku (Sanskrit: Maitreya), and Seishi (Sanskrit:

Mahāsthāmaprāpta). The names of minor Buddhist deities, such as Fudō and other Myō-ō were also found among the *bonji*, together with those of Daikokuten (Sanskrit: Mahā-kāla), Benzaiten or Benten (Sanskrit: Sarasvatī) and Bisha-monten (Sanskrit: Vaiśravana), also known as Tamonten or Kubera (Kubira), three of the Seven Gods of Luck.

Among the purely Hindu deities we find Marishi (Marīcī), Seiten or Suiten (Varuṇa), Taishakuten (Indra) and Kōjin (Rudra). The last two are gods of war, brute force and destruction in the Hindu mythology. We may note that the Buddhas and bodhisattvas whose names appear among the *bonji* represent mercy, healing and salvation, and that the other deities also possess characteristics auspicious for a warrior, e.g. valour, forcefulness and steadfastness. The presence of the *bonji* on the blade served a dual purpose. It offered the owner of the sword protection from evil influences and helped to imbue him with a firm sense of purpose and a warlike spirit, like that of Fudō Myō-ō for example, and it also provided him with the chance of a favourable rebirth if he met his death in battle grasping the hilt of his sword.

Another common inscription on the tang of a blade was the record of a test carried out with the sword. It was customary to test the quality, especially of new blades, on the corpses of executed criminals. This was known as *tameshigiri*, the corpse being called a *tameshi mono* (chopping block). *Bushi* used to go to the execution ground, bringing with them blades they wanted to try out, and the servants in charge of the place would pile corpses on one another. A blade of exceptional quality could cut through the corpses of three men with one blow, according to the records, and it was certainly possible with a good blade to cut the body of an adult man in half. A sword which could not cut off a man's head with one stroke was considered useless. Some of the early foreign travellers in Japan in the sixteenth and seventeenth centuries record having seen corpses by the roadside which had been used for the testing of blades, and although it was discouraged, and indeed forbidden by law, the practice of *tsuji-giri* (cross-roads cutting) the cutting down of an innocent wayfarer in order to test a sword, did occur when the opportunity arose.

One of the most famous of the early Western observers

of Japan, and the only one to have given a comprehensive account of the country as it was before the Tokugawa *Bakufu*, the Portuguese Jesuit priest João Rodrigues (1561-1633) described the testing of swords in his *História da Igreja do Japao*: 'They wonder at the civil practice of killing tame and domestic animals and things of that sort, for they show great pity and compassion in this respect. But they do not feel this when they kill men in a bloodthirsty way and test their swords on the corpses, and they excuse this. Some lords may ask other nobles for some men who have been condemned to death in order to see whether their sword cuts well and whether they can trust it in emergencies. They often sew up bodies which have been cut up by swords and put together the severed parts so that they may once more cut and see whether their sword passes through a body with one blow. They indulge in this and other types of slaughter and leave the bodies in the fields for the birds and dogs and do not bury them. The delight and pleasure which they feel in cutting up human bodies is astonishing, as is also the way that young boys sometimes indulge in this.'[35] The Swede Olof Eriksson Willman, who travelled to Japan in Dutch service in 1651-1652, and who was a member of the party which made the journey to Edo, mentions seeing what may have been a victim of a *tsuji-giri* while travelling from Suruga to Hakone along the *Tōkaidō* (Eastern Sea) road: 'We saw along the way (. . .) a man who was cut down with one blow from the shoulders to his midriff; he lay dead on the road since no-one wanted to burn him up'.[36]

Swords were sometimes given names in order to commemorate some particular feat which had been performed with them, the manner of their acquisition by a certain family, or the circumstances in which they had been forged. Such well-known swords were highly valued and became treasured family heirlooms. We have already mentioned the sword by Munechika called *Ko-kitsune* (Little Fox), which was handed down through the centuries among the descendants of Emperor Ichijō. The great heirloom of the Taira clan was the sword known as *Ko-garasu* (Little Crow), which according to family legend was said to have been brought from Ise Shrine by a gigantic crow with a wingspan of eight feet.

Among swords owned by the Minamoto clan two blades, the *Higekiri* and *Hizamaru*, have already been mentioned. The most celebrated sword of the Minamoto was however called *Shishi Ō* (Lion King). It was given by the Emperor Konoe (regnavit 1151-1153) to Minamoto Yorimasa as a reward for the killing of a monstrous spirit which haunted the Emperor. In the *Heike Monogatari* we are told how Minamoto Yorimasa invoked Hachiman, and with one arrow, which he shot into a threatening black cloud, felled a *nue*, a chimaera with the head of a monkey, the body of a badger, the tail of a snake, and the feet of a tiger. This fabulous creature was thought to be able to steal the soul of a human being away from the body. As a token of his gratitude the Emperor gave Yorimasa the *Shishi Ō*, a famous sword, and it was presented to him by the *Sadaijin*, the Minister of the Left, the highest court official below the *Daijo-Daijin* or 'Great Chancellor', who received the sword from the hands of Emperor Konoe and descended halfway down the steps in order to hand it to Yorimasa, who was also asked to choose one of the court ladies for himself.[37]

The swordsmith was considered to instil something of his own personality into the sword he was forging, hence the importance given to his mental preparation for his work and the prayers said during the actual process. The great fourteenth-century swordsmith Masamune (born 1264) had a reputation for making swords which were benevolent and would avoid shedding blood if possible. His mentally unstable disciple Muramasa, on the other hand, is said to have made blades which were particularly malevolent and bloodthirsty. There are many stories about the testing of blades made by these two swordsmiths, and how their inherent power was revealed. According to one account the blades were suspended from a bridge into a stream where fallen leaves came floating by. The leaves seemed to avoid the Masamune blade, floating on unscathed, but when the Muramasa blade was put into the water the leaves were drawn to it and cut in half. Indeed Muramasa's swords were said to drive their owners to commit murder or suicide, and this sinister reputation was so powerful that the wearing of these swords became subject to legal regulations. Thus owners of Muramasa blades were not allowed to wear them except in battle.

Generally speaking, it may be said that swords became famous and were treasured for three reasons: because of the skill and reputation of the smith, because of a particular feat which was performed with them, or because of the position of the donor or the circumstances surrounding their acquisition. Swords were exchanged as tokens of friendship, and a girl of such remarkable ugliness as to be considered unmarriageable might be asked for in marriage on condition that an especially fine sword form part of her dowry.

In his memoirs, *Oritaku Shiba no Ki* (Told Round a Brushwood Fire), written in 1716-17, Arai Hakuseki mentions a suit of armour which he had bought with a large sum of money given by his lord, the *Daimyo* of Kai, who later became the sixth Tokugawa Shōgun, Ienobu (1662-1712, regnavit 1707-1712), when his house had been devastated by a fire. Arai kept the armour and a sword which had been a gift from his lord constantly by his side, thus saving them when his house burned down again. He asked his heirs likewise to preserve these momentoes of his lord and pass them on to their descendants. From his father Arai had received a sword called *Shishi* (Lion), with which a friend of his father had sliced off the top of a man's head with one blow. His father had asked him never to part with this sword and to let it remain in the family. Arai describes his father as a man of great and uncompromising character, who lived his entire life according to the strictest *bushi* standards, adhering to old-fashioned ways. Their conversations, as recorded by Arai, are an interesting example of how the principles of *Bushidō* were transmitted from father to son.

We may trace Arai's reverence for the gifts from his lord to his father's account of how Arai's grandfather always used the same pair of chopsticks at his meals. They were kept in a black lacquer box with gold decorations, and had been a gift from his general, who had offered him his own meal tray after a battle as a reward for an important enemy head taken on the battle-field that day. Concerning swords Arai's father told him, with an example from his own impetuous youth, never to discuss the quality of his blade in public. It ought to be self-evident that no samurai would wear a sword of inferior quality. This way of reasoning is quite similar to the code of European chivalry, where the mere mention of honour was to imply the possibility of its opposite.[38]

The markings on the blade, resulting from the tempering process which produced a wave pattern along the cutting edge, were regarded as lucky or unlucky, depending on their shape, and it was thought possible to tell the fortune of the wearer by the markings on his blade. The proportions of the blade, i.e. the length of the tang in relation to that of the entire blade, were adjusted to produce a propitious figure. The signing of the finished blade was the moment when the sword was invested with its *tama* (vital spirit), and for this ceremony the swordsmith wore the robes of a Shinto priest. Armour could indeed also be imbued with a spirit of its own. Of the famous eight suits of armour which were among the heirlooms of the Minamoto clan, one of them, known as *Hizamaru* (Knee Suit of Armour), was always inherited by the eldest son. The plates of this suit were laced together with thongs made from the sinews of the knees of one thousand bulls, and the armour was said to be possessed by the spirit of a bull. The spirit would appear to the owner of the armour, manifesting displeasure if he had eaten meat, and the person who cleaned the armour had to abstain from meat and purify himself before undertaking the work.[39] It was also believed that a suit of armour and a helmet left in a house afforded protection against evil spirits.On the eleventh day of the first month it was the custom for a *bushi* to make an offering of a *mochi*, rice dumpling, to his suit of armour.

The sword was regarded as a powerful protection against evil spirits. This idea closely resembles the folk beliefs of Europe, as well as other parts of the world, that steel, and especially an implement with a sharp cutting edge such as a knife, dagger, or sword, offers protection against evil, witchcraft and sorcery. When a samurai died, a sword was placed by the bier before the corpse was taken from the house, and a sword was also put in the room of a newly-born child.

As the chief weapon of the *bushi* the sword came to be regarded almost as part of the man and as an extension of his personality, and there was a great deal of truth in the saying 'The sword is the soul of the samurai'. To confirm the taking of a vow, the *bushi* would strike his sword so that it gave off a ringing sound. It was constantly about his person, since no *bushi* would be out of reach of his sword for a moment, not even in his own house and in the company of his family. The state of the sword reflected the honour of its wearer, whose duty it was to polish his blade and keep it spotless at all times.

Sword furniture was one of the very few luxuries a *bushi* could permit himself. As mentioned earlier, blades were occasionally reworked to suit the current fashion, while mountings were more frequently changed. The hilt was usually covered with *same*, shagreen, which, being knobbly, afforded a secure grip, and laced with silk cord in a criss-cross pattern. The scabbard was made of wood, usually lacquered, sometimes covered with leather, and some early illustrations show *bushi* carrying swords in fur-covered scabbards. The upper part of the scabbard had silk cords attached, with which it could be secured to a suit of armour or other garments, and a number of small appurtenances were fastened to the hilt and scabbard. The two pommels, *kashira* and *fuchi*, one at each end of the hilt, were usually decorated, often with inlaid patterns in gold or silver. Small metal ornaments, *menuki*, miniature representations of animals, landscapes or mythological scenes, were threaded into the laces on the hilt to provide an even more secure grip. A small skewer, *kōgai*, a dirk, *kozuka*, or a pair of metal chopsticks, *wari-bashi*, with handles decorated in similar style, were frequently attached to the scabbard. The *kōgai* was used by the *bushi* for arranging his hair in the characteristic top-knot. In a feud the *kozuka* could be used as a 'visiting card', and was left stuck in the ear of the severed head of an enemy who had been killed, in order to show who had done the deed.

The *tsuba*, swordguard, provided great scope for decoration and was often inlaid in gold or silver with animal or flower motifs, landscapes, or scenes from mythology and legend. The decorative appendages and the colour of the scabbard and cords were considered to be so indicative of the owner's personal character and taste that people were not infrequently able to identify the owner merely by seeing his swords. In a famous anecdote Toyotomi Hideyoshi, who admittedly appears to have possessed more than the ordinary share of psychological insight, is said to have been able to identify correctly the respective owners of five pairs of swords left on the sword-rack, *katana-kake*, outside a reception room at his palace, guided by his knowledge of their owners' characters and temperaments.

Being so closely identified with its owner, the sword was treated with the utmost reverence. With everyday clothes the pair of swords was worn stuck into the sash on the left side, and two samurai passing each other in a city street or on a narrow bridge always kept to the left, so that there would be no chance of their scabbards knocking against each other. This was considered a deadly insult, and cause for a duel, unless the offending party apologised immediately. Two *bushi* could, however, confirm mutual vows of friendship by touching swords, a practice called *kinchō*. Once a sword had been fully drawn it could not as a rule be returned unused to the scabbard without dishonour to its owner. Even in poverty and adversity it was a matter of honour for the *bushi* to look after his blade, which needed regular cleaning and polishing in order to remain bright and free from rust, especially in the damp summer months. It was the last possession a poverty-stricken samurai would part with, and he would rather starve than sell his swords.

When visiting a superior a *bushi* would usually leave his swords outside the room on the special wooden rack, *katana-kake*, which was often lacquered and inlaid with mother-of-pearl and a work of art in itself. The short sword, *wakizashi*, could however be brought into the room by a *bushi* visiting another of equal rank. It was then always placed on the owner's right, with the hilt towards his host, to demonstrate that his intentions were friendly and to ensure that it could not be easily drawn. When a blade was offered for examination it was customary to hand it to the person inspecting it with the cutting edge facing the person handing it over. A similar procedure is of course prevalent in the West, where one always hands over knives or scissors or any implement with a point or sharp edge with the handle towards the person one is giving it to.

The awe in which the common people held the samurai generally applied also to their swords, which were regarded as extensions of the owner's person as well as insignia of his social status. An anecdote told by an acquaintance of the author's, who visited Japan in the 1930s, will illustrate how tenacious this custom was. Before the Second World War all Japanese officers carried swords when in uniform. On one occasion the visitor and a Japanese officer were the first to arrive at a small rural ferry which was to take them across a river. Waiting for the ferryman and other passengers to appear they stepped onto the boat. The officer laid his sword along the railing, and the two men then stood talking, looking across to the other shore. When they happened to turn around after some time they discovered a queue of prospective passengers waiting on the shore. None of them had dared to embark, as this would have entailed stepping over the officer's sword, an act of gross disrespect.

Swords were considered eminently suitable gifts among the *bushi*, and they were commonly given by feudal lords to their vassals. As we shall see below concerning *bushi* loyalty, there existed in feudal Japan nothing like the legally binding contract drawn up between lord and vassal in medieval Europe. The sword, however, was one token of the feudal relationship in Japan, and it was also given as a reward for outstanding acts of bravery on the battle-field or other services rendered. One of the privileges of a *bushi* was the exclusive right to be executed with a sword if found guilty of a crime. Commoners were executed by means of crucifixion or other methods. Although it was regarded as shameful to be executed by the public headsman, a form of punishment which resulted in the head being gibbetted for a period, with a tablet giving an account of the nature of the crime committed, the fact that a sword was used at least set the samurai apart from and above the common people, even *in extremis*. An honourable form of execution was the performance of *seppuku*, suicide by cutting open the abdomen, a punishment to which *bushi* could be sentenced if there were extenuating circumstances. This practice will be discussed below.

Swords played an important part in early Japanese mythology. In the *Kojiki* and the *Nihongi* we learn how Susanoo no Mikoto, God of the Storm and turbulent younger brother of the Sun Goddess, Amaterasu Ō Mikami, vanquished a dragon which had terrorised the countryside. When cutting the monster open from heads to tails (it had eight of each), Susanoo found a sword in the middle tail. This became one of the three Imperial regalia of Japan, the other two being the sacred mirror kept in Amaterasu's shrine at Ise and the sacred *magatama*, often translated as 'jewel', a comma-shaped jade bead of the traditional type found already in a late Jōmon context.

The sacred Imperial sword, said to be the very one found by Susanoo in the dragon's tail, was known as the *Ame no Murakumo no tsurugi* (The Village Clouds under Heaven Sword), or *Kusanagi no tachi* (The Grass-slashing or Herb-quelling Sword). This sword was an important symbol of the ruling Emperor's power and regarded as an embodiment of his military protection. During the *Gempei* War this sword was brought into the field with the child-Emperor Antoku, grandson of Taira Kiyomori, and was lost in the sea when the Taira forces were defeated at Dan-no-ura. In the *Heike Monogatari* there is a vivid account of how the Emperor's grandmother threw herself into the sea clasping the little Antoku and the sword.

The disappearance of the sacred sword created great confusion, and in the *Heike Monogatari* it is explained that there were in fact three Imperial swords, one kept at the Iso no kami Shrine, one at Atsuta Shrine, and one at the Imperial court. The sacred sword kept at Iso no kami Jingū was said to have the power to maintain peace in the country. It was used in a dance performed by the *Mikanko*, Palace medium, in the *Chinkonsai* ceremony for the 'veneration and pacification of the souls of the Emperor and Empress', *Mitama o agame shizume*. Since the soul of the sovereign was considered especially numinous and imbued with power this ceremony took place during the lifetime of the Emperor and Empress in order to ensure that they would enjoy long and prosperous lives. Illness was believed to be due either to the soul of another having taken possession of the body, or to the person's own soul having temporarily left it. The 'pacifying' or 'fixing' of the soul was thus a means of restoring or maintaining health. The text of the *Chinkonsai* ceremony contains a direct reference to the sword of the Iso no kami Jingū: '*Iso no kami, furu yashiro no, tachi mo ga to, negafu sono ko ni, sono tatematsuru*' — 'The great sword of Furu Iso no kami, which she says she wants, we present it to her with respect'.[40]

The commentaries appear to agree that the sword which was lost at Dan-no-ura was the *Ame-no-Murakumo* or *Kusanagi*, but there are conflicting accounts whether this sword was kept at the Atsuta Shrine. The *Heike Monogatari* claims that Yamato Takeru bequeathed this sword, which he had used to quell a rebellion in Suruga, to the Atsuta Shrine, but from the time of Emperor Temmu it is said to have been kept at the Imperial court. Already while at the Atsuta Shrine the sword manifested its supernatural powers. A Korean, Dōkyō, who stole it and attempted to take it to his own country, was forced to return the sword when a violent storm threatened to wreck his ship. The Emperor Yozei, who was ill, is said to have unsheathed the sword one night and to have been frightened when looking at the blade, which flashed like lightning and returned of its own accord to its scabbard when he threw it down.

After the battle of Dan-no-ura there were many rumours concerning the sword lost at sea. There were claims that Emperor Sujin had had replicas made of both the sword and the mirror, and that the sword lost in the sea was in fact not the original. *Ama*, women pearl divers, were however sent down repeatedly in order to search for the sword, although their efforts were of no avail.

There was much discussion among contemporary scholars concerning the significance of the disappearance of the sacred sword, one of the central problems being the question why Amaterasu, supreme protectress of the Empire, had permitted this turn of events. The *Heike Monogatari* quotes an anonymous scholar who gave the event a numerological interpretation: 'The great serpent that was killed by Susanoo-no-Mikoto long ago at the upper part of the Higawa River must have borne a grudge because of the loss of the sword. Therefore with his eight heads and eight tails, he has entered into the eight-year-old emperor after eighty generations, and has taken the sword back to the depths of the sea'.[41] Jien (1155-1225), author of the *Gukanshō* (Miscellany of Ignorant Views), a history of Japan written around 1220, discussed the loss of the sacred sword at some length and regarded the event as a divine sign indicating the shift in political power which occurred during his own lifetime. 'The birth of this sovereign (Emperor Antoku) was an act of divine grace performed by the Great

Shining Kami of Itsukushima Shrine in the province of Aki, an act brought about by the prayers of Taira Kiyomori. Word has come down to us that the Kami of this Itsukushima Shrine was a daughter of the Dragon King. In response to Kiyomori's faith, this Kami was incarnated as Emperor Antoku. People acquainted with the situation said: 'At last she has returned to the sea!'[42]

These ideas are very close to those quoted above from the *Heike Monogatari*, but Jien then went on to express his own conclusions. 'The loss of the Imperial Sword was a really sad thing for Imperial Law. In turning over the thought that a Principle had probably been created which would enable us to understand this event, I have come to the conclusion that since present conditions have taken such a form, and soldiers have emerged for the purpose of protecting the sovereign, the Imperial Sword turned its protective function over to soldiers and disappeared into the sea. One reason for reaching this conclusion is that a sword called the long sword (*tachi*) was a soldier's original military weapon, and so the Imperial Sword became the Emperor's military talisman.

'The nation's sovereign rules the state by following two ways: the way of military might (*bu*) and the way of learning (*bun*). The way of learning is associated with the Emperor in the phrase: "He inherits the throne and protects learning", and so a Confucian scholar is customarily attached to the Emperor. (. . .) With respect to the military way of ruling the state, the two ancestral Kami of the Imperial House have provided protection—until these final reigns—with this Imperial talisman. But then the Sun Goddess and the Great Hachiman Bodhisattva reached this agreement: "Clearly there is now a time fate (*jiun*) which makes it impossible, since great military Shoguns have definitely gained control of the state, for the country's ruler to survive if he openly opposes the wishes of the great military Shoguns." Consequently, the Imperial Sword no longer has a function to perform. Emperor Takakura was placed on the throne by the Taira clan in 1168, and the Imperial military talisman was finally lost in 1185. Understanding clearly why the Imperial military talisman was lost, I have come to feel deeply about conditions of the present age.'[43]

Having lived through the downfall of Imperial power and

the rise to glory of the Minamoto Shōguns, and being himself related to the newly adopted infant Shōgun Yoritsune, Jien appears to have been striving for a conciliatory interpretation of recent historical events. He argued that while the supreme symbol of Imperial power might be lost, its inherent significance had been passed on to the new ruler. 'After the Imperial Sword sank to the bottom of the sea, military Shoguns seized control of Japan and, doing as they pleased, placed Land Stewards in various provinces. (. . .) After the Imperial Sword was lost, was not its virtue (*toku*) passed to a human Shogun?'[44]

The sacred sword has been used in the enthronement ceremony of a new Emperor since the beginning of historical records. The practice probably goes back to prehistoric times. The concept of the sword as a symbol of the ruler's power is very ancient, and can be found in many parts of the world. We have already seen that the sword was also regarded as a powerful antidote against evil spirits and malignant influences of various kinds. In the *Ō-harai* (Great Purification) ceremony, a Shinto rite performed by the Emperor twice every year for the benefit of the entire Empire, a sword was symbolically touched by the sovereign and then removed. By breathing on or touching the sword the Emperor transferred to it any impurities adhering to himself, or indeed to his realm and people, and purified them. The Emperor received swords as gifts or forms of tribute from his subjects, and himself gave swords to temples and shrines, sometimes as votive offerings. The *Kojiki* and the *Nihongi*, as well as the early legal codes, provide a wealth of instances of this, which appears to have been standard practice.

If we consider the religious significance of swords in general, and the importance which the samurai gave to his chief weapons, which were also the insignia of his status in society, it seems a natural consequence that the actual use of the sword was also surrounded by religious ideas, many of them esoteric in nature. The *bushi* were trained in swordsmanship and sword-fighting techniques from boyhood. Tuition was, as is customary in Japan, largely by example, transmitted from father to son and from older to younger member of the household. Very few *bushi* lived in isolation, as those in the service of a *daimyo* or other feudal lord were attached to the household of their lord, living on the estate or nearby.

From the *Sengoku jidai* onwards there were the so-called *jōkamachi* (castle towns), literally 'town below the castle', which grew up around major fortresses. They were populated by the *bushi* of different rank in the *daimyo's* employ, as well as by menial servants of various kinds. Thus we must imagine large 'extended families' of *bushi*, all living in close proximity, working together as guards and administrative officials. Their sons were educated together in the local school, or, if they were of sufficient rank or showed exceptional promise, with the sons of the feudal lord under special tutors.

The first actual treatises on sword-fighting techniques were written down only during the early part of the Tokugawa *Bakufu*. The earlier House Laws contain certain hints on strategy and general behaviour, but it seems clear that like so many other skills the art of sword-fighting was taught rather like the martial arts in today's Japan, e.g. Judō and Kendō, through practical example and instruction by a master of the art. The tradition of 'scriptureless transmission' belongs to Zen Buddhism, and the earliest treatises on the art of the sword were strongly influenced by Zen Buddhist ideas. Typical among these ideas was the quality known as *fudōshin* (immobility of heart) which had been cultivated by the *bushi* from the introduction of Zen Buddhism during the early Kamakura *Bakufu*. The warrior stood in special need of an unperturbable mind which could remain calm and collected regardless of his surroundings and circumstances or the pressure of events, and *fudōshin* became a central tenet of swordsmanship. The *bushi* must above all learn to act coolly and after due deliberation, since a hasty word would lead to immediate action, and a sword once drawn could not be returned to the scabbard unused.

The famous master of sword-fighting Miyamoto Musashi (1584-1645?) who fought in the battle of Sekigahara, then wandered around the country as a *rōnin*, practising his theories on swordsmanship, and in his later years lived the life of a recluse, wrote his *Go Rin Shō* (Book of Five Rings), in 1645 as a kind of philosophical treatise on the mental as well as the physical art of swordsmanship. Mental discipline and physical training were considered to be equally important. The same applied to another celebrated master of the sword, Yagyū Tajima no Kami Munenori (1571-1646) who composed a treatise on swordsmanship for the use of his sons in 1632. Technical skill without the correct mental attitude was a waste of time, and both Miyamoto and Tajima urged a severe mental discipline which entailed a constant alertness and awareness which bordered on the attainment of a sixth sense. Both authors employed terms such as *mushin* (no-mind), *munen* (no-thought), *tomaranu kokoro* (the mind that knows no stopping), and *fudōshin* (immobility of heart), to describe the state of mind and mental preparation required of the man who wanted to be able to survive a duel with an adversary or, equally important, to carry out his own suicide with dignity and equanimity.

The masters of sword-fighting generally displayed a remarkable psychological insight, and an ability to sum up and anticipate the mood and intentions of an adversary in an instant. Like the masters of Zen Buddhism the masters of sword-fighting advocated emptiness. The mind had to be cleansed of all plans, schemes, and pre-conceived notions until it was like a mirror, reflecting instantly whatever crossed its surface. Having attained this state, the mind was free to act immediately without the slightest hesitation or hindrance. 'To attain the Way of strategy as a warrior', wrote Miyamoto Musashi, 'you must study fully other martial arts and not deviate even a little from the Way of the warrior. With your spirit settled, accumulate practice day by day, and hour by hour. Polish the twofold spirit heart and mind, and sharpen the twofold gaze perception and sight. When your spirit is not in the least clouded, when the clouds of bewilderment clear away, there is the true void.'[45]

Another treatise from the 1630s, the anonymous *Heihokadenshō* (A Book on Strategy and Tactics in Victory and Defeat), again shows a strong Zen Buddhist influence. The eternal problem of the *bushi* acting against the precepts of religion is dealt with from the point of view of righteousness, and the end is said to justify the means. 'It was said of old: 'The fighting man is an ill-omened instrument; the Way of Heaven has no love for him, yet has to make use of him, and this is the Way of Heaven.' (. . .) Ten thousand people are oppressed by the wickedness of one man, and by killing that one man the other ten thousand are given new life. So there the sword which kills is indeed a blade which gives life. There is righteousness in using the arts of fighting in this way. Without righteousness, it is merely a question of killing other people and avoiding being killed by them.'[46]

Concerning training, we find the ideas of Miyamoto Musashi and Yagyū Tajima no Kami echoed again: 'Forgetting the training, throwing away all minding about it so that I myself have no idea about it—to reach that state is the peak of the Way. This state is passing through training till it ceases to exist.' (. . .) 'There is a Zen saying, "the great action is direct and knows no rules". "Direct" means that the action of a man of full inner awareness appears directly; and the fact that the action of a man of such awareness is not bound by any of the training principles he has learned, or by any established ways of doing a thing, is expressed by the words "knows no rules".' (. . .) 'Awareness means never to lose inner clearness, to see in everything its real point.'[47]

A treatise published in 1730 by a man called Tamba, who wrote under the *nom-de-plume* Chissai, goes under the title *Tengugeijutsuron* (Treatise on the Tengu Art of Fighting), a name no doubt chosen for its superior connotations. As we have already noted, the *Tengu* were reputed to possess, among their other supernatural skills, a complete mastery of sword-fighting techniques. Under exceptional circumstances, such as in the case of youthful Minamoto Yoshitsune, a lonely and exiled scion of a house of legendary warriors, they could even be prevailed upon to impart their skills to mere mortals. The *Tengugeijutsuron* contains a succinct definition of swordsmanship which gives a clear indication of the *bushi*'s traditional attitude towards life and death. 'Swordsmanship is an art at the meeting of life and death. To throw away life and die is easy; to make no distinction between death and life is difficult.'[48]

These instances of mental discipline are quite straightforward, displaying acute psychological awareness and insight. Other techniques, of an esoteric nature, were however also advocated. The *kiai* (spirit-meeting) shout which is still used today in the martial arts, was seen not only as an expression of concentrated mental and physical energy but also as a means of achieving feats of a supernatural kind. The master of the *kiai* technique was thought to be able to actually stun his opponent, disarm him, stop him in his tracks, or petrify him in an exposed striking position. The technique was even claimed to make the expert capable of seeing in the dark and of being able to break his opponent's sword by sheer will-power. Ideas of this kind have found their way into the many stories concerning the allegedly supernatural powers of the *ninja*, hired spies and assassins who dressed in black and carried out night raids. They were trained as cat-burglars and able to scale seemingly impossible walls, and their mastery at concealment and stealth led to numerous legends about their supposedly magical feats. Needless to say, the genuine and highly skilled exploits of the *ninja* became magnified out of all proportion with every subsequent telling of the tale, until their real qualities were obscured by a cloud of fantasy.

PART II: SEPPUKU, JUNSHI AND THE TAK-ING OF HEADS

His pair of swords provided the samurai with a powerful weapon of attack and defence as well as an honourable means to end his own life, should this be necessary. *Seppuku*, the unique form of suicide practised by the *bushi*, was performed with the shorter of the two swords, the *wakizashi*. It was carried out by cutting open the abdomen, usually with a crosswise cut, first from left to right across the abdomen and then upwards towards the navel. This method was known as *jūmonji* (in the style of the figure ten), the character for 'ten' being shaped like a cross. No vital organs were damaged by this method, and the victim might have to wait for hours before death occurred.

The first *bushi* to commit *seppuku* in this manner was supposedly Minamoto Tametomo in 1170. This doughty warrior (he is described as having been seven feet tall) had been banished after the *Hōgen* Disturbance of 1156 with the sinews of his right arm severed. In his exile he took to piracy, and when facing defeat by a punitive force sent by the government he is said to have disembowelled himself. Another of the earliest instances of this form of suicide is meantioned in the *Heike Monogatari*. This *seppuku* was performed by the septuagenarian Minamoto Yorimasa in 1180, after the defeat of the Genji troops in the battle at Uji Bridge near the Byōdōin Temple. Having seen his two sons fall in the battle, and being himself wounded in the knee by an arrow, Yorimasa summoned his attendant Watanabe Chōjitsu Tonau, and ordered him to cut off his head. Watanabe refused to do so while his lord was still alive, and Yorimasa turned towards the west, chanted the *nembutsu* (*Namu Amida Butsu*, i.e. 'Hail Amida Buddha') of the Jōdō School ten times, and composed his *jisei no ku* (valedictory poem): ' "Like a fossil tree/Which has borne not one blossom/Sad has been my life/Sadder still to end my days/Leaving no fruit behind me." Having spoken these lines, he thrust the point of his sword into his belly, bowed his face to the ground as the blade pierced him through, and died. No ordinary man could compose a poem at such a moment.

For Yorimasa, however, the writing of poems had been a constant pleasure since his youth. And so, even at the moment of his death, he did not forget. Tonau took up his master's head and, weeping, fastened it to a stone. Then, evading the enemy, he made his way to the river and sank it in a deep place.'[49]

In the early Heian period the custom seems to have been for defeated or wounded warriors to kill themselves by falling on their swords, and in the many battles of the *Gempei* War a number of *bushi* committed suicide by jumping into the sea in full armour. Throughout Japanese history there are also many examples of people setting fire to their houses and perishing in the flames. A *bushi* in this situation usually committed *seppuku* while the building burned. As will be discussed in greater detail presently, it was the custom to take the heads of fallen enemies on the battlefield. Wounded and helpless warriors left on the scene of a battle preferred to take their own lives rather than be beheaded or mutilated by enemy soldiers, possibly of lower rank than themselves. To be taken prisoner alive was a great dishonour, and cowards who survived by hiding or running away were ostracised. As we can see from the account of Minamoto Yorimasa's death, his second, Tonau, did not act before his master was dead when he cut off his head. In this particular case, since Yorimasa was a high-ranking member of a famous clan, the head was sunk in the river to prevent it from falling into the hands of the enemy and being gibbeted.

Later, the custom of having a second known as *kaishaku-nin* became more widespread, especially in the case of *seppuku* being performed as a form of execution, a practice which began during the late Ashikaga *Bakufu*. The second would stand behind the person about to commit *seppuku* who was seated in a crosslegged position, and the head would be struck off once the first incision had been made. During the Tokugawa *Bakufu* this practice was further modified so that the *kaishaku-nin* let the blow fall when the person to be executed leaned forward to grasp a fan placed before him, or when he had poured water from one dish into another. It was however considered more honourable to perform the act alone, slowly bleeding to death, and those who did so, composing their *jisei no ku* in the meantime and writing it down with a brush dipped in their own blood, were highly praised for their admirable self-control.

Seppuku, in fact, became the only honourable death for a *bushi* who was accused of a crime, whether he was guilty or innocent. It was also regarded as an honourable way out of an impossible situation, the only solution to overwhelming and insurmountable problems. A *bushi* who had acted in a headstrong and impulsive manner could atone for his carelessness and imprudence through *sokotsu-shi* (expiatory death) and indignation and hatred could be expressed through a form of *seppuku* known as *munenbara* or *funshi* (death out of mortification and chagrin). For a *bushi* who had actually committed an offence against the law *seppuku* was regarded as a lenient form of punishment which allowed him to die with honour and with his property intact. This privilege, known as *shi o tamau* (granting death), was as a rule only available to fairly high-ranking *bushi*.

Although the *bushi* alone were entitled to be executed by decapitation with a sword, *zanzai*, a public execution was regarded as a disgrace. The convicted criminal was paraded through the streets to the common execution ground, with placards recording his crime carried before him. He had to kneel on the ground in order to be dispatched by the public headsman, and his severed head was then gibbetted for a certain period, with a wooden sign proclaiming his name and the nature of the crime. The head might or might not later be returned to his family for interment. This ignominious form of public exposure was utterly distasteful to the *bushi*, who were careful to maintain their distance from the populace. Only samurai proper could be sentenced to commit *seppuku* as punishment for a crime, which meant that *rōnin* who, although *bushi* by birth, were no longer in the service of a feudal lord were technically excluded from his honour. Notable exceptions to this rule however occurred, as we shall see in the case of the Akō *rōnin*.

One reason for this peculiar form of suicide was the fact that the soul or spirit of a person was thought to have its seat in the abdomen. Indeed the word *hara*, 'belly', also means 'spirit', 'courage', 'resolution'. The vulgar term *harakiri*, literally 'cutting the belly', which is still widely used in the West to denote *seppuku*, was never commonly used in *bushi* circles in Japan. By cutting open his abdomen the *bushi* could 'lay bare his soul' and show his resolution to expiate his crime, or demonstrate his innocence and sincerity. There was also a kind of 'corrective' *seppuku*, *kanshi*, used as a final form of remonstrance when all else had failed. A teacher or mentor could resort to this means to correct a wayward disciple, and Oda Nobunaga's teacher is said to have committed *seppuku* in order to prevail upon his pupil to curb his violent temper. A samurai might commit *seppuku* after having felt duty-bound to give his lord sensible but unwelcome advice, as a means of demonstrating his absolute sincerity.

In the *Heike Monogatari* we are told how a retainer remonstrated with his lord, Kiso Yoshinaka, who was reluctant to go into battle because of an amorous involvement with a lady. When his efforts were fruitless, the retainer committed *seppuku*, saying that he wanted to precede his lord on the journey of the dead to the other world, waiting for him on Mount Shide which the souls of the dead have to cross, whipped on by the servants of one of the Buddhist hells. This act brought Kiso Yoshinaka to his senses, and he immediately left the lady. The anecdote is indeed one of the extremely rare instances of the love for a woman preventing a *bushi* from carrying out his duties, and it may have well have been included in order to discredit Yoshinaka, a cousin of Minamoto Yoritomo who became his enemy.

Seppuku as a form of execution carried out by the condemned man himself continued to be used until modern times. The young British diplomat A.B. Mitford, later Lord Redesdale (1837-1917) who served in the British Embassy in Japan during the turbulent years around the Meiji Restoration, was obliged to witness an instance of *seppuku* in 1868. The man who carried out his own death sentence, Taki Zensaburo, had been in charge of an attack on a foreign settlement, and Mitford was called in, with other foreign representatives, to see that justice was done. He described the gruesome event in minute detail, both in his famous *Tales of Old Japan* and in a letter to his father.[50] As a way of demonstrating sincerity and firmness of purpose, albeit for a lost cause, the death of the famous author Mishima Yukio in 1970 provided a startling contemporary example.

Suicide by other means, often by jumping out of windows or in front of trains, continues to be an honourable way of expiating crime or protesting innocence in today's Japan. Mishima's death in the traditional *bushi* manner, with his closest friend and ally acting as second, seems to have shocked his compatriots who tended to regard his outspoken militaristic and nationalistic views as smacking too much of the 1930s. This failed attempt to stir up a martial revival reminded the Japanese of the abortive military coup of 1936 whose chief protagonists also ended their lives by committing *seppuku*, and public opinion seems to have regarded Mishima's last gesture as not only futile but also in bad taste.

In his reminiscences Mitford discussed a debate held in the first Japanese Imperial Parliament, modelled on its British counterpart, which opened in 1869. The motions under discussion were whether *seppuku* ought to be abolished, and whether the carrying of two swords should be optional. W.G. Aston, another of the famous British scholars on Japan who began his career in the diplomatic service, translated the debates. The former motion was almost unanimously defeated (200 against, 3 for, 6 abstentions) and some of the arguments against it are highly illuminating. *Seppuku* was referred to as 'the very shrine of the Yamato Damashii, the spirit of old Japan, and the embodiment in practice of devotion to principle.' Different speakers claimed that 'We ought to maintain a custom which fosters a sense of shame in the military caste and in the existence of which doubtless consists the superiority of Japan over other countries.' — 'Why should this custom be prohibited in imitation of the effeminacy of foreign nations?' — 'In this Country of the Gods it is not necessary to discuss such a law.' The motion against the compulsory carrying of the two swords was unanimously defeated, one of the arguments being the familiar idea that 'It is a good maxim for the soldier in peace time never to forget war.'[51]

After the *Gempei* War *seppuku* became an established custom, not only for defeated and incapacitated warriors on the battlefield but also for disgraced officials in the *Bakufu*. Rules were established which determined how it should be carried out, down to details of dress and precedence. When a group of samurai performed *seppuku* together, the person who had the highest rank killed himself last. On occasions when *seppuku* was performed as an execution, a suitable space was prepared, with a red cloth for the condemned man to sit upon, and four chief witnesses, one at each corner of the square made by the *tatami* mats which formed a sort of dais. The *wakizashi* of the man about to commit *seppuku* was laid out on a small table, the hilt usually covered with white paper. The victim stripped to below the waist, tucking in the sleeves of his kimono under his legs so that he would be sure to fall forwards when he died and not backwards. Once an act of *seppuku* had begun it could not be interrupted for any reason, even if a note of pardon were to arrive at that instant, and the act was carried out with the utmost solemnity and dignity by all the participants. A valedictory message was customarily written, and the *jisei no ku*, a poem summing up the life of the man about to die, an *apologia pro vita sua*, was the ideal. Also *bushi* who died of an illness or old age were expected to compose a farewell poem summing up their lives.

In addition to the reasons for *seppuku* discussed above, there were other important causes which compelled the samurai to commit suicide. Most common of these was *junshi* (following the lord in death), which was practised until the early Tokugawa period. *Junshi* was committed by a number of the chief retainers of a *daimyo* or feudal lord upon the death of their master. There were no fixed rules for *junshi*, and to some extent it depended on the circumstances, the importance of the lord and the esteem in which he was held by his followers, as well as the manner of his death. *Junshi* could be carried out irrespective of whether the lord had died of an illness, fallen on the battlefield, or committed *seppuku*. A retainer might decide to accompany his lord in death if he felt that his master had been unjustly condemned to death, for example, as a demonstration of loyalty.

Another rather special form of suicide was the practice of *hito-bashira* (human pillar) whereby a *bushi* would kill himself to protect the foundation of his lord's residence or castle. When the hole had been dug for one of the supporting pillars or the corner-stone of the new building, the person about to become a *hito-bashira* would climb down into the hole and commit *seppuku*. The foundation stones would then be laid upon his corpse, and it was thought that his spirit would become a guardian of the building. Other kinds of building sacrifices also existed in Japan, for example at the construction of bridges over particularly difficult rivers or streams, but in these cases the victim would be chosen among strangers who happened to pass through the village.

This kind of building sacrifice, often seen as a pacification of disturbed local spirits, occurred the world over, and there are numerous examples from Medieval Europe of similar practices having been carried out from time to time. The *hito-bashira* practised by a samurai in order to become a guardian spirit and protect his lord and his family for as long as the building would remain standing was certainly a voluntary act on the part of the victim. It must be remembered, however, that on the occasion of important fortifications or a castle being constructed there would certainly be a strong general opinion demanding that suitable volunteers come forth. An element of competition in demonstrating loyalty towards the lord should also not be excluded.

Junshi, the ultimate demonstration of loyalty towards the feudal lord, was seen by the cautious Tokugawa *Bakufu* to contain certain elements of sedition. A number of followers of a feudal lord who committed *junshi* upon his death might by their exemplary devotion incite others among his retainers to rebel. We find therefore, in the version of the *Buke Sho-Hatto* promulgated in 1663 by the fourth Tokugawa Shōgun, Ietsuna (regnavit 1651-1680) the first prohibition of *junshi*, read out to the assembled *daimyo* as an additional article of the code. The enforcement of this law was strict, and worked in the customary Japanese way by laying the blame for an instance of *junshi* on the son or successor of the deceased lord whose death had occasioned it. While showing their loyalty to their dead lord by following him in death, his retainers would at the same time seriously jeopardise the career of his successor, and quite possibly ruin his entire house through the confiscation by the authorities of the fief.

The prohibition of *junshi* was subsequently repeated in every new promulgation of the *Buke Sho-Hatto*, reflecting the strict precautions taken by the Tokugawa *Bakufu* to maintain law and order and prevent conspiracies and un-rest. As we shall see below in the discussion of loyalty, the Tokugawa *Bakufu* was vociferous in its insistence that loyalty to the Shōgun must supersede all personal loyalties among the *daimyo* and their retainers. Needless to say, the legal prohibition against *junshi* did not prevent it from taking place, and the old values appear generally to have been stronger than the laws of the *Bakufu*, so that the deed was usually highly praised and approved of by public opinion. One of the most celebrated and sensational cases of *junshi* took place in 1912, when General Nogi Maresuke, hero of the Russo-Japanese War, accompanied the late Emperor Meiji in death. His house in Minato Ward in Tokyo, between Aoyama and Akasaka, still stands, a de-serted and dusty memorial, permeated with *sabi*, the Japa-nese concept of loneliness and *vanitas vanitatum*. Here the General committed *seppuku* the moment a cannon salute announced that the funeral procession had left the Impe-rial Palace grounds. His wife accompanied her husband in death by severing her jugular vein in an adjacent room. Today *shimenawa* ropes, festooned with *gohei*, white folded paper pendants, hang across the doorways of the two rooms in accordance with Shinto beliefs. A tiny shrine is set up in the garden of the house, and next to the main building is a flourishing Shinto shrine, the Nogi Jinja, a popular venue for weddings.

It was quite common for wives to follow their husbands in death, and this practice, which had no political implica-tions, was never prohibited by law. All *bushi* women car-ried a knife for the purpose of committing suicide and were instructed from girlhood how to sever the jugular vein. Before doing so, they had to tie their legs together so that their clothing should not be disturbed in an unseemly way in their death-throes. The *Kojiki* and the *Nihongi* as well as the *Manyōshū* (The Collection of a Thousand Leaves), an early anthology of poetry, all contain numerous references to women sacrificing themselves or being sacrificed, usu-ally by drowning. These were peasant women, and some of these practices indicate the presence of ancient ideas of human sacrifice, e.g. a young girl killed in a rice paddy as a sacrifice to the god protecting the water supply.[52]

In the *Gunki Monogatari*, however, there are several

instances of *bushi* women accompanying their husbands in death, again by drowning. The most famous example of this was Nii-dono, the widow of Taira Kiyomori, who threw herself into the sea with her grandson, Emperor Antoku, and the sacred sword during the battle of Dan-no-ura, when it became clear that the Heike forces were losing. She too, like Minamoto Yorimasa above, first prayed to Amida Buddha, telling her little grandson that they were going to Amida's Western Paradise. The *Nihon Shoki* contains some examples of widows committing suicide, and what seems to have been quite a widely practised custom was forbidden after the Taika Reform.[53]

Local folklore and place names in different parts of Japan also bear witness to the exposure of elderly peasant women who could no longer contribute to the family economy by working in the fields and who thus became a burden on their relatives. They appear to have been left exposed to starve to death, or to have committed suicide by throwing themselves from a cliff, practices which are well attested also in other parts of the world in communities living on the margin of subsistence. In the context of *bushi* women, however, the act of suicide in order to follow their husbands in death was considered as a kind of *junshi*.

In marriage the wife became her husband's subordinate, according to the Five Relations of Confucianism, and *bushi* women extended the same kind of loyalty to their husbands and masters as that of vassals to their feudal lord. Thus we learn in the *Heike Monogatari* that the wet nurse and another female attendant on the eight-year-old Taira Yoshimune, son of Taira Munemori and grandson of Taira Kiyomori, followed the child in death when he was executed on the orders of Minamoto Yoshitsune after the defeat of the Heike. The women were allowed to carry away with them the corpse and head of the boy, and were later found to have drowned themselves in the Katsura River. The wet-nurse had only done her duty by following her lord in death, whereas the other woman was considered to have shown a devotion out of the ordinary.[54]

Fallen and defeated enemies were as a rule beheaded on the battlefield, dead or alive. This custom is mentioned in the *Gunki Monogatari* as the usual procedure for dealing with enemies among the *bushi*. The *Kojiki* and the *Nihongi* contain little mention of severed heads, a fact which may be at least partly due to the lack of detail when battles are recorded. The Heian period was characterised by peace and prosperity until the first stirrings of the provincial *buke* in the eleventh century, and apart from campaigns against the Ainu and raids against pirates or rebellious peasants there was no large-scale general warfare in the country. The late eleventh century collection of tales on various subjects, *Konjaku Monogatari*, often translated as 'Tales of Times Past' from the opening words of each tale: '*ima wa mukashi*' (Now it is a long time ago), contains stories set in India, China and Japan. Among the tales set in Heian Japan are a number dealing with warriors and warlike exploits, usually campaigns against rebels and pirates. In the tale relating how the pirate Fujiwara no Sumitomo and his son Shigetamaro were killed in 941 it is related how their heads were brought to the capital. The Emperor, Shujaku-In, and the Court officials were keen to inspect the heads. They could not be brought to the Emperor, however, for reasons of defilement, and a famous artist, Kanimori no Arikami, was sent to the place where they were gibbetted in order to make a drawing. This was then shown to the Emperor, and the likeness is said to have been remarkably accurate.[55]

The *Gunki Monogatari* and the historical chronicles of the early Kamakura *Bakufu*, such as the *Gukanshō* and the *Azuma Kagami*, contain innumerable references to the taking of heads in battle and the parading of the heads of enemy commanders and high officers. This practice continued until the end of the Tokugawa *Bakufu*, although with the cessation of actual warfare after the *Sengoku jidai* it became confined to enemies of the state, those convicted of a crime, and victims of acts of private vengeance. Heads of enemies defeated on the battlefield were taken as trophies and displayed in public. During a battle they might sometimes be attached by the hair to the armour or saddle of the warrior who had taken them. The heads of fallen enemy generals or other leading figures would be taken to the capital or the military headquarters for identification. During the *Gempei* War the custom of parading the heads of fallen enemies through the streets of the capital seems to have begun.

There is an account of one of the first instances of this practice on a larger scale in the *Heike Monogatari*: 'It was on the twelfth day of the second month of the third year of Juei/1184/that the heads of the Heike cut off during the battle at Ichi-no-Tani in Settsu Province were returned to the capital.' (. . .) 'Noriyori and Yoshitsune demanded of the cloistered emperor that they be allowed to parade the heads north on the wide street of Higashi-no-Tōin and then hang them on the trees to be exposed to public view.' The retired Emperor, Go-Shirakawa (1127-92, regnavit 1155-58), was unwilling to comply with this request, and held a council with his chief ministers. The council decided unanimously to refuse the request: 'From of old there has been no precedent for this—that the heads of nobles and courtiers should be paraded on the streets of the capital. Above all, these people were related to the Emperor Antoku on his maternal side, and it is with this status that they have served the imperial family for many years. Therefore we think that it is advisable for His Majesty to reject the demand of Noriyori and Yoshitsune.'

The Minamoto, however, repeated their request several times with the motivation that 'These beheaded men of the Heike were the enemies of our grandfather Tameyoshi at the time of the Hōgen Insurrection, and of our father, Yoshitomo, at the time of the Heiji Insurrection. We obtained their heads at the risk of our lives to calm His Majesty's wrath and avenge our father and grandfather. If we are not allowed to parade them, how shall we be able to fight courageously against the rest of the Heike?'[56] Their persistence was finally rewarded, the retired Emperor Go-Shirakawa had to comply with the request, and the heads of the Heike were paraded through the streets of Kyoto. The Heike themselves, however, had transgressed against custom on an earlier occasion, and even flaunted the religious rules which forbade such displays during the period of mourning for an Emperor, when Minamoto Yoshimoto's head was paraded in the capital in 1181, after the death of the retired Emperor Takakura. On that occasion they claimed a precedent for this irregularity by referring to an earlier instance, when the head of a rebel, the former governor of Tsushima, Minamoto Yoshichika, had been displayed just after the death of Emperor Horikawa in 1108.

The main reason given by Minamoto Yoshitsune and Noriyori in their request for permission to parade the heads of the Taira after Ichi-no-Tani was that the heads were meant as an offering of appeasement of the retired Emperor's wrath (Go-Shirakawa was opposed to the Taira and a champion of the Minamoto) and as concrete proof that the deaths of their father and grandfather had been avenged. On his deathbed, in 1181, Taira Kiyomori made the following request of his wife, according to the *Heike Monogatari*: 'But I cannot die in peace, for I have not yet seen the head of Yoritomo, who is now in exile in Izu Province. When I die, do not build a temple or pagoda. Do not perform any ceremonies for me. Instead you must send an army at once to vanquish Yoritomo; you must cut off his head and hang it before my tomb. I ask for nothing more.'[57]

The sentiments of Taira Kiyomori reflect the belief in vengeful spirits which was, and still is, prevalent in Japan. The spirit of someone who died with feelings of hatred or a wish for revenge in his mind would not find peace unless Buddhist rites for the pacification of his soul were accomplished, or until his enemy had been vanquished. The tomb was the place where the errant spirit should be laid to rest, and the idea that someone's death was only avenged when the head of his enemy was brought to his tomb was to recur throughout history until modern times. In 1702 the Akō *rōnin* placed the head of his enemy on the tomb of their former lord together with a document stating that their intention was to bring peace to his spirit.

The severed head of an enemy or rebel was as a rule treated with great reverence, and presented for inspection in a formal manner and according to fixed rules. Heads collected on the battlefield were washed, and the hair was arranged in the proper manner if dishevelled. The head was then placed in a specially constructed receptacle, a round box of unvarnished wood with a deep lid covering a tray used for the presentation of the head. Until modern times head-boxes were part of the standard utensils of a samurai household. If the head was to be transported some distance it was preserved in *sake*, rice wine, in order to prevent putrefaction, and before presentation it was washed and combed. The taking of the heads of high-ranking enemy officers in a battle would be a cause for promotion or even conferment of land or a stipend in the form of a certain number of *koku* of rice, and low-ranking *bushi* struggled to obtain the heads of important enemies.

After a battle it was customary to make out a list of the warriors who had distinguished themselves during that day, and the one who had taken the head of the highest-ranking enemy would have his name at the top of the list, a great honour in itself, and one which would be quoted by generations of his descendants. In the heat of the fray a warrior might not always know the identity of the enemy with whom he grappled, and whose head he cut off. The same applied to some of the corpses left on the battlefield. There are instances in the *Gunki Monogatari* of warriors refusing to give their names if their opponents were of inferior rank, and of warriors being cut down and only later identified by their belongings or a poem found on their person.In full armour, with a helmet and visor obscuring the face, warriors were not easily identified. In order to distinguish friend from foe the Taira wore red pennants attached to the back of their body armour, and the Minamoto wore white. The splendour of the armour and the trappings of his horse would also betray the high birth or rank of a *bushi*, as would the colour of his teeth.

There is a famous episode in the *Heike Monogatari* in which the Minamoto samurai Kumagai no Jirō Naozane intercepts the young Taira Atsumori, unseats him and removes his helmet in order to cut off his head. When Kumagai sees that the youth has blackened teeth and wears face-powder, he realizes that his opponent is a high-ranking Taira and introduces himself. Since Kumagai is far inferior to him in rank Taira Atsumori refuses to give his name, and only when he presents the head to Minamoto Yoritomo and his entourage does Kumagai learn who his adversary was. The blackening of teeth with a concoction made of iron filings, powdered gallnuts (*fushi*) and *sake* or urine, was practised by the *kuge* of both sexes during the Heian period. In the *Gempei* War blackened teeth became a sign of recognition among the Taira warriors. The Minamoto did not blacken their teeth, but under the Hōjō *shikken* in the Kamakura *Bakufu* the custom was taken up again by their followers. By the *Sengoku jidai* the only males who blackened their teeth were members of the Imperial family and the *kuge*.

A matter-of-fact account of the handling of severed heads during the *Sengoku jidai* exists in the brief memoirs of Yamada An, a lady of *bushi* stock. In 1598, when she was a young girl, she was staying with her parents in the Castle of Ōgaki in Mino Province, which was under siege by the troops of Tokugawa Ieyasu. The women of the besieged castle made themselves useful by casting bullets for their garrison. 'And then, too, our soldiers would bring to us in the turret the heads they had taken, and make us label them for reference. They would also often ask us to blacken the teeth with powder, the reason being, you see, that in old days "tooth-powder heads" were those of men of rank, and therefore more prized, so that a soldier would bring you a plain head and ask you to do him the good turn of giving the teeth a rub of powder. We weren't a bit afraid of the heads, and used to sleep in the midst of the nasty smell of blood that came from them.'[58]

It is interesting to note that the soldiers of Ōgaki-jō must have got their ideas of 'men of rank' with blackened teeth from the *Gunki Monogatari* and from vague notions of customs at the Imperial Court in the capital. Married *bushi* women blackened their teeth with *tesshō* (iron juice), or *dashigane* (iron extract), popularly known as *o-kane* (honourable metal), or *o-haguro* (honourable tooth-black), at this time, however, hence the ready availability, even in a besieged castle, of the substance. One only wonders what the reaction was on the part of the commanding officers to the multitude of heads with blackened teeth which they found presented to them accompanied by claims for substantial rewards.

The *Heike Monogatari* also relates how Imai no Shirō Kanehira, the foster brother of Kiso Yoshinaka, pleaded with him to retreat when it became clear that his side was losing what was in fact to be his last battle: 'Whatever fame a warrior may win, a worthless death is a lasting shame for him. You are worn out, my lord. Your horse is also exhausted. If you are surrounded by the enemy and slain at the hand of a low, worthless retainer of some unknown warrior, it will be a great shame for you and me in the days to come. How disgraceful it would be if such a nameless fellow could declare, "I cut off the head of Yoshinaka, renowned throughout the the land of Japan!" ' Yoshinaka refused to retreat, and was surrounded and killed, and his head was indeed brandished on the tip of the sword of his assailant, who declared: 'Kiso no Yoshinaka, renowned throughout the land of Japan as a valiant warrior, has been killed by Miura no Ishida Jirō Tanehisa!'

When Kanehira heard that his foster brother was dead he stopped fighting and killed himself by putting the point of his sword in his mouth and throwing himself from his horse.His last words, according to the *Heike Monogatari*, were: 'You, warriors of the east, see how the mightiest warrior in Japan puts an end to himself!'[59] We find here that the idea of honour dictated that the warrior should be matched against an adversary worthy of his rank, and consequently that the prestige which adhered to a warrior who managed to defeat a *bushi* of superior rank was great indeed. In Kanehira's death we have an example of the older form of suicide which preceded *seppuku*, as well as a demonstration of the indomitable spirit so lauded in a *bushi* who would taunt his enemies with his last breath.

In the *Gempei* War, as already mentioned, the heads of fallen enemies were paraded through the streets of the capital. After the Battle on the Uji River, when the Heike were victorious, five hundred Genji heads were carried in procession on the points of swords and halberds, including the head of Go-Shirakawa's son, the belligerent Prince Mochihito, and those of the monks of Mii-dera, one of the major Buddhist temples. The head of Minamoto Yorimasa did not suffer this ignominy, however, since his faithful retainer had weighted it with stones and sunk it in the Uji River after his lord's *seppuku*.

The heads of defeated enemies were often suspended from trees outside the prison gates in late Heian times, and later they were gibbetted outside the prison or the execution ground, or exposed at a major thoroughfare such as a bridge. People above a certain rank, usually the third court rank, were supposed to be exempt from this shameful treatment, although exceptions occurred. While severed heads of enemies were as a rule treated with a certain reverence and were preserved for presentation to the victor, there were instances of heads being thrown away by the roadside. Thus, during the *Gempei* War, Kiso Yoshinaka is supposed to have told a *bushi* who had taken the head of one of his opponents, the turbulent Abbot Myōun: 'I don't care what is done with such a man!', whereupon the head was thrown into a river.[60]

Kiso Yoshinaka was notoriously uncouth, but in this particular instance his shocking disregard of the clerical status of the victim can perhaps be explained by the fact that the Abbot was himself a man who took to the sword in an argument. Myōun had fought a pitched battle with his colleague and predecessor as Abbot of Mount Hiei, Kaishū, in 1167, with the result that forty-eight lives were lost before Myōun gained his abbacy. This kind of behaviour on the part of clerics was not unique, and as late as at the Battle of Mikata-ga-hara in 1572, when Takeda Shingen defeated Tokugawa Ieyasu, the latter's private secretary, a Zen monk named Denchorō, distinguished himself by taking three heads. He was rewarded by Tokugawa Ieyasu by the bestowal upon him of a family crest, *mon*, of three black stars in commemoration of his feat.

In the *Gunki Monogatari* there are several references to heads being sacrificed to the God of War. The *Heike Monogatari* tells of the battle in 1184 when Kiso Yoshinaka's forces were defeated by those of Minamoto Yoritomo. The young warrior Shigetada grappled with one of Kiso Yoshinaka's men, saying, 'Let me cut off your head and make it the first sacrifice today to the god of war!'[61] He is then said to have unseated his opponent, cut off his head, and attached it to his saddle.

There are many mentions of prayers being addressed to Hachiman for victory, of vows made to him, and of prayers of thanksgiving. Once the *Gempei* War was over, and the political power safely in the hands of Minamoto Yoritomo, he turned against his half-brother Yoshitsune, driving him into exile while plotting his death. At the outset of his flight from Yoritomo's troops Yoshitsune had a minor skirmish with his new enemies. After defeating them, according to the *Heike Monogatari*, he cut off the heads of his fallen foes and hung them on the trees as an offering to the God of War and thus 'celebrated a victory at the start of his journey.'[62] The idea that an enemy, sometimes the first one encountered on the battlefield, should be offered as a sacrifice to ensure victory, is not unique to Japan, but can be found in many cultures throughout the world.

The head is generally considered as the seat of the intellect and the epitome of the personality, and on its own it can be regarded as a symbol of the entire person, the most important *pars pro toto*. There are a number of practical reasons for the presentation and exposure of the severed heads of defeated enemies or executed rebels in feudal Japan. A head could be reasonably well preserved from putrefaction and transported over long distances with relative ease. It also provided absolute proof of identity, although both the heroic and popular literature provide many instances of mistaken identity, for example the head of a retainer's child being substituted, at his own behest, for that of the son of his lord.

In the case of executed criminals the gibbetting of the head of a *bushi*, albeit ignominious, must he regarded as a gesture of some courtesy, compared to the exposure of the entire corpse as was the case with executed commoners, who were usually crucified. The taking of heads on the battlefield, however, many of which were neither formally presented or exposed, since their owners were not of sufficiently high rank to warrant this attention, would seem to have been at least partly due to other reasons. By taking the head of a fallen enemy his spirit was also subjugated and would be laid to rest with the burial of the head. The opposing sides usually interred each others' captured heads, with the exception of those of high-ranking *bushi* which were either exposed or returned to their own families for burial. Disrespectful treatment of captured heads was, as we have noted, a rare occurrence and due to special circumstances. As late as during Toyotomi Hideyoshi's Korean campaign, 1592-94, the ears of his fallen enemies were brought back to Japan and buried outside Kyoto in what became known as *Mimizuka* (Ear Mound). In this case practical reasons must have prevented the entire heads from being transported from Korea.

For an example of the many different implications of taking the head of an enemy in combat we may look at the death of Taira Tadamori, as described in the *Heike Monogatari*. When challenged by a Minamoto *bushi*, Okabe Tadazumi, to declare himself he refused, and in so doing revealed his Taira origins by his blackened teeth. Having lost his right arm in the ensuing sword fight, he asked permission to say his death prayer, and turned towards the West chanting: 'O Amida Buddha! Thy light shines upon all the ten quarters of the world. Thou saveth all sentient beings who seek thee calling thy name.' His opponent then struck off his head, and his identity was revealed through a signed poem found in his quiver. Tadazumi then raised the head on the point of his sword, calling loudly: 'The head of one of the most prominent Heike courtiers, a lord named Tadamori, Governor of Satsuma Province, has been obtained by Okabe no Rokuyata Tadazumi.' When they heard this, says the *Heike Monogatari*, both friends and enemies wept at the sad fate of one who was of such high renown both in martial arts and in the art of poetry.[63]

Arai Hakuseki (1657-1725) in his historical chronicle *Tokushi Yoron* (Lessons from History), quotes a Muromachi period work, the *Yasutomi-ki*: 'In the winter of the previous year/1447/the heads of the supporters of the southern emperor in Kii Province were sent to Kyoto. They were presented by Hatakeyama himself to the shogun. It was regarded as a good omen that these heads of the shogun's enemies were presented at the beginning of the year. Therefore, everyone, regardless of rank, presented swords to the shogun on this day as a token of congratulation.'[64] The Shōgun in office at this time was Ashikaga Yoshimasa (1436-1490, regnavit 1443-1473), and the incident referred to was a rising in Kitayama, Kii Province, begun by the Abbot of Emman'in Temple, En'in, who was defeated by Hatakeyama Mochikuni.

The helmet of a Japanese suit of armour was designed in such a way as to give the wearer a fierce and awesome aspect. The traditional shape was that of a rather shallow bowl, with flaps covering the cheeks and the back of the neck, and a visor covering either the entire face or the nose, mouth and chin. The interior of the helmet was usually lacquered red, in order to give the wearer a ruddy complexion. The colour red was considered to indicate fierceness, and it may be remembered that the red aspect of Fudō Myō-ō the so-called *Aka-Fudō*, was the most common. The visor was often quite grotesque in appearance, with a large, hooked nose and thick wrinkles, adorned with long horse-hair moustaches or a beard. The uneven surface of the visor was specifically designed to deflect and break the force of a sword cut.

Ornaments in the shape of antlers or horns, as well as other shapes such as discs or crescents, were usually attached to the front of the helmet. Some of the very early helmets, found with pieces of body armour in a Kofun context, had a peak at the front, making them resemble a cricket cap. The traditional helmet had a round aperture at the crown, probably for the purpose of ventilation, called the *Hachiman-za* (the seat of Hachiman). This could prove a hazard in battle, and in the *Gunki Monogatari* older and more experienced warriors would warn young *bushi* to keep their heads down when charging the enemy, in order to protect their throats, but not to bend too far forward lest they be struck by an arrow through the *Hachiman-za*. The idea that the soul or spirit leaves the body through the top of the head at the moment of death is common in Asia, and among warriors it seems appropriate that the crown of the helmet should be regarded as being under the special protection of the God of War.

PART III: ALLEGIANCE, OATHS AND BUSHI ORGANISATIONS

The feudal system of Japan bears a superficial resemblance to the organisation of feudal Europe, and certain parallels can be drawn between knights and *bushi*. The differences, however, are more significant than the similarities. Loyalty towards the feudal lord in Japan was hereditary, voluntary and absolute. We have already noted the importance of lineage and heredity where service of a feudal lord went from father to son, so that the relations of lord and retainer existed between many families for generations. This arrangement, in theory indissoluble, was at the same time a voluntary one, in that there was no binding agreement between the two parties. The European feudal contract, which was a legal document spelling out the obligations of lord and vassal respectively, never existed in Japan, where the relationship was more arbitrary, resembling the dictates of filial piety.

The nature of feudal allegiance changed considerably in Japan during the course of history. After the *Gempei* War all vassals owed their allegiance directly to the Shōgun, a system which became gradually eroded with the decrease in central power during the latter part of the Kamakura *Bakufu* and the Ashikaga *Bakufu*. Local *bushi* usually became the vassals of their provincial *daimyō*, and the latter increased in power and prosperity until many of them were in a position to be able to oppose the shogunate and join the power-struggle of the *Sengoku jidai*. As we have seen, one of the first actions of Tokugawa Ieyasu after having gained control of the political situation was to ensure that all the *daimyō* swore allegiance to him personally as Shōgun. Strictly centralised power was the backbone of the Tokugawa *Bakufu*.

The basis for the relations between lord and vassal was the Confucian idea of the Five Relations. In theory it was a one-sided arrangement, in which the vassal owed total allegiance to his lord, like a son to his father, and where the lord was free to treat his vassal well or badly according to his whim. A vassal who failed to exercise his duties could be dismissed by his lord or have his fief confiscated. In reality the Confucian ethic stresses the fact that the obedience on the part of the vassal should be reciprocated by benevolence on the part of his lord, but there were certainly no legal means by which this could be enforced.

To the rules of the Confucian ethic were added the Buddhist ideas of reincarnation, so that it became common to speak of a *bushi*'s allegiance to his lord as lasting for the duration of three lives, *shūjū sanze no katame*, meaning his past existence, the present one, and the next life. Occasionally, one comes across expressions of devotion and service to the lord for seven lives, but three was the customary formula. The life of a vassal was not his own, but belonged entirely to his lord, and it was the duty of a *bushi* to consider this at all times. Thus his fierce pride in his own dignity was not so much in defence of his own honour as that of his lord. Likewise, in displaying patience and caution in looking after his own life and the affairs of his household, the vassal was acting in the best interest of his lord, who would then, in an emergency, be able to make use of his vassal and his dependents. Not only the life of a *bushi* himself was at the disposal of his feudal lord, but also those of his wife and children, as a matter of course. As we shall see when dealing with the concept of *Bushidō* below, the one question which might present a problem in certain cases was whether the loyalty owed to one's own father ought to take precedence over that to one's lord.

The indissoluble bond between lord and vassal, and the absolute and unquestioning loyalty by which the vassal put himself, body and soul, at the disposal of his lord, constituted the ideal. Reality, however, sometimes displayed the reverse of the coin, and deviations from the norm did occur, particularly during periods of unrest, notably the *Sengoku jidai*, when it was far from uncommon for *bushi* to change their allegiance. As Joüon des Longrais points out, the transfer of allegiance was not necessarily seen as a form of treachery, and the vassal would devote himself as sincerely and wholeheartedly to his new master as he had to his former lord.[65]

Although no formal contract existed between lord and vassal in Japan, a certain ceremony came to be observed from late Heian times, reminiscent of similar customs in

Europe. From the beginning of the Kamakura *Bakufu* Minamoto Yoritomo used to receive personally the *bushi* who came to Kamakura to offer him their services with a request to be made his vassals, *go-kenin*. The honorific prefix, '*go*', distinguished these direct vassals of the Shōgun from the *kenin*, who owed their allegiance to a local feudal lord. It was the ambition of all *kenin*, however, to become *go-kenin* under the Shōgun. Later, the vassals of the Shōgun came to be known as *hatamoto*, literally 'bannermen', while those who were the vassals of a *daimyō* were referred to as samurai. The act of presenting oneself at Kamakura, asking to become the Shōgun's direct vassal, was known as *genzan*, a term which in the Heian period had indicated the act of paying a formal visit to a superior.

Under Yoritomo the *genzan* developed into a ceremony, and the *bushi* who presented himself as a new vassal received a gift in recognition of his acceptance, usually sword, a suit of armour or a horse. Later, especially during the Tokugawa *Bakufu*, it became customary for the lord and vassal to exchange toasts in *sake*, a custom similar to that which occupies a central place in the traditional marriage ceremony. During the Kamakura *Bakufu* the practice of writing a *kishōmon*, sworn oath, was resorted to in moments of crisis. The *kishōmon*, in the form of a sworn statement to protect the rules of a Buddhist temple, had appeared in the tenth century, calling down divine retribution on those who acted against it. The *kishōmon* in use under the Kamakura *Bakufu* took the form of a written confirmation of land rights or official appointments. It was also used for oaths in which the *bushi* promised to fulfil their duties loyally and with justice. Hachiman was usually the principal deity called upon to witness the sincerity of the oath and to strike the violator of it with terrible vengeance. This type of *kishōmon* was only used on special occasions, in times of acute crisis, and must not be confused with a formal oath of fealty, the latter being always oral.

During the *Sengoku jidai* the *kishōmon* became more common, and indeed took on a certain aspect of reciprocity, so that the lord promised in his turn to protect the vassal who swore him allegiance. In the turbulent and disturbed times of the *Sengoku jidai*, when old feudal ties were frequently severed and it was more than ever before a case of every man for himself, the custom of affixing a *keppan* to the *kishōmon* arose. This so-called 'blood-seal' was a fingerprint, made with the signatory's own blood, under his written signature. A person who used his own blood to sign a document demonstrated both the seriousness of the matter and the fervour of his wish. The contract signed with one's own blood is a concept known all over the world and commonly endowed with magical properties, for good or evil. Blood is the vital force, and its use in this context means that the person pledges his life for the desired outcome, or forfeits it if he should break his promise.

The Emperor Sutoku, as we have seen above, wrote a curse in his own blood in one of the sutras he had copied before sinking the books into the sea. In the *Heike Monogatari* there is an account of how Taira Kiyomori had a vision prophesying future prosperity while praying in a temple on Mount Kōya. In order to commemorate this event, and also no doubt to ensure that the prophecy would come true, Kiyomori ordered an artist to paint a mandala for the great hall of the temple and painted another one himself. This was a picture of Amida Buddha, and Kiyomori painted the crown with his own blood, taken from the neck.[66] When a number of *bushi* of equal status signed a document, it was also common to put the signatures in a circle, so that no-one appeared to take precedence. As we have already seen, Tokugawa Ieyasu was the first Shōgun to exact a written oath of fealty from all the *daimyō* of Japan. The first was a preliminary oath after the Battle of Sekigahara in 1600, and then a final version appeared in 1611 for the *daimyō* of the West and in 1612 for the *daimyō* of the East.

The personal reception of a new vassal by the Shōgun, the gift of weapons, armour or horses, and the written document, *jō*, which confirmed his fief, constituted the formal guarantee of his vassalage, and, as Joüon des Longrais points out, there was no special ceremony marking the vassal's first taking possession of his domain. Under the Tokugawa *Bakufu* the Shōgun ensured the loyalty of his *daimyō* by instituting the *sankin kōtai* system, which meant that the *daimyō* had to spend a certain part of each year in their residences, *yashiki*, in the shōgunal capital, Edo, and that their families had to be left there as a kind of hostage when they returned to their fiefs periodically. The *daimyō* were obliged to provide troops for the Shōgun in relation to the size of their fiefs. Thus a fief of 100.000 *koku* per annum had to furnish 30 mounted samurai.

The military service which the vassal owed his lord took the form of guard duty as well as regular armed service in times of war. Since Heian times the gates of the capital and the gates of the Imperial Palace compound in its centre had been guarded by provincial *bushi*. Minamoto Yoritomo saw to it that his own vassals, the *go-kenin*, were in charge of guarding the Imperial capital, taking turns of six months each for three successive years, a tour of duty later changed to periods of three months. The *bushi* also mounted guard during periods of one month each, at the Shōgun's Kamakura residence, and there were also garrisons in the provinces, especially in Kyushu, where the threat of foreign invasion was greatest.

During the Mongol invasions of the late thirteenth century the guard forces in Kyushu were increased, but about a century after the failed second invasion of 1281 they were disbanded. The barriers, *seki*, which were established at strategic points between the provinces and at major thoroughfares, regulating the movements of people and goods, were likewise guarded. Fortresses, and later the fortified castles, *jō*, built under the influence of the first Europeans in the latter half of the sixteenth century, had their own garrisons, consisting of vassals on guard duty in the service of their lord.

The duties of the vassal extended beyond military obligations, and he must be prepared to advise his lord on matters of administration as well as strategy, according to his proficiency. He was not to proffer advice unless asked to do so, and like the mentor of Oda Nobunaga he might, if he volunteered an admonition, be forced to underline its importance, demonstrate his sincerity, and at the same time expiate his guilt over this breach of conduct, by means of committing *seppuku*. The loyalty of the vassal went as far as to follow his lord in death, as we have seen above when discussing *junshi*, although this practice was discouraged by the authorities in the Tokugawa period. It was

considered to be the duty of a samurai, however, to avenge
the death of his lord if he had been killed in a fight or died
as a result of some treacherous action on the part of
another. *Katakiuchi*, best rendered in Western terms as
'vendetta', was regulated in the legal code, and was only
permitted after due notification of the authorities, as is
apparent from the different editions of the *Buke Sho-Hatto*
promulgated during the Tokugawa *Bakufu*.

It was strictly forbidden for outsiders to become involved
in a case of *katakiuchi*, which was regarded as a private
matter between the two parties concerned. This worked to
the advantage of the Akō *rōnin* when they avenged the
death of their lord in 1702. They had not requested permission for their *Katakiuchi*, knowing full well that it would
not have been granted by the authorities, since their lord
had been condemned to commit *seppuku* after having attacked another man with a drawn sword inside the Shōgun's
palace and was thus considered guilty of a crime. When
they attacked the house of his enemy Kira, however, one of
the forty-seven *rōnin* climbed onto the roof of one of the
buildings and shouted to the neighbours that this was a
case of a private vendetta. As a result, none of Kira's
neighbours came to his assistance, and the *rōnin* were able
to fulfil their mission.

It was only possible for a vassal to avenge his lord, and
a person of higher rank could not avenge the death of one
of his subordinates. The Japanese system of loyalty rested,
as Joüon des Longrais has pointed out, 'on real faith, a
mutual confidence which establishes itself between two
persons unequally placed, but both of them belonging to
the same social category, still small in numbers.'[67] The
parties might have been unequal, in the sense that one was
lord and the other one vassal, but between them they
formed an exclusive group which imposed its rules throughout society. Faith, indeed, in its immutable rules and iron
discipline, cemented it, and provided the necessary conti-
nuity which lasted for nearly a millennium, overcoming
both violent internecine warfare and threats from alien
forces. Ideals were not always adhered to, and practice
might vary considerably from the established theory, but
the basic ideas of loyalty between lord and vassal were
never questioned and never altered.

The very close bonds between lord and vassal and the entire fabric of feudal relationships contained elements which are reminiscent of those commonly found in men's societies in many cultures. Japanese folk religion has several examples of men's societies. One of the best known is an annual festival, the *namahage*, in north-eastern Japan, in which some of the young men in the village dress up in straw raincoats and grotesque demon masks and enact a visit by the dead, usually described as dwelling in the mountains or across the sea. Many other similar festivals are recorded, and in some of them the young men go through the village at night, striking the walls of the houses with sticks. While this visitation lasts none of the villagers dare leave their houses or even look out.

This type of festival, now virtually obsolete, contained an element of violence not to be found in the Buddhist *Bon*, still celebrated all over Japan in the late summer. In this festival the spirits of the dead, especially those of recently deceased relatives, are received in the homes with food and drink, dances are held in the open, and when the spirits depart they are lighted on their way by candles or lanterns in miniature boats cast adrift on rivers or by the sea. The men enacting the visits of the spirits to their home village, however, were members of a secret, or at least exclusive, society formed for this purpose.

With the *bushi* the idea of belonging to an exclusive group was extremely strong, and, although we have seen examples of commoners rising to *buke* rank, the *bushi* appear generally to have been very conscious of the fact that they were born into their position, as were the *kuge*, and that membership was not as a rule open to outsiders. The son of a *bushi* was initiated in his future warrior status at the age of six or seven, when the ceremony of *yoroi-ki-zome*, the first wearing of armour, was celebrated, whereas his coming of age ceremony, *genbuku*, was a much more solemn occasion. The *genbuku* was usually celebrated at the age of fifteen or sixteen, when the young samurai was considered an adult man, and it took the form of a solitary vigil during a night spent in a Buddhist temple. In the morning the young man was dressed in the formal robes of an adult *bushi*, and his *eboshi-oya* (hat godfather) usually an older male relation or friend of the family who held a senior position, tied on the young man's *eboshi*, the stiff black gauze hat traditionally worn with the formal costume of the Heian court, for the first time. In the Heian period the young man also had his teeth dyed black for the first time on this occasion. The *genbuku* ceremony had been practised among the *kuge* before the *buke* nobility came into existence, and ceremonies marking the transition from adolescent to adult were also celebrated among the common people.

Homosexual relationships between an older and a younger *bushi* who were attached to one another as knight and page, were virtually the rule in feudal Japan. In Buddhist monasteries and temples the same form of attachment tended to exist between monks and acolytes, *chigō*, young boys of *kuge* or *bushi* families. Homosexuality tends to be particularly prevalent in warrior communities, where the love of women is considered a sign of weakness, classical Greece being a typical example. Usually, however, the homosexual attachment, which was regarded as the ultimate form of friendship between men, was a passing phase which lasted during the period of the warriors' active service. In Japan this would have been the time of guard duty, in the capital or in the provinces, and once the *bushi* returned home to the fief of his lord he was expected to marry and raise a family of his own. Marriage was an important means of establishing ties of kinship, and hence alliance, between different families, and a *bushi* was not free to contract a marriage outside the fief to which he belonged, or without the consent and approval of his lord.

In the latter part of the Ashikaga *Bakufu* and during the *Sengoku jidai*, organisations of *bushi*, usually low-ranking, were a common feature. These so-called *ikki*, 'organisation of one goal', were groups founded for a specific purpose or a particular campaign, and the members were as a rule unrelated both where ties of kinship or vassalage were concerned. The group signed an oath of loyalty to a common cause, valid until the task had been accomplished. Groups of peasants followed the example of the *bushi*, forming bands, *tsuchi-ikki*, *tsuchi* meaning 'land', for the purpose of trying to obtain economic aid from the authorities in a crisis. *Tsuchi-ikki* often took the form of revolts against heavy taxation, or campaigns for the cancellation of debts, and they were rarely directed against the local landowners. *Bushi* not infrequently joined forces with the peasants in these revolts, in spite of the fact that they were liable to have their property confiscated for doing so.

When the old *shōen*, or estate, system was replaced during the Ashikaga *Bakufu* by a village organisation where the individual peasants gained a certain amount of autonomy within the village unit, the cause for peasant risings was removed. The local *daimyō* were however anxious to prevent the *bushi* from making common cause with the peasants, and the turbulent political situation made it necessary for them to have their vassals under control and close at hand. Thus many *bushi* were compelled to leave the land where they had farmed alongside the peasants and move to the precincts of the fortified castles. Here they lived in the so-called *jōka-machi* (town below the castle), more than ever dependent on their *daimyō* for their subsistence. The move was frequently opposed, and *kuni-ikki* were formed by the *bushi* in order to provide organised resistance.

Behind both the *kuni-ikki* and the *tsuchi-ikki* was the popular and powerful *Ikkō* (Single-Minded) sect of the *Jōdō Shinshū* (True Pure Land) school of Amidist Buddhism. The teachings of the *Jōdō Shinshū* promised an easy salvation for everyone who prayed to Amida Buddha, and the school had a great appeal for the common people. Many *bushi* also adhered to the *Jōdō Shinshū*, and the *Ikkō* sect, which was hierarchical in organisation and exceptionally militant, seems to have attracted them in considerable numbers. The *Ikkō-ikki*, rebels belonging to the *Ikkō* sect, acted on the precepts of Shinran (1173-1262), the founder of the *Jōdō Shinshū*, among whose utterings are such famous pronouncements as 'If even good people can be reborn in the Pure Land, how much more a wicked man!', and 'The mercy of Buddha should be recompensed even by pounding flesh to pieces. One's obligation to the Teacher should be recompensed even by smashing bones to bits!'[68] The *Jōdō Shinshū* adherents gained great political power, and in 1531 the whole province of Kaga was thrown into a state of anarchy and civil war due to factional quarrels among the leaders of the *Ikkō* sect there. Among the influential and antagonistic Buddhist establishments suppressed by Oda Nobunaga in the 1570s and 80s, the *Ikkō* sect must be considered as one of his most troublesome adversaries.[69]

Taking into consideration both the power and virulence of the *ikki* and the very large number of *rōnin* produced by the two decisive battles of Sekigahara in 1600 and Osaka Castle in 1615, it is not surprising that the Tokugawa *Bakufu* legislated with great vehemence against all forms of associations and sworn confederacies. There was indeed only one notable insurrection during the Tokugawa *Bakufu*, the Shimabara Rebellion of 1637, a peasant revolt consisting largely of Christians, which was soon quelled in blood, and one attempted coup, the so-called *Rōnin* Conspiracy of 1651. The latter was accidentally revealed while still at the planning stage, and the conspirators were arrested and executed.

In spite of the legal decrees of the *Buke Sho-Hatto*, however, organisations of *bushi*, mainly young men, were formed during the Tokugawa *Bakufu*, and there were also groups of townsmen who banded together, as well as what could best be described as gangs of outlaws and people from the criminal underworld of the large cities. These men were known as *otokodate* (self-disciplined men) or 'stalwarts', the latter rendering being favoured by nineteenth-century Western translators. The original ideals of the *otokodate*, whether made up of *bushi* or townsmen, were to protect the weak from violence and injustice. Among the townsmen, the merchants had the lowest status and frequently needed to defend themselves against the *bushi*, who treated them with arrogance and were, as we have seen, quite capable of cutting down a commoner in the street at the slightest pretext.

All *otokodate* dressed conspicuously, often in kimonos of the same pattern of large checks, carried especially long and ornate swords, wore their hair in special styles, and generally liked to attract attention. The commoner *otokodate*, who were not allowed to carry swords used heavy iron fans, not unlike the *gunsen* (war fan) which formed part of the traditional *bushi* armour, and especially large and heavy metal pipes for smoking tobacco, a custom which had come to Japan with the first Europeans in the sixteenth century. Both the iron fans and the pipes could be wielded as lethal weapons, and the use of the fans soon became prohibited. Although there were some famous early groups of *otokodate* led by *hatamoto*, shōgunal vassals, organisations of townsmen, often led by a *rōnin*, soon became common. Most, not to say all of them, seem to have degenerated into bands of criminals, which were, however, strictly and hierarchically organised. Absolute obedience to the leader was the main rule, and the gangsters, *yakuza*, of modern Japan, who maintain a similar organisation along hierarchical lines, can be said to be heirs to this criminal tradition.

Unhindered travel was never possible in Japan in historical times. Travellers were checked and questioned at the barriers, and people were not allowed to accommodate strangers even for a night without notifying the authorities. Pilgrims, monks or nuns collecting alms, and other legitimate wayfarers had to present documents stating their identity, place of origin and business. These regulations were strictly enforced during the Tokugawa *Bakufu*, and one of the most perceptive foreign travellers in Japan, the Swedish Linnaean scholar and Doctor of Medicine Carl Peter Thunberg (1743-1828) who visited the country while in Dutch service between 1775 and 1776 and formed an intelligent and largely accurate opinion of the country and its government, likened Tokugawa Japan to a police state. The police of the country is as vigilant, and order and manners are as carefully observed, as the laws are strict. The effect of this is rather remarkable and important, because there is hardly any country where fewer excesses occur. And since no notice is ever taken of the person, and the laws are ancient without any change, explanation or explication, the subjects grow up not only with sure knowledge of what is done or not done, but they are also inspired by the example and unblemished conduct of their elders. Most crimes are punished by death, not because of the greatness or smallness of the crime, but because of the audacity in violating the sacred laws of the realm and insulting justice, which together with the doctrine of the gods is considered the country's holy of holies.'[70]

Among those members of religious orders who were able to move about the country were the *komusō*, monks of the Zen Buddhist school called *Fuke*. The origins of this school are obscure, although it is said to have originated in the thirteenth century. Its monks were chiefly known for their curious headgear, a deep, basket-shaped reed hat which completely covered the face of its wearer. In front of the wearer's eyes there was a grille of somewhat larger spaces between the strands, so that he could see without being himself recognised. The *komusō* wandered about the country playing a bamboo flute, the *shakuhachi*. This is a large, clarinet-shaped instrument, about half a metre in length, which is held vertically. Like other Zen monks many of the *komusō* were of *bushi* stock, and not a few of them seem to have travelled the country as spies in the employ of the Tokugawa *Bakufu*. They enjoyed complete freedom of movement, and were not answerable to local authorities but directly to the shōgunal office in charge of temples and shrines, the *Jisha-bugyō*. The fact that their identity was concealed, combined with their religious vocation which gained them entry everywhere, and their capacity to provide musical entertainment, would have made them ideally suited for the purpose of acting as informants and intelligence agents, and some *komusō* fulfilled this function until the end of the Tokugawa *Bakufu*.

After the political upheavals marking the beginning of the Tokugawa *Bakufu*, large numbers of masterless samurai (it has been estimated that there were 50,000 *rōnin* after the battle of Sekigahara) were forced to find a means of subsistence. Holy orders, particularly in one of the Zen schools, held great appeal. Not a few *rōnin* joined the ranks of the *komusō*, and were able to preserve their anonymity as well as the right to carry arms, i.e. the *wakizashi* and a staff, while requesting alms. The *komusō* were known only by their religious names amongst themselves and did not engage in conversation with strangers. Few people would refuse to give money or food to a Buddhist monk, and the *komusō* commanded respect through their masterful and warlike demeanour, like the *yamabushi* who also carried a sword.

Some *rōnin* living on the fringes of society banded together under the convenient guise of *komusō* and joined the criminal underworld which flourished in the large cities in spite of the vigilance of the authorities, and this would have been a contributing factor in bringing the *Fuke* school into disrepute. The romantic appeal of the *komusō* proved irresistible to writers, story-tellers and artists, however, and together with the *otokodate* they became popular figures in the *Kabuki* plays and woodcut prints, *ukiyo-e*, of the last two centuries of the Tokugawa era. After the Meiji Restoration of 1868 the *Fuke* school was prohibited, a fact which would seem to corroborate the theory that the *komusō* were Tokugawa partisans.

The *komusō*, like the *yamabushi*, wore distinctive clothing and carried swords and staffs and other implements which immediately distinguished them from Buddhist monks belonging to the more conventional schools. While the *Fuke* school cannot be defined as a secret society, some of the *komusō* employed in intelligence work must have formed secret groups. The borderline between extralegal, illegal and outright criminal activities tends to be a tenuous one, and it is not difficult to understand why certain *komusō* became involved with the criminal urban subculture, and why the characteristic *tengai* basket-headgear provided welcome cover for those whose affairs did not bear close scrutiny by the authorities.

Distinctive clothing and appurtenances are important criteria of men's societies, second only to the ceremony marking the formal acceptance of the individual into the group. The *otokodate*, as we have seen above, tended to wear kimonos of exceptionally loud and eye-catching patterns, usually checks, and outsize swords. Some however went as far as to have one of their front teeth replaced by one of gold or silver, or to have it inlaid with one of these metals. This practice signalled their membership of one of the groups or gangs known as *kin-gin-gumi* (gold or silver associations).

Criminals other than *bushi* were commonly punished by tattooing. The tattoo marks could vary somewhat locally, but the most common form was a stripe around the convict's upper arm. For the next offence another stripe might be added, and the offender sometimes had a character, usually that representing *inu* (dog) tattooed on his forehead, again in instalments, so that the strokes would be added one at a time with each conviction. The custom of tattooing spread to the *otokodate*, as well as to prostitutes and other categories living on the fringes of society. Sometimes the entire torso would be covered with polychrome tattoos representing mythical scenes or auspicious mythological animals such as dragons.

One explanation given for this practice has been that convicted criminals wanted to hide their penal tattoo markings under a wealth of figurative motifs, and this may well have been true in some cases. The distinguishing factor, however, must have been more important. By tattooing his body the *otokodate* demonstrated his membership in the group, albeit in a somewhat less conspicuous manner than by having a gold or silver front tooth, since the body tattoos would be invisible when their wearer was fully clothed. The tattoos became a means of expressing one's affiliation with the criminal element in society, and they must have served the dual purpose of intimidating ordinary law-abiding citizens and eliciting a favourable response among other members of the confraternity of outlaws.[71]

Like the *yamabushi* and the *komusō*, the *otokodate* were favourite subjects of popular stories and *Kabuki* plays as well as *ukiyo-e* prints, and with repeated telling of the stories they tended to assume legendary and heroic proportions. In contrast to the *bushi*, who represented an awe-inspiring and unattainable ideal, and who were to be treated with the utmost respect, however penurious or down-at-heel, these other categories were somewhat more accessible. Although feared by the common people, the *yamabushi* for their reputed mastery of the occult, the *komusō* for their reputation as government spies and agents as well as for their position as Buddhist monks, and the *otokodate* for their criminal associations, these three categories were largely made up of commoners even if the *rōnin* element was fairly strong among the former two. Their popularity was due to their strong appeal as objects of identification, and great vicarious pleasure was taken in their more remarkable exploits, whether real or fabled.

4

Bushidō: The Concept of Chivalry

PART I: EARLY NOTIONS OF CHIVALRY AND ITS LEGAL ASPECTS

The term *Bushidō* (Way of the Warrior), was first used by the Neo-Confucian *jusha* Yamaga Sokō (1622-1685) who began codifying the concept of chivalrous behaviour in his writings on *bukyō* (the warrior's creed), and *shidō* (the way of the samurai), in the first century of the Tokugawa *Bakufu*. We must distinguish, however, between the late use of this term to denote the attitude and deportment expected of a *bushi*, and the concept of chivalry itself. Unwritten rules governing the life and every action of the *bushi* had been in existence since the Heian period. Minamoto Yoritomo expressed some of them in writing in his House Laws, which regulated the living conditions and subsistence of his vassals. His example was later followed by local *daimyō*, and the emphasis of the different House Laws was on practical matters.

The concept of chivalry, which encompassed spiritual as well as practical values, was referred to in the *Gunki* -

Monogatari and other chronicles of the early Kamakura *Bakufu* by terms such as *bushi no kokorogiwa* (the warrior's heart or spirit), *chūgi no michi* (the way of loyalty), and *kyūba no michi* (the way of bow and horse). In the following, the term *Bushidō* will be used to denote the *bushi* concept of chivalry, also prior to the Tokugawa *Bakufu*, together with other terms which the warrior nobility employed about their own way of life.

The origins of the concept of *bushidō* appear to coincide with the establishment of the *buke* nobility as a power factor in society. The early warriors and heroes mentioned in the *Kojiki* and the *Nihongi* vanquished their foes by fair means or foul, totally unencumbered by notions of chivalry. Susanoo, the wilful younger brother of Amaterasu, is seen in the early chronicles to have acted in a manner which could by no standards be described as chivalrous. From the *Kojiki* we learn how he defeated the Eight-forked Serpent of Koshi by means of treachery. This monstrous creature, with eight heads as well as eight tails, which had devoured seven maidens in as many years, was lured into drinking *sake* from eight large vats. While in a drunken stupor, the dragon was slain by Susanoo, who then proceeded to cut the body into pieces. In doing so, he found the sacred sword, *Kusanagi no tachi* (The Herb-quelling sword), which later became one of the Imperial regalia, in one of its tails.[72]

Earlier, Susanoo had annoyed his sister Amaterasu, who was his senior in age as well as in rank, by his exceedingly rude behaviour in her palace, culminating in the throwing of a newly flayed horse through the roof of the hall where she sat weaving, an event which so startled her that she injured herself on the shuttle. This would not in itself count as unchivalrous behaviour in Japan, however, where courtesy to women has never been included among the male virtues. Although the rules of the Confucian Five Relations demanded that a woman, as the inferior in any relationship, should be treated with kindness and consideration, there was never a trace in Japan of the exalted awe and adoration accorded to women in the European tradition of chivalry and courtly love.

Yamato Takeru, the great semi-divine culture hero, who is credited with the pacification of the land of Yamato and the quelling of various tribal insurrections, began his career by murdering his older brother. His father, the Emperor Keikō, had complained that the older brother did not appear at the morning and evening meals, whereupon Yamato Takeru hid in the privy and tore his brother limb from limb when he entered. He then proceeded to kill various insurgents, also by devious means. In order to slay the two brothers picturesquely known as the 'Kumaso bravoes' in Chamberlain's translation of the *Kojiki* (the Japanese word translated as 'bravo' being *takeru*) he dressed in women's clothes borrowed from his aunt and appeared uninvited at a feast thus disguised.

His impersonation of a young girl was so convincing that he attracted the attention of the two brothers and was placed between them. At the height of the festivities Yamato Takeru drew his sword which he had concealed about his person, and cut down the Kumaso bravoes, the younger of whom bestowed upon him with his dying breath the name of Yamato Takeru, in recognition of his prowess.

Having travelled to the province of Izumo, Yamato Takeru set about eliminating the local trouble-maker, known as the Izumo Bravo. In this task he displayed to the full his consummate skill in treachery. He began by making friends with the Izumo Bravo, and then secretly manufactured a sword with a wooden blade. Wearing this sword he suggested to the Izumo Bravo that they should go for a swim in a river. Yamato Takeru then got out of the water first, put on the Izumo Bravo's sword while suggesting that they exchange swords, and challenged him to a little friendly sword-play. He then made swift work of cutting down the defenceless Izumo Bravo with his own blade.[73]

Yamato Takeru is celebrated throughout Japanese history as the first exponent of *Yamato damashii* (the spirit of Yamato), the name of the province here denoting also the concept of 'old Japan'. To be said to possess *Yamato damashii* was the highest accolade for a *bushi*, and meant that he embodied all the most highly valued qualities of the country as it had been in the age of the gods. These qualities, e.g. bravery, loyalty and perseverance, were regarded as being unique to Japan, and vestiges of these claims to uniqueness are to be found among the Japanese to this day.

In the Heian novels and diaries written by the ladies of the *kuge* there is, as we have already noted, very scant mention of *bushi*, and warriors do not figure as objects of admiration. During the Heian period the ladies of the Imperial court came closest to being treated with respect and courtesy than any other women, possibly with the exception of some notable figures such as Hōjō Masako, before or since in Japan. Life at the Heian court was an elaborate ritual, hedged around by rules of etiquette and religious prohibitions and requirements. Polygamy was the rule, and women were regarded as chattels rather than as independent individuals, but the rules of etiquette were strict, and both men and women obeyed them.

Already by this time the idea was firmly implanted in the Japanese mind that to act against the established rules of polite behaviour befitting one's station in society, was not only to subject oneself to criticism, but to ostracism and indeed personal disaster. With this atmosphere at the Imperial court and among the *kuge*, it seems only natural that similar ideas of proper and suitable demeanour should also develop among the provincial *bushi*. Their geographical distance from the capital, as well as the difference in their lifestyle, meant that these ideas took longer to penetrate into the consciousness of the provincial warriors. Once a tradition had been adopted, however, it tended to last. The tenacity with which ideas as well as customs were adhered to was greater among the *buke* than among the *kuge*, who as the elegant élite of the Imperial capital were exposed to constant changes in fashion.

From the *Gunki Monogatari* of the early Kamakura *Bakufu* we learn a great deal about the *bushi* code of behaviour at the time of the *Gempei* War and during the disturbances of the eleventh and twelfth centuries which preceded it. One of the central themes of the *Gunki Monogatari*, especially the *Heike Monogatari*, was the contrast between the by then thoroughly gentrified Taira warriors and the uncouth and rustic Minamoto warriors from the Eastern provinces. Although some of the Minamoto *bushi* were ignorant of the finer points of court etiquette and ceremonial, both sides were conscious of the already well-established code of behaviour.

Genealogy is of great importance in a society based on

a clan system, and a significant feature of any battle at this
time was the formal challenge, by the commander of the
troop or some especially renowned warrior. This man would
advance somewhat from his troop and call out his name
and rank, reciting his lineage back to his most famous
ancestor, usually an imperial prince or emperor. This was
known as *ujibumi o yomu* (to read the lineage of one's
clan). It was customary for a *bushi* to give his name and
parentage when asked to do so, for example while engaged
in hand-to-hand combat in the middle of the fray, but there
were occasions when he might decline to reveal his identity, particularly if his opponent was considerably his inferior in birth or rank.

The very detailed nature of the recital of lineage is demonstrated by the following example: 'A man who seemed
to be their leader stood forth. He was wearing a long, light,
silk coat of the kind then worn exclusively by noblemen,
and the cords which laced his armour together were of dark
blue and white which had been dyed yellow. His arrows
had black feathers, and he carried a bow whose close
bindings of rattan had been lacquered with black. He rode
a saddle-horse of the colour of yellow earthenware. "I", he
said, "am but an ignorant sort of person, but I am not
without what might be called a family line. My name is
Unohichiro Minamoto no Chikaharu. I am the son of
Shimozuke Gon no Kami Chikahiro, the grandson of
Nakatsukasa no Jo Yoriharu, who was a descendant of the
fourth generation in a branch line from Yamato no Kami
Yorihika, the younger brother of Settsu no Kami Yorimitsu,
who was the seventh descendant of Rokuson-Ō, the tenth
in descent from Seiwa Tenno. I have been living for a long
time in Oku Gori in Yamato Province, but have not yet lost
a reputation for military art. I am on my way to visit
Sutoku-In in obedience to the commands of the Sadaijin.
As men of Minamoto clan never serve two masters, even
though you are the Emperor's messenger, I shall not take
sides with the Court." '[74]

The outer appearance of a *bushi* was of great importance, as we find from the detailed accounts in the *Gunki
Monogatari* of the colour combinations and patterns of
armour, helmet, cloak, saddle and horse, including the
colour and pattern of the feathers on the arrows in his

quiver. 'Ashikaga no Tadatsuna wore a lattice-patterned orange brocade battle-robe and over it armour laced with red leather. From the crown of his helmet curved two long ox horns, and the straps were tied tightly under his chin. In the sash around his waist was a gold-studded sword, and in the quiver on his back were arrows with black-and-white spotted hawk feathers. He gripped a bow bound thickly with lacquered rattan and rode a dapple grey. His saddle was of gold and was stamped with his crest: an owl on an oak bough. Now, thrusting hard with his legs, he rose in his stirrups and cried out in a thunderous voice: "Men in the distance—hear me! Men near at hand—behold me! I am Matataro Tadatsuna, aged seventeen, the son of Ashikaga no Tarō Toshitsuna, tenth-generation descendant of Tawara no Tōta Hidesato, a warrior who long ago won great fame and rewards for destroying the enemies of the emperor. A man with no rank and title such as I may risk the wrath of the gods when he draws his bow against a prince of the royal house. Nevertheless let the god of the bow judge which side is in the right. May his sympathy be with the Heike! Here I stand, ready to meet any among the men of the third court rank nyūdō Yorimasa. Who dare to face me? Come forward and fight?" '75

This preoccupation with the warrior's clothing and accoutrements was a reflection from the Heian Court, where personal appearance was of paramount importance, and the wrong colour combination in the costume of a *kuge* was a *faux-pas* which might affect his career prospects. Sartorial elegance in the *Gempei* War was by no means confined to the Taira warriors, and even the notoriously rustic Kiso Yoshinaka rode to his last battle splendidly attired: 'That day he wore armour laced with twilled silk cords over a red battle robe. His helmet was decorated with long golden horns. At his side hung a great sword studded with gold. He carried his quiver a little higher than usual on his back. Some eagle-feathered arrows still remained. Gripping his rattan-bound bow, he rode his famous horse, Oniashige.

Rising high in his stirrups, he roared at the enemy: "You have often heard of me. Now take a good look at the captain of the Imperial Stables of the Left and governor of Iyo Province—Rising-Sun General Minamoto no Yoshinaka, that is who I am! I know that among you is Kai no Ichijōjirō

Tadayori. We are fit opponents for each other. Cut off my head and show it to Yoritomo!" '76

The authors of the *Gunki Monogatari* appear to have been very keen to retain something of the atmosphere of the Heian period, which when they wrote had been irrevocably supplanted by the austerities imposed by the Kamakura *Bakufu*. They seem torn between nostalgic longings for the glorious past and admiration for the military valour and prowess of the new masters, and the same sentiments are echoed in the *Gukanshō*, Jien's historical chronicle of 1219.

Much attention was given to the individual warrior in the *Gunki Monogatari*. Hand-to-hand combat was frequently sought, and opponents of particular fame and merit tended to be called upon by name to appear and fight their challenger. Before a battle there was frequently a prolonged exchange not only of challenges of named enemies, but also of arrows. Especially powerful archers or particularly skilled marksmen would be called upon to shoot at the enemy force standing opposite, attempting to hit the commander or some other easily recognisable enemy of note. In a famous incident just before the final battle at Dan-no-Ura the Taira fixed a red fan decorated with a golden sun disc to a pole on one of their ships just off the coast. One of the Minamoto *bushi* managed to hit the fan with an arrow from the shore so that it fell into the sea, a feat which was applauded by Taira and Minamoto *bushi* alike. One of the Taira warriors on the ship was so impressed by this display of marksmanship that he got up and executed some steps of a ceremonial dance. Yoshitsune ordered the marksman, Nasu no Yoichi, to shoot this man as well, and he managed to hit him in the neck. This time there was no applause from the Taira side, and while some of the Minamoto *bushi* applauded the shot, others considered this to have been a deed of unwarranted cruelty. Generally speaking, it is evident from the *Gunki Monogatari* that acts of exceptional military skill or great courage were universally praised and equally admired in foes as well as in friends.

The *ujibumi o yomu* and the general self-presentation before a battle, in which the individual warrior would draw the attention of the enemy to his own excellence and skill as a warrior, was a feature seemingly quite out of character

with the traditional Japanese reticence and tendency towards self-effacement. The individual *bushi*, however, regarded himself, and was seen by others, as the representative of his clan at that particular time. Thus, when
Minamoto Yoshitsune dropped his bow into the sea during
a battle between mounted Minamoto troops and Taira
warriors in boats in the shallows, he retrieved it himself at
the risk of being killed by the surrounding enemies. When
his senior retainers complained that he had taken an un-
necessary risk, he replied: 'It was not because I grudged the
loss of the bow. If it were one that required two or three
men to bend, a bow like that of my uncle Tametomo, then
I would gladly let it fall into the hands of the enemy. But
if a weak one like mine were taken by them, they would
laugh at it and say, "Is this the bow of Yoshitsune, the
commander-in-chief of the Genji?" That would be unbear-
able. I had to recover it even at the risk of my life!'[77]

Bravery in fighting was held in very high esteem, and
many suicidal charges straight into the thick of the fray are
recorded in the war chronicles as laudable feats. Especially
in a hopeless situation, outnumbered by his enemies and
far from his own men, a *bushi* would make one last charge,
trying to kill as many enemies as possible before being
himself killed. Cowardice, which nearly always entailed a
breach of loyalty as well, was seen as a particularly hei-
nous crime, and most *bushi* would prefer to die rather than
endure even the suspicion of cowardly behaviour. In the
Heike Monogatari we learn how Morinaga, the foster brother
and retainer of one of the Taira generals, Shigehira, de-
serted his lord, who was subsequently taken prisoner,
when they were pursued by Minamoto horsemen. Removing the red pennant signifying that he was fighting on the
Taira side, Morinaga fled to Kumano province, where he hid
in the house of a priest.

Many years later, when the priest had died, Morinaga
accompanied his widow to Kyoto, but was recognised and
subjected to scornful remarks: 'Shameless Morinaga! He
received many favours from his master, Shigehira, but in
an hour of need he would not risk his life and refused to
help his master escape. How disgraceful he is to come back
to the capital with the widow of Priest Onaka. This is an
intolerable act!' According to the *Heike Monogatari* the

shame of Morinaga was so great that he could not show his face, but had to hide it behind a fan.[78]

Hereditary retainers who deserted their lords were a rare exception, whereas mercenaries hired from other parts of the country than their lord's home province did not always feel themselves bound by the laws of loyalty. To plead for one's life was considered extremely disgraceful, and a *bushi* who found himself overpowered would urge his opponent to cut off his head. When the Taira warrior Etchū no Zenji Moritoshi had the Minamoto warrior Inomata no Koheiroku Noritsuna at his mercy, however, the latter tried to strike a bargain to have his life spared. 'As I examine the trends of this world,' he said, according to the *Heike Monogatari*, 'I can see that the Genji are winning over the Heike. Therefore, even if you present an enemy head to your lord, you will be rewarded only when he is prosperous. I pray you to unbend and spare my life. In exchange for any honours I may receive at the conferment ceremony, I will plead for the lives of you and your retainers, if you let me go.' This plea profoundly shocked Moritoshi: 'However humble, I am still a Heike. I have no intention of pleading with the Genji for my life. I cannot believe that you, a Genji, would ask me to intercede with the Heike for your life. What disgraceful words you speak!' Noritsuna persisted, and managed to put Moritoshi off his guard by claiming that it would be an infringement of the rules of chivalry to cut off the head of an enemy who had surrendered. When Moritoshi had released him, Noritsuna attacked him, killed him, and cut off his head. Seeing a warrior from his own side approaching, and fearing that he might try to claim part of the honour of the captured head, he hastened to put the head on the tip of his sword and declare the names of his slain enemy and himself. 'By this singular deed,' the *Heike Monogatari* goes on to tell, 'Noritsuna was given the first place on the list of awards for the battle that day.'[79]

This incident clearly demonstrates that there were flaws in the behaviour of the *bushi*, and that blatant disregard of the rules of *Bushidō* occurred among opportunists who would resort to treachery and deceit for personal gain. This episode may perhaps be regarded as an exception which confirms the general rule, and also as an example of the tendency of the author or authors of the *Heike Monogatari* to give the account a pro-Taira slant. The Minamoto are admired and revered throughout the work as the victors and new holders of power, but the sympathies are with the Taira, who fought so nobly and lost. These feelings come to the fore in the account of the death of the young Taira Atsumori, which in contrast to the previous example shows both parties acting according to the tenets of chivalry. Splendidly attired and riding a fine mount, Taira Atsumori was challenged by the Minamoto *bushi* Kumagai no Jirō Naozane and overcome by him. Naozane wrestled his opponent to the ground and removed the helmet in order to cut off his head. Discovering that he was only a boy of sixteen or seventeen, Naozane remembered his own son and asked for his opponent's name, saying that he would spare him. The youth demanded to know Naozane's name and upon learning that he was not a high-ranking *bushi* declined to give his own name. Naozane understood that the youth must be of high rank, but even so felt disinclined to kill him, thinking; 'The slaughter of one courtier cannot conclusively effect this war. Even when I saw that my son, Naoie, was slightly wounded, I could not help feeling misery. How much more painful it would be if this young warrior's father heard that his son had been killed. I must spare him!'

Seeing a group of Minamoto warriors approaching, however, he said aloud: 'Though I wish to spare your life, a band of my fellow warriors is approaching, and there are so many others throughout the countryside that you have no chance of escaping from the Genji. Since you must die now, let it be by my hand rather than by the hand of another, for I will see that prayers for your better fortune in the next world are performed.'—'To this,' the *Heike Monogatari* continues, 'the young warrior replied simply: "Then take off my head at once!" So pitiable an act was it that Naozane could not wield his blade. His eyes saw nothing but darkness before him. His heart sank. However, unable to keep the boy in this state any longer, he struck off his head. Frenzied with grief, Naozane wept until the tears rushed down his cheeks. "Nothing is so bitter as to be born into a military family! Were I not a warrior, I should not have such sorrow! What a cruel act this is!" He covered his face with the sleeves of his armour and wept. But he could no longer

1

1. *Bushi* in full armour with visor, carrying bow and arrows as well as swords, from *Honchō kōkenroku* by Kaji Eiryō and Sugimoto Yasunaga, 1782. (Nordenskiöld Collection, Royal Library, Stockholm)

2. Fighting scene : *bushi* in armour, some holding severed heads, from *Ōjō yōshū* by Genshin (942-1017). This edition ca. 1840. (Nordenskiöld Collection, Royal Library, Stockholm)

3

4

3. The tomb of Minamoto Yoritomo on the hillside behind the Tsurugaoka Hachiman-gu, Kamakura. (Photograph by the author)

4. The tomb of Ōishi Kura-no-suke Yoshio, leader of the 47 Akō *rōnin*, in the Sengakuji temple in south-west Tokyo which is also the burial place of Asano Takumi-no-kami Naganori whose vassals the 47 *rōnin* had been. (Photograph by the author)

5

5. Fighting scene, from *Kokon bushikagami* by Mukunashi Issetsu, 1696. (Nordenskiöld Collection, Royal Library, Stockholm)

6

6. Fencing practice with halberds (*naginata*), from *Bukōron*, by Kashiwabuchi Yūgi, 1768. (Nordenskiöld Collection, Royal Library, Stockholm)

7

源
滿
仲

7. Minamoto no Bitchū, warrior portrait from *Honchō hyakushōden*, 1656. (Nordenskiöld Collection, Royal Library, Stockholm)

8

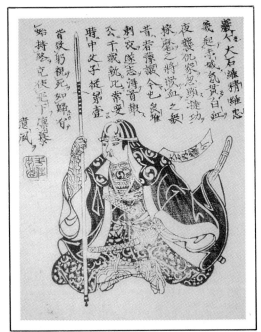

8. Ōishi Kuranosuke, leader of the 47 Akō *rōnin*, from *Sekijō gishinden*, by Katashima Shinenshi, 1868. (Nordenskiöld Collection, Royal Library, Stockholm)

stand there weeping. Then as he was wrapping the head in a cloth, he found a flute in a brocade bag tucked into a sash around the boy's waist. "What a tragedy! At dawn I heard the sound of a flute from within the Heike lines. It was this youth who was paying. Among the hundred thousand warriors on our side, there is no one who has carried with him a flute to a battlefield. What a gentle life these nobles and courtiers have led!" ' It was only when the head was presented to Minamoto Yoritomo for inspection that it was recognised as having belonged to Atsumori. The flute was a famous instrument called Saeda, 'Small Branch', and had been a gift from Emperor Toba to the boy's grandfather, Taira no Tadamori. According to the *Heike Monogatari*, this event so affected Naozane that he took the tonsure and became a disciple of the famous Buddhist teacher Hōnen under the name of Rensei.[80]

This episode demonstrates several of the traits typical of *bushi* thought. There is empathy with the victim, or in this case with the victim's father, an overriding sense of duty, in that he has to be dispatched for the sake of honour, and a strong sense of tradition, in that Naozane assures his victim that he will have prayers said for a favourable reincarnation. It was far from unusual for *bushi* to take the tonsure in later life in order to pray for their victims, and in this case the famous flute and Atsumori's musicality are said to have been the deciding factors which compelled Naozane to take holy orders.

Just as it was the duty of a retainer to die for his lord, so it was the lord's duty to see to it that prayers were said for his fallen brother in arms. A typical example of their respective feelings is to be found in the account of the death of Tsuginobu, Minamoto Yoshitsune's faithful aide. According to the *Heike Monogatari*, Tsuginobu's last words to his lord were: 'The only thing I regret is that I shall not live to see you flourish. Except for this, I have no desires. It is the fate of a man of bow and sword to fall by the shaft of an enemy. I am content with this death, for they will say in days to come that Tsuginobu died in place of his master at the battle on the beach of Yashima in Sanuki Province during the war between the Genji and the Heike. This is a great honour for a warrior, and it is something that I will carry with me on the shaded path to the world beyond.'

Yoshitsune immediately gave orders for a Buddhist priest to be brought, telling him: 'This wounded man is dying. I wish you to gather as many of your disciples as possible and let them write out a copy of a sutra within a day and pray for this soldier's better lot in the next world,' and presented him with a finely caparisoned steed as a remuneration for his services.[81]

Buddhist priests usually accompanied the troops in the field in order to pray for the souls of those who fell during a campaign. The fear of malevolent spirits was, and remains, strong in Japan, and the soul of someone who died without prayers or burial rites was thought to be condemned to wander aimlessly forever. Such a spirit was very likely to turn evil and wreak havoc either on its own living relations or descendants, or on total strangers. We have already noted that a severe earthquake in the Kansai region, including Kyoto, at the time of the *Gempei* War was attributed to the vengeful and unappeased spirits of the Taira *bushi* who had been drowned at Dan-no-Ura. Epidemics were also commonly attributed to similar causes.

The central tenets of what later became known as *Bushidō* were thus present already before the establishment of the Kamakura *Bakufu*. Minamoto Yoritomo had gained control not only of the political situation but also over the lives of his vassals even before being formally appointed to the office of Shōgun in 1192. His system was simple and effective. The personal bond between lord and vassal was strong, and his basic idea was to keep his government at Kamakura safely removed from the capital and its weakening influence on *bushi* morale. The differences in attitude between *buke* and *kuge* were stressed, and the *bushi* were exhorted to remember their warlike origins and lead lives of austerity and frugality, caring little or nothing for the effeminate comforts of the Imperial court. Once the Taira faction had been eliminated or suppressed life continued much as before at the courts of the Emperor and the retired Emperors, but the great artistic, literary and aesthetic achievements of the Heian court were never to be attained again, except perhaps during the 25 years of the Momoyama period, 1574-1600, when Chinese, Japanese and European art forms mingled under the enthusiastic patronage of Toyotomi Hideyoshi and his circle.

With the assassination of the third Minamoto Shōgun, Sanetomo, in 1219, the political power passed into the hands of Hōjō Tokimasa, the father of Yoritomo's widow, Masako, and later to his son, Yasutoki, who succeeded his father as *Shikken*, 'power-holder', in 1225. After Sanetomo's death there had been an unsuccessful attempt at Imperial restoration, the Shokyu Insurrection 1219-1221, but the Hōjō clan had no difficulty in retaining its position. The actual power was held by the *Shikken* on behalf of the Shōgun, who was usually a minor and a Hōjō grandson. The so-called *Jōei* Code, named after the reign in which it originated, also known as *Go-seibai Shikimoku* (Customs of Civil and Criminal Legislation), was promulgated in 1232. This was the first written legal code designed specifically to deal with the affairs of the *bushi*, and the text contains many references to laws which had been in force from the beginning of the Minamoto Shōgunate. In fact the *Jōei* Code constantly refers to Minamoto authority and strives to uphold the rights of those who had been invested with fiefs during the life-time of Minamoto Yoritomo, his sons, or his widow, Hōjō Masako, who died in 1225, but makes it clear that false claims to Minamoto authority are not to be tolerated.

In this context it is interesting to note that women were entitled to hold fiefs in their own right, for example after being widowed or divorced, if they had not been found guilty of misdemeanour. *Bushi* loyalty and honour were important issues, and of those who had taken part in the Shokyu Insurrection the vassals of the Shōgun were held especially culpable, having acted disloyally. Those apprehended at the time had been executed and their fiefs had been confiscated, but the text goes on to say that some who had managed to escape punishment were to be let off with only a partial confiscation of their fiefs, and that no further action would be taken against those who had not been shōgunal vassals.

The arbitrary nature of Japanese legal codes is amply illustrated by the fact that distinctions were made between *bushi* of the Kantō region, i.e. the Eastern Provinces including Kamakura, and the Kansai region, i.e. the Western Provinces including Kyoto. In several instances fathers and sons had taken opposite sides during the Shokyu Insurrection, in itself a flagrant breach of the rules of filial piety. Where Kanto *bushi* were concerned, they had been rewarded or punished individually, but in the case of Kansai *bushi* the one who did not take part in the insurrection was held to be as guilty as the one who did, being regarded as an accomplice, however passive. Only in special cases, where two relatives had been physically separated by such a distance that it seemed unlikely that they could have been in communication over the matter, were they considered not to be implicated. This idea of guilt by association pervaded the Japanese legal system until modern times, and it is still widely held by popular opinion. The wife and children of a convicted criminal would frequently be executed with him, and until the Meiji Restoration no-one would touch a corpse found by the roadside, or even report the find to the authorities, for fear of being accused of having killed the dead person.

In the case of a father and son being regarded as responsible for each other's actions, this was an idea based on the Confucian principle of the Five Relations, which regulated all human intercourse in society. The *Jōei* Code contains strict injunctions against those who attempted to gain promotion to higher rank or office by asking their superiors to recommend them, as this practice violated both the rules of hierarchical order and seniority. Those who tried to obtain preferment or even a fief by means of slander and false accusations were guilty of still more serious violations of the Confucian principles, and punished by banishment or by having their own fief confiscated and given to the person whom they had slandered.

It is clear from the *Jōei* Code that the honour of a *bushi* was a matter of paramount importance. Abusive language was punishable by partial confiscation or banishment, since it might easily lead to an armed quarrel, usually with fatal outcome for at least one of the parties involved. The striking of a *bushi* by another was an insult of such gravity that it could only be atoned for by the life of the offender, or at the very least serious physical injury, and the punishment was confiscation of the fief, or, in the case of a low-ranking *bushi*, banishment. Already at this stage we also recognise a clause which was to be repeated throughout the pre-Meiji legislation, namely the injunction against interfering in a fight between *bushi*. The law states that the circumstances of the individual case should be taken into account, but the interference of bystanders was clearly discouraged, and anyone who stepped into the fight to assist one or the other of the parties without knowing the reason for the quarrel was liable to find himself accused of being an accomplice of the person eventually considered guilty.[82]

The Kamakura *Bakufu*, under Hōjō rule, came to an end in 1333, and after a few years of civil war during which the Emperor Go-Daigō (regnavit 1318-1339) attempted to overthrow the *Bakufu* and grasp the political power for himself, the Ashikaga family founded a new dynasty of Shōguns. Go-Daigō's attempt at imperial restoration had been aided by Ashikaga Takauji, who had installed his younger brother Tadayoshi as *Shikken* in Kamakura. When, however, the last Hōjō managed to recapture Kamakura in 1335, Ashikaga Takauji marched on the city, took it, and proclaimed himself Shōgun. The continued civil war developed into protracted internecine warfare within the Imperial family, and until the end of the fourteenth century there were in fact two rivalling courts in Japan, the *Nanchō* (Southern dynasty) under Go-Daigō and his heirs of the Daikakuji imperial line, and the *Hokuchō* (Northern dynasty) under the other imperial line known as the Jimyōin. Both courts claimed to be in possession of the genuine imperial regalia, mirror, sword and jewel, and only on the occasion of the reconciliation of the two lines in 1392, when the *Nanchō* Emperor, Go-Kameyama, surrendered the regalia to the *Hokuchō* Emperor, Go-Komatsu, did it transpire that the Emperor Go-Daigō had surrendered a set of replicas to Emperor Kōmyō in 1336, and that the genuine sacred regalia had in fact been in the possession of the *Nanchō* all along.

Although the Imperial imbroglio continued for decades before the office returned to one legitimate incumbent only, the military power remained firmly in the hands of Ashikaga Takauji, and with it the political power. In 1336 Takauji promulgated the so-called *Kemmu Shikimoku*, named after the *nengo* (era name) of the Imperial reign of its promulgation. The *Kemmu* Code was brief, and followed the tradition of the *Jōei* Code, being likewise directed to the *buke* and *bushi*. The fact that it contains seventeen articles links it also to the first and most famous Japanese legal code, *Jūshichijō no kenpō*, the 'Seventeen-Article Constitution' attributed to Shōtoku Taishi, Prince Shōtoku, who is said to have published his edict for the government of the country in 604 A.D. Recalling venerable traditional precedent has been a favourite method of acquiring legitimacy for government documents in both China and Japan since time immemorial. Like the *Jōei* Code, the *Kemmu* Code put great emphasis on the fact that promotion to government offices should be made on the basis of merit and competence, and repeated the injunctions against appeals to the Emperor for preferment on the part of private individuals as well as the Buddhist clergy.

As in the aftermath of the Shokyu Insurrection more than a century previously, the questions of restitution of property to the rightful owners, and the confiscation of the fiefs of those who had taken sides with Emperor Go-Daigō, presented major problems, and the *Kemmu* Code advocated careful investigations into the individual cases. Distinctions ought to be made between the leaders of the insurrection and their subordinates, i.e. their vassals, whose duty it was to follow their lords. Where requests and claims by temples and shrines were concerned, these were to be treated under the same careful rules of investigation as were cases concerning private persons, and the investigators were urged not to be overawed by the religious nature of these institutions.

Fifty years previously, after the two invasion attempts by the Chinese navy under the Mongol rule of Kublai Khan, in 1274 and 1281, the Kamakura *Bakufu* had carefully investigated the claims made by temples and shrines. Particularly those dedicated to Hachiman put in requests for grants of fiefs or offices as rewards for the *bona officia* of the deity, who was claimed to have assisted the Japanese army and navy by producing the typhoon winds which wrecked the enemy fleet. The that the flags of the shrines had been pointing in the direction of the invaders was quoted as proof of the intervention of the divine wind, *kamikaze*, of Hachiman, according to these religious establishments. Each individual claim was painstakingly examined and investigated by the authorities in Kamakura before any reward was forthcoming, and many petitioners never received any official recognition of the validity of their claims. This attempt at scepticism on the part of the government is an interesting example of Confucian pragmatism, especially when regarded in contrast to the prevailing notions of *onryō*, vengeful spirits, which permeated all strata of society.

The *Kemmu* Code, however, contained a new feature which was to figure prominently in Japanese legislation until the end of the Tokugawa *Bakufu*, namely the sumptuary laws. In fact the first article of the *Kemmu* Code contained an exhortation to practise universal economy, criticising the fashionable tendencies of the times, which seem to have encompassed an inordinate fondness for figured brocades, embroidered silks, and elaborately mounted swords. The love of luxury and ostentation was condemned as detrimental to the fabric of society, giving rise to envy and to a mad race to keep up appearances and outdo one's rivals. Drinking and gambling were next on the list of vasteful pastimes which ought to be suppressed, and later in the text bribery was severely condemned. A person who accepted a bribe was suspended from office for an indefinite period of time, and if the crime was serious the suspension was for life. Any presents sent to officials at the Shōgunal residence were to be returned immediately, especially gifts of curios from China. Chinese goods, being rare and of excellent craftsmanship, were particularly valuable and sought after, especially after the breach in contact between the two countries which had been a consequence of the Mongol invasions.

Ashikaga Takauji also insisted, in the *Kemmu* Code, that formality, ceremonial and etiquette should be strictly observed, firmly upholding the Confucian principle that each person should behave in a manner befitting his station in life and treat others in accordance with their private and public circumstances. Distinctions between superior and inferior were deemed to be of the utmost importance, and they should be scrupulously maintained in the way of address as well as in manner. The hierarchical structure of Japanese society is also reflected in the language, which provides ample opportunities for subtle distinctions between persons of superior, inferior or equal rank. Ashikaga Takauji's emphasis on the importance of maintaining dis-

tinctions in matters of ceremonial etiquette demonstrates
the development of their own code of behaviour among the
samurai.[83] With the establishment of the Kamakura *Bakufu*
the *buke* also established their own etiquette, partly based
on the ceremonial of the Heian Imperial court. As we have
already noted, the traditional court offices and titles were
retained under *bushi* rule, and in all their dealings with the
Imperial court the minutiae of court etiquette were observed. When Minamoto Yoritomo set up his *Bakufu* at
Kamakura, the amount of ceremony required was adapted
to the simple lifestyle of the *bushi* as well as to the warlike
conditions. There was a conscious effort to dissociate the
Bakufu from the Imperial court, and an emphasis on simplicity which brings to mind the continuous struggle of the
ancient Roman patricians against the weakness for luxury
displayed by the Greeks, to whom they stood in the same
relationship as did Japan to China, the source of all its
cultural refinement. From the wording of the *Kemmu* Code
it is apparent that with the passage of time *buke* and *kuge*
forms of etiquette had begun to show a tendency to become
confused.

The legal codes regulating the affairs of the *bushi* not
only controlled matters of property, public office and criminal offences, but also their standard of living, including
their apparel. The power of example was, and is, extraordinarily great in Japan, and in the *Kemmu* Code there are
to be found several references to this phenomenon. Those
in a position of authority were considered to have special
responsibilities, as their subordinates would attempt to
emulate their behaviour and attitudes, and the character
and actions of his vassals tended to reflect on the character
of their lord, since a man was judged according to the
qualities of the people who surrounded him either as friends
or as servants. Personal attendants on the Emperor and
Shōgun were to be chosen for their upright character, and
the Code even issued a serious warning against admitting
artistic performers of different kinds to the immediate circles
surrounding the Emperor and Shōgun, where they might
gain influence through their elegant costumes, manners
and accomplishments.

PART II: WARRIOR ETHICS EAST AND WEST

Thus a *bushi* was trained from childhood for his future position in society by being taught to observe his father and his male elders and imitate their behaviour. Formal education consisted of the teaching of the Confucian Classics, but *bushi* of low rank were often illiterate until the time of the Tokugawa *Bakufu*, when literacy became exceptionally widespread in Japanese society. The military arts were the most important part of the training of a *bushi*, and were constantly practised from boyhood. Horsemanship, archery and sword-fighting techniques were taught to males, whereas girls of *bushi* stock learned how to use the *naginata*, a halberd with a curved blade, in self-defense. *Bushi* women were also instructed in the use of the dagger which they always carried about their person, in order to be able to commit suicide by severing the jugular vein should the need for such action arise. The education of the *bushi* was referred to from the early Kamakura *Bakufu* by the term *Bun-Bu* (Letters and military arts). The study of letters encompassed the five traditional Chinese Classics and the four Confucian books.

The study of martial arts included a theoretial side as well as a practical one. The nature of the theory of *Bushidō* before it was recorded in the seventeenth century can only be gauged from literary references, and as we have seen the *Gunki Monogatari* provide many instances of the *bushi*'s philosophy of life and death. First of all he was aware of the fact that by fulfilling his duties as a professional warrior he was acting against the central principles of both Buddhism and Shinto. By taking life the *bushi* condemned himself to the existence of an *asura*, infernal spirit, in one of the Buddhist hells, of which there are ten cold and ten hot varieties, instead of being able to gain a favourable rebirth and eventual salvation in the Western Paradise of Amida Buddha. The knowledge of this certain damnation did not deter the samurai from giving loyal service to his lord, however, and it was frequently stressed by the authors of the *Gunki Monogatari* that the carrying out of duty was its own reward. This attitude was considerably elaborated upon and much discussed in later writings on *Bushidō*.

The *kuge* and *buke* continued to lead separate lives after the establishment of the Kamakura *Bakufu*, although members of the *kuge* and the Imperial family occasionally were impressed or influenced by the warlike spirit of the new rulers. Jien wrote with evident disapproval in his *Gukanshō* of the abdicated Emperor Go-Toba (1180-1239, regnavit 1183-1198) who displayed an unusual interest in such pastimes as archery and horsemanship. Go-Toba established his own guard force, the *Saimen Bushi* (Westface Warriors) modelling it on the *Hokumen Bushi* (Northface Warriors) of Go-Shirakawa, a private guard which had been disbanded by Minamoto Yoritomo. These imperial guard forces became a disruptive element which tended to disregard the *Bakufu*. There were instances of *Bakufu* officials being arrested in Kyoto, and of court titles being conferred directly, without the customary recommendation and approval of the Kamakura government.

The author of the *Tsurezure Gusa*, a title which can be translated as 'Idle Jottings' or 'Adiafora', Yoshida no Kaneyoshi, also known as Kenkō, (1283-1350?) was a *kuge*, descended from the ancient clan of Court diviners, *Urabe*. Having served at the court of Emperor Go-Uda, he took the tonsure on the death of the Emperor in 1324 and lived as a recluse in a hermitage in the country for many years, although he is said to have returned to Kyoto for a period. His book contains a random collection of anecdotes, miniature essays on various topics, and reflexions on the state of the world. Yoshida clearly deplored the tendency of his contemporaries among the *kuge* to take an interest in warlike pursuits. 'Any man is soldier enough to crush the foe when fortune favours him, but War is a profession where he cannot make his name until, his forces exhausted, his weapons at an end, he seeks death at the hands of the foe rather than surrender. So long as he is living he cannot boast of warlike fame. What then does it profit, unless one is of a military family, to devote oneself to conduct removed from human principles and approaching that of the beasts?' Such behaviour did not suit the *kuge*'s station in life, and should be left to those born into the ranks of the *bushi*.

He could not, however, refrain from expressing admiration for those who lived and died as befitted warriors, as is evident from an anecdote he recorded. This concerned a party of *komusō*, Zen monks of the Fuke school, who were praying in an Amida temple. Another *komusō* entered, demanding to know whether a man whose name he gave was among them, and explaining that he wanted to avenge the death of his master. The man who had killed his master was present, answered in the affirmative, and arranged to meet his challenger outside the temple, so as not to pollute it or disturb the service in progress. The two men met outside, sword in hand, and fought a duel in which both of them died. 'Wilful and determined, they appear to be devoted to the Way of the Buddha, but they make strife and quarrel their business. Though dissolute and cruel in appearance, they think lightly of Death, and cling not at all to Life. The bravery of such men having impressed me, I set this down as it was related to me.'[84] This, albeit somewhat reluctant, expression of admiration is rather far removed from the unmitigated disdain shown by the Heian literary ladies four centuries previously. It demonstrates how by this time the attitudes of the *bushi* had at least become accepted as a viewpoint which, even if it was not to be emulated, was regarded as worthy of consideration as an alternative to the *kuge* way of life. The *kuge* continued to regard themselves as the only true nobility, while the *buke* saw them as exponents of the remote and largely inconsequential court system.

The ethics and morals governing the life and thought of the *bushi*, and forming the guidelines for warrior comportment, bore a striking resemblance to contemporary European codes of chivalry. If we examine one of the most famous European works on the subject, *Libre del Orde de Cauayleria* (The Book on the Order of Chivalry), written in Catalan by Raymond Lull around 1280, we find a way of reasoning which is similar to many of the ideas and sentiments expressed in the *Gunki Monogatari* and the legal codes of the Hōjō and Ashikaga rulers. These similarities are entirely fortuitous, but nevertheless interesting and illuminating when we take the widely differing background and development of the two feudal systems into account.

Not unlike different religions, which display affinities of ideas arrived at from diametrically opposed standpoints, the ethical and practical demands of the two types of chivalry demonstrate a certain universality in human thought and endeavour. It must be remembered also that when dealing with European chivalry as well as *Bushidō* we are contemplating an ideal whose attainment might vary quite considerably, according to circumstances, and from one individual to another, and that far from every knight or *bushi* even attempted to attain this ideal although he was certainly aware of its requirements.

Religion was at the back of both kinds of chivalrous behaviour. The European knight was constantly reminded that he was a Christian knight, and that his duty at all times was to uphold the principles of charity, loyalty, truth, justice and virtue, protecting the weak against the strong and defending widows and fatherless children. Lull went to great lengths in his treatise to explain the religious and symbolic significance of the knight's arms, pointing out the resemblance of both his sword and dagger to a cross. The *bushi*, on the other hand, was not expected to uphold justice, truth and virtue *ad majorem Dei gloriam*, but because the quality of *gi* 'duty' or 'righteousness' was demanded of him by the Confucian doctrine to which he adhered.

Whereas the Christian knight could obtain absolution from his sins, e.g. of taking life, through confession, the *bushi* accepted with fortitude that he was condemned according to the tenets of Shinto as well as Buddhism. When we consider the sword of the *bushi* we find that it also had religious connotations, being dedicated to and protected by Buddhas, Bodhisattvas and minor Buddhist deities. The most significant difference between Europe and Japan, however, lay in the fact that not every man born of a knightly family in Europe actually entered an order of knighthood, while in Japan every male of the warrior nobility was a *bushi* by birth. In Europe the new knight was invested in a religious ceremony, usually held on one of the major feast days of the church, and we may compare this ceremony with the *genbuku* (coming of age) ceremony of the young *bushi*.

While keeping the cultural and ideological gulf separating Japan and Europe in the Middle Ages in mind, some of Lull's treatise provides interesting material for comparison.

In the first chapter an old knight, now living as a hermit, gives advice to a young squire concerning the rules of chivalry, culminating in one sentence which sums up his ideas: 'For just as chivalry gives to a knight all that appertains to it, in like manner a knight ought to give all his forces in order to honour chivalry.'[85] Lull extols the nobility of knighthood, which demands that the knight is worthy of his station in life and behaves accordingly, being trained from boyhood in horsemanship and the use of arms. He stresses the point that every knight should serve as a squire in his youth, so that having learned servitude he will later be fit to be a master. The use of arms is not enough, however, and the young squire should also be taught the doctrine of chivalry from books, which in fact is the reason why Lull himself has written his treatise. 'The office of a knight,' says Lull, 'is to maintain and defend the holy Catholic faith. (. . .) As our lord God has chosen the clergy to uphold the holy Catholic faith with scripture and reason against the wicked and the unbelievers, in like manner the God of glory has chosen knights in order that by force of arms they may vanquish the wicked who daily labour to destroy the holy Church.'[86]

Although this is far removed from the tenets of *Bushidō*, we soon find a convergence of ideas. 'The office of a knight', continues Lull, 'is to uphold and defend his worldly or earthly lord, for neither a king nor any high baron has the power to maintain righteousness in his men without aid and help.' Lull also stresses the importance of the knight's taking active part in jousts and tournaments as well as hunts in order to keep himself fit and in training, while taking care of his soul by means of practising the virtues of 'justice, wisdom, charity, loyalty, truth, humility, strength, hope, quickness.'[87] The faithless knight who opposes his lord wrongs not only his own lord, but also all the faithful knights who fight and die in order to maintain justice, says Lull. 'Nobility of spirit cannot be vanquished by man—and when it is in its full strength, it cannot be surmounted by all the men who exist.' Cowardice is a betrayal of all the principles of chivalry, whereas a strong spirit and a noble appearance in the face of adversity does honour to the order. 'No man honours and loves chivalry more than he who dies in order to love and honour the order of chivalry, nor can any act contribute to chivalry more than death.'[88] This sentiment is one which we will presently see echoed in the writings on *Bushidō*, particularly in the famous dictum found in the *Hagakure*: '*Bushidō to wa shinu koto to mitsuketari*' (*Bushidō* consists in dying—that is the conclusion I have reached).

Lull also sees the knight as an upholder of public order, and the guardian of the land and the peasants who work on it. He should support artisans and craftsmen, protect the people against robbery and other crime, and look after the weak, especially women and children, and the infirm. Similar ideas existed in Japan, largely through the influence of Confucianism, since there is no exact parallel to Christian compassion in Buddhism, and certainly none in Shinto. Lull emphasises the importance of lineage, and strongly discourages the admittance to knighthood of any man not born into the peerage. The knight must be worthy of his station, be of good character and manners, truthful and honest, ablebodied and modest. One who seeks to enter the knighthood for reasons of self-aggrandisement or vanity is not suited for it and will bring dishonour to the order of chivalry. We have seen similar ideas in the *Gunki Monogatari*, where lineage was of paramount importance, and where every *bushi* endeavoured to honour his name and clan.

In Japan the only refuge for a man of *bushi* stock who did not wish to lead the life of an active warrior was to take holy orders and enter the Buddhist priesthood. Buddhist temples and monasteries served as sanctuaries for young survivors of clan feuds, such as Minamoto Yoshitsune, whose life was spared by Taira Kiyomori after the execution of his father on the condition that he enter the Buddhist priesthood where he would be unable to avenge the death of his father. The same course of action was not infrequently taken also in Europe. Although Christianity and Buddhism are religions devoted to peaceful pursuits and spiritual needs, there existed in Japan as well as in Europe a powerful *ecclesia militans*. In Japan the so-called 'warrior monks', *sōhei*, who first appeared in the Heian period, were a notable feature in the *Gempei* War as well as during the *Sengoku jidai*. Already in 970, Ryōgen, the abbot of the Hieizan monastic complex, laid down rules designed to curtail the activities of armed monks who disrupted the religious services.[89] These regulations seem to have been largely ineffective, if we consider the amount of political power wielded by the armed clerics towards the end of the Heian period, and also the very serious disturbances created during the *Sengoku jidai* by the *Ikkō-ikki*.

The *sōhei* appear to have originated as a result of disputes over the ownership of land rather than over matters of doctrine, and many fights took place between two monasteries belonging to the same school of Buddhism. The warrior monks were not recruited among the high-ranking ecclesiastics, and quite a few laymen were also employed by the temples and monasteries to provide armed protection. Prior to the Kamakura period the *sōhei* wore the ordinary habit of a Buddhist monk, with the addition of a long scarf-like piece of cloth which was wound around the head and neck, covering the face and leaving only a space open for the eyes. They originally carried a staff and a sword, and only during the *Gempei* War did they begin to wear armour and other weapons. The *Heike Monogatari* provides vivid pictures of warrior monks, especially of one who took part with distinction in the Battle on Uji Bridge in 1180, fighting on the Minamoto side. 'Among the warrior-monks was one Tsutsui no Jōmyō Meishū. He wore armour laced with black leather over a deep blue battle robe. The thongs of his helmet with five neck-plates were tied tightly under his chin. He carried a sword in a black lacquered sheath, twenty-four black-feathered arrows, a bow thickly bound with lacquered rattan, and his favourite wooden-shafted sickle-bladed halberd. He stepped forward onto the bridge and thundered: "You have heard of my fame as a valiant warrior. Take a good look at the pride of Mii-dera, I am Tsutsui no Jōmyō Meishū—among the dōju I am worth a thousand soldiers. Is there any among you who thinks himself a great warrior? Let him come forward!" '

The *Heike Monogatari* then goes on to tell how he performed outstanding feats of marksmanship, killing twelve enemies and wounding eleven more with as many arrows, and swordsmanship, cutting down five men with his halberd and eight more with his sword. After these extraordinary exploits Jōmyō retired to the Byōdōin temple nearby, where he counted the sixty-three dents in his armour and his five wounds, which he cauterised by applying burning grass to them. 'Then', says the *Heike Monogatari*, 'he wrapped a piece of cloth around his head, donned a white robe, and took up a broken bow for a staff. Chanting "Hail Amida Buddha", he went off toward Nara.'[90]

We may compare the important part played by the warrior monks in the Japanese civil wars with the not dissimilar phenomenon in Medieval Europe of the spiritual orders of knights, notably the Templars, Hospitallers, and the Teutonic Order. The Order of the Knights of the Temple was founded in 1118 for the protection of pilgrims on their way to Jerusalem, and the other orders soon followed. They established a network of hospices and churches all over Europe and the Near East, and became a factor of the utmost importance in the Crusades through their knowledge of the countries around the Mediterranean and their languages and customs. Although their origins and the conditions which brought about their foundation were widely different, the Japanese warrior monks and the military orders of Europe shared one fundamental trait, namely the fact that they had to justify the taking of life. The *sōhei* were either laymen serving in a temple or monastery, or low-ranking monks, and the Knights Templar and Hospitaller were members of religious orders within the Roman Catholic church, and subject to rules of poverty, chastity and obedience like monks and clerics.

The problem was one of morals and ethics, and the main question was whether the ultimate end could be said to justify the use of means which were theoretically forbidden. Buddhism, like Christianity, categorically forbids the taking of all life, going indeed a step further than Christianity by forbidding also the killing of animals, including insects. The person who instigates, or even condones, a killing, is as guilty as the person who carries it out, according to Buddhist doctrine, and in war all soldiers are equally guilty of taking life, whether they actually kill an enemy or not. The negativism of Buddhism, however, which teaches that all is suffering and that nothing really exists, can easily be interpreted as inimical to life itself. The idea of reincarnation may seem to favour the ending of the present existence in order to try again under different and perhaps better circumstances. This is not possible, however, owing to the belief in *karma*, the sum total of the individual's actions, which adheres to its bearer throughout the cycle of reincarnations. There is no getting away from the influence of *karma*, and only by leading a virtuous and pious life and refraining from sinning, can the individual hope to improve his chances of a more favourable rebirth in the next existence.

In Buddhism, as in Christianity, however, there is a considerable divergence between philosophical speculation on doctrine and dogma and popular ideas, and it is not difficult to see that the taking of life could be condoned under special circumstances, even among members of the clergy. The *sōhei* developed parallel to the *bushi* in a society which became increasingly dependent on warlike qualities for maintaining stability, and in the end the *bushi* were forced to eliminate the *sōhei* in order to gain political supremacy and unify the country.

Most of the *sōhei* appear to have been recruited from the popular Amidist schools of Buddhism. Zen Buddhist monks played a more ambivalent part. The Zen schools were introduced in Japan in the early years of the Kamakura *Bakufu*, and Zen monks seem to have taken an active part in the power struggles between the Hōjō *Shikken*, the Imperial court, and the Ashikaga *Shōguns*. As we have seen, the mental discipline taught by Zen came to influence the art and techniques of fighting, especially swordsmanship, to a very large extent. The Zen masters seem to have gone in for theory rather than practice, however, and Zen monasteries did not figure prominently among the religious institutions which were annihilated in Oda Nobunaga's purge of the politicised clergy of the *Sengoku jidai*.

One line of defence adopted by the Buddhist clergy to justify their taking up arms was the simple and apparently irreproachable fact that they were defending their religion against the enemies of the faith. Since they were fighting against their co-religionists of other Buddhist schools, this meant that they considered themselves as defenders of the true religion against false or heretical doctrines. In Europe, the religious orders reasoned in a similar vein, and in the Crusades they felt called upon to rescue one of the most sacred monuments of Christendom, the Holy Sepulchre, from infidel dominance. There is a comprehensive Buddhist tradition of armed divinities protecting the faith against all forms of evil influences, including the *Niō-ō*, the *Shi-tennō*, and the *Myō-ō*, as well as Bodhisattvas like *Monju*. The profound influence of the *bushi* on the militant side of Buddhism did not fail to impress the Buddhist clergy, and the prevailing atmosphere was one of warlike exploits rather than peaceful pursuits, however pacifist the Buddhist doctrine may have been originally.[91]

The Christian attitude is well illsutrated by a sermon written by Bernard of Clairvaux in the early twelfth century. Bernard had written the rules of the Order of the Knights Templar after the council at Troyes in 1128, and in his sermon, addressed 'To the Knights of the Temple, a book in praise of the new chivalry', he dealt especially with the problem of taking life. He contrasted the old, secular, chivalry, whose knights lived in luxury and vainglory and were guilty of murder when they killed an enemy in battle, with the new, spiritual, chivalry, the *milites Christi*, as he called them. 'I say that this is a new sort of chivalry, unknown through the centuries, because it tirelessly wages an equal and double war, both against flesh and blood and against the spiritual forces of evil in the other world.' (. . .) 'Surely, it is an intrepid knight, protected on every side, who clothes his body with the armour of iron and his soul with the armour of faith. Thus supremely protected by arms of both types, he fears neither demon nor man. Nor indeed does he who wishes to die fear death. He whose life is Christ, and for whom death is profit, what should he fear in life or death?' (. . .) 'However, death in battle is so much the more precious, since it is the more glorious.' (. . .) 'I say that the soldier of Christ kills in safety and dies in greater safety. He profits himself when he dies, and he profits Christ when he kills.' (. . .) 'Truly, when he kills a criminal, he commits not homicide but, as I would call it, malicide, and clearly he may be considered the avenger of Christ in those who do wrong, and a defender of the Christians.' (. . .) 'Therefore, the just man will always rejoice when he sees this just vengeance.'[92]

In his sermon Bernard also mentioned the monastic discipline of the Knights Templar. 'Both in food and in garment all excess is avoided, and only necessity is considered. They live in common, in a cheerful and sober manner,

without wives and without children. And lest they fall short
of evangelical perfection, they keep no private possession,
but they live as a single community in a single house, eager
to preserve unity of spirit in a bond of peace. You would say
that in the entire throng there is but a single heart and a
single soul. The individual by no means seeks to follow his
own will but rather to obey his commander. At no time do
they sit in idleness or wander about in curiosity.' (. . .)
'Among them there is no distinction of persons; noble
deeds, not noble birth, gain respect.' (. . .) 'Insolent speech,
useless actions, immoderate laughter, even a low grumble
or whisper never, when they are noticed, are left unpun-
ished. They detest chess and dice; they abhor hunting and
take no pleasure, as is customary, in the silly chase of
birds. They detest and abominate actors, magicians, story-
tellers, immodest songs and plays; these for them are
vanities and follies.' (. . .) 'Finally, in a marvellous and singular fashion, they are seen to be meeker than lambs and
more ferocious than lions, so that I nearly hesitate in
deciding whether I should call them monks or knights.'[93]

We see here that Bernard of Clairvaux himself considered the Knights Templar as a spiritual order, nearly on a
par with the religious orders proper. The discipline which
the knights were subjected to was not unlike that of any
Christian, or indeed Buddhist, monastery, and the rules
concerning clothing and lifestyle are strikingly reminiscent
of the sumptuary laws for the *bushi*, enforced by the Hōjō
Shikken in Japan two centuries later. The major difference
lies in the equality practised by the Knights Templar, whose
nobility rested in their acts, not in their birth. Nothing like
this was ever possible in the hierarchical society of Japan,
where lineage was never forgotten. The Buddhist monasteries, especially of the Zen schools, came closest to equality in this sense, but even there pedigree was never completely disregarded.

The most important and influential Buddhist monasteries, nunneries or temples, as well as the major Shinto
shrines, as a rule chose their abbots and abbesses or chief
priests and priestesses among junior members of the Imperial family until modern times. Among the *bushi*, for
whom lineage was of the utmost importance, the possibility
of entering their ranks from below did however exist until

the late sixteenth century. Later, in the latter half of the Tokugawa *Bakufu*, adoption for men and marriage for women became other means of gaining admittance into a *bushi* family. Even such a very powerful man as the autocrat Toyotomi Hideyoshi, who was given a family name and pedigree by Imperial decree, was never able to forget or conceal his plebeian origins. He was greatly feared and in complete command, but nevertheless despised by the old *kuge* and *buke* families. There is no doubt that some families over the centuries managed to get away with spurious and newly fabricated pedigrees, but despite the prevalence of natural disasters such as earthquakes and typhoons, Japan is a country where families have managed to preserve their documents and records from the early Heian period until this day to a remarkable degree.

PART III: EARLY CONFUCIAN INFLUENCE

The five cardinal virtues of Confucianism, *gojō*, i.e. benevolence, *jin*, justice, *gi*, propriety, *rei*, wisdom, *chi*, and fidelity, *shin*, have provided the basis for the Japanese outlook on life since Heian times and before, in conjunction with Buddhist ideas of compassion in the face of the vanity of human wishes and the fatalism inherent in the belief in inexorable *karma*. One of the most lucid analyses of the Confucian virtues in a Western language was written by the remarkable Jesuit missionary João Rodrigues (1561-1633), who lived in Japan from 1577 until his expulsion in 1610. In his account of the country and its inhabitants he enumerates the five virtues, giving a definition of each of them. 'The first is compassion, observance, benevolence, love and kindness, for it embraces all these virtues. The second is justice, fairness, equity and integrity. The third is reverence, courtesy and politeness. The fourth is wisdom. The fifth is loyalty and truthfulness in social matters and agreements.'[94]

These virtues were embraced by the entire population in varying degrees, depending on education and social position as well as on circumstances. They were emulated by the *bushi*, for whom the principle of *giri* 'duty' or 'obligation' which included loyalty to the feudal lord, was of fundamental importance. The observance and upholding of *giri* was essential for maintaining the elaborate system of interdependence between lord and vassal, between vassals of the same lord, and within the immediate family as well as the clan. *Giri* was a key principle in *Bushidō*, and the total devotion and unswerving loyalty given to the hereditary head of the clan was one of the most important factors in the political ascendancy of the *bushi*.

In the *Mutsu Waki* (A Tale of Mutsu), we encounter fully developed ideas of loyalty well over a century before the *Gempei* War. This precursor of the later *Gunki Monogatari* is a contemporary attempt to chronicle the famous campaign of Minamoto Yoriyoshi (988-1075) against the rebel Abe Yoriyoshi (who changed his name to Yoritoki when his Minamoto namesake was appointed governor) in the north-eastern province of Mutsu. This campaign, in which Minamoto Yoriyoshi's son Yoshiie (1041-1108), the famous Hachiman Taro, first showed his mettle as a warrior, lasted from 1051 to 1063. The *Mutsu Waki* was written in Chinese, apparently soon after the events it records, probably by a *kuge* official in the capital.

The author's admiration for *bushi* values is apparent in several passages in the text. During one battle, which ended in a defeat for Minamoto Yoriyoshi, one of his men, Saeki Tsunenori, lost sight of his commander and feared that he had fallen. ' "For thirty years now I have been in Yoriyoshi's service", said Tsunenori. "I am sixty and he is almost seventy. If he must die, I intend to share his fate and go with him to the underworld." He wheeled and entered the enemy cordon. Two or three of Tsunenori's retainers were present. "Now that our lord is about to die honourably by sharing Yoriyoshi's fate, how can we stay alive? Although we are merely sub-vassals, we are men of principle too," they said.'[95] Another retainer of Yoriyoshi's, Fujiwara Shigeyori, also believed that his lord had fallen when the latter remained missing for several days after the battle had been lost. ' "Let me at least recover his body to give it a proper burial. Nobody but a monk can enter an armed camp on such an errand, so I'll have to shave my head before I go," said Shigeyori, weeping bitterly. He made haste to renounce the world and become a monk. Then as he was going towards the battlefield he encountered Yoriyoshi himself, and so returned with him, rejoicing and lamenting at the same time. He had embraced the religious life in a rather cavalier manner, perhaps, but his loyalty was praiseworthy.'[96]

An interesting example of the importance of propriety at all times, and the reverence which was accorded the lord in death as well as in life, is found in the *Mutsu Waki*'s relation of the circumstances of the presentation of the head of Sadatō, Abe Yoritoki's son, who had become the leader of the rebels after his father's death. 'Before this, some of Sadatō's surrendered followers told their new leader—the warrior sent by Yoriyoshi to present the heads— that they needed a comb. "Dress his hair with your own combs", he replied. The man carrying Sadatō's head took out his comb and dressed the hair, sobbing bitterly as he said, "When my lord was alive, I looked up to him as to heaven on high. How could I ever have dreamed that one day I would presume to dress his hair with my filthy comb?" Everyone wept with him. Though he was only a porter, his loyalty was commendable.'[97]

However, when a warrior who had been taken alive by the rebels was released because he was the brother-in-law of one of their chieftains, the followers of Minamoto Yoriyoshi regarded this turn of events as disgraceful. It is notable that from the earliest times the *bushi* were supposed neither to give nor ask for quarter. To be captured alive by the enemy in a battle was a misfortune which brought dishonour. A true warrior died fighting when outnumbered, and those who became incapacitated and unable to leave the battlefield came to prefer committing *seppuku*, as we have seen in the *Gunki Monogatari*.

The life of a *bushi*, in fact, was not his own to be squandered recklessly, but should at all times be at the disposal of his lord. For a vassal to kill his own lord was the ultimate act of treason. Minamoto Yoritomo, who clearly realised that there could be no deviation from the principles of loyalty and faithfulness when he established his *Bakufu*, refused to receive among his vassals a former Taira partisan who had killed his own lord and brought his head to Yoritomo. The man was executed on the orders of Yoritomo, who stated that he did not wish to have among his retainers someone who was so lacking in principles as to even contemplate treachery against his lord, let alone kill him. In the end Yoritomo accused his own half-brother Yoshitsune of treason and drove him to commit *seppuku*. The quarrel between the two brothers, who together had defeated the Taira, is one of the most famous episodes in Japanese history.

Volumes have been written about the relationship between the brothers, who had never met before Yoshitsune joined his older brother in fighting the Taira. There is no evidence of treacherous intent on the part of Yoshitsune, but since he appears to have been the greater military strategist of the two, and was also very well liked by his troops, Yoritomo may have had reason to fear that a strong rivalling faction might eventually appear. In putting a price on his half-brother's head Yoritomo acted contrary to the

Confucian precepts, although he justified his action by claiming that Yoshitsune had turned traitor and was trying to grasp the power himself. That Yoritomo was aware of having acted unjustly is clearly demonstrated by his bad conscience, which, as we have already seen, may have caused his death by a fall from his horse. On that occasion, according to legend, Yoritomo's mount shied away from the ghostly apparitions of Minamoto Yoshitsune and Yukiie and the child-emperor Antoku, all three of whom could be said to have been innocent victims of his jealousy or hunger for supremacy.

The *Jōei* Code of the Hōjō successors of Minamoto Yoritomo and his sons contained Yoritomo's ideas on proper *bushi* behaviour, and we have also seen that the *Kemmu* Code of 1336, although brief, repeated the rules concerning restraint in personal behaviour, the observance of strict etiquette, and indeed the duty of a *bushi* always to set an example through his actions. Beside the actual legal codes other written regulations concerning *buke* and *bushi* began to appear. The Shōgun Ashikaga Yoshimitsu (1358-1408, regnavit 1368-1395) commissioned a collection of regulations regarding general deportment and etiquette, the so-called *Ogasawara-ryū*. This was written in 1396 by Ogasawara Nagahide, Imagawa Noritada and Ise Sadayuki, and strongly influenced by Zen Buddhist ideas. The Ogasawara family remained hereditary teachers of etiquette to the Shōgun until the Meiji Restoration, and to this day provide private tuition in archery, etiquette and deportment.

The name of Imagawa likewise became associated with rules of conduct for the *bushi*, through the so-called *Imagawa-jō* (Imagawa Letter). This was probably written in 1412 by Imagawa Sadayo, also known as Ryōshun (1325?-1420?), for his younger brother Nakaaki, whom he had adopted as his heir. Imagawa Ryōshun's laconic reprimand, although personal in tone, was considered generally applicable. It first became a sort of manual on questions of ethics for the Imagawa clan, and soon caught the interest of other warrior families. Tokugawa Ieyasu knew it and made use of it for his House Laws, and during the Tokugawa *Bakufu* it was used in schools, either in its original form or annotated and adapted for the use of children or common-

ers. A version for women, *Onna Imagawa*, was published in
1700.

In a nutshell, the letter calls for Nakaaki to remember his
position and birth and conduct himself and his official
affairs (he was a *shugo*, provincial military governor) in
such a way, according to Confucian and Buddhist principles, that his subordinates and the people of Tōtōmi
would look up to him and find his character worthy of
emulation. Ryōshun was emphatic in stressing the equal
importance of martial accomplishments, strategy and Confucian learning, claiming in fact that one without the other
was useless. Many injunctions were identical to those
found in the legal code in force at the time, the *Kemmu
Shikimoku*, e.g. the warnings against harrassment or unjust treatment of the people, and the stern reflexion that
the company a person keeps is indicative of his own morals
and character, sentiments which we also recognise from
the nearly one century older *Tsurezure Gusa* by Yoshida no
Kaneyoshi.[98]

At the time when the Imagawa Letter was written in the
early fifteenth century the country had recovered something of a precarious equilibrium after the period of the
Northern and Southern Imperial courts, 'The Great Age of
Turncoats', as the historian James Murdoch with his un-
rivalled talent for a poignant *mot* called it, although the
party in support of the Southern Emperor attempted to
rally again in 1422 under Shinnō Moroyasu. The Ashikaga
Shōguns had moved back to Kyoto, disregarding Minamoto
Yoritomo's cardinal rule for a strong government, namely
that the *Bakufu* should be kept geographically separate
from the political intrigues which flourished in the proximity of the Imperial court. With the waning of Ashikaga
power the political situation gradually became untenable,
however, as the number of peasant revolts, *ikki*, increased
and local *daimyō* were able to gain increasing autonomy in
their provinces.

Between the years 1467-1477 the so-called *Ōnin* War
raged, chiefly in the Kyoto area. The war was fought between rivalling *daimyō*, who were at this time strong enough
to attempt to wrest authority from the Ashikaga government. Large parts of the capital were laid waste by the war,
and, although the Ashikaga continued to hold the office of

Shōgun for another century, the name *Sengoku jidai* (The period of the Warring Country) given to the period 1477-1573 by Japanese historians, aptly sums up the state of the country in the later Ashikaga/Muromachi period.

The fourteenth, fifteenth and sixteenth centuries in Japan, plagued by intermittent warfare and general turmoil, constituted a period of considerable social change. Not even the Imperial house was exempt from trials and tribulations, and the fact that Emperor Go-Kashiwabara, who succeeded to the throne in 1500, had to wait for 21 years until enough money could be scraped together for his enthronement ceremony, is a good example of the state of society at large. The peasant rebellions offered opportunities of advancement for those of ability and talent. Not a few peasants became mercenary soldiers in the employ of local *daimyō*, and for those who possessed the necessary qualities chances to rise in the ranks presented themselves.

Already in the first half of the fourteenth century the author of *Tsurezure Gusa* lamented the passing of old values and standards and the rapid rise of upstarts, *nariagari*. Rapidly changing fortunes became a characteristic of the *Sengoku jidai*. Old *buke* families lost their fiefs and lapsed into obscurity, while men of peasant origin were able to grasp power, titles and offices. The act of overthrowing one's lord and replacing him as *daimyō* was known as *gekokujō*, and was resorted to by many vassals who wished to rise in the world. In spite of the chaotic conditions, especially during the sixteenth century, the basic tenets of *Bushidō* however remained the guiding principle for warrior relations. There were serious and quite frequent infringements of the rules, legal and political as well as religious and ethical, during the years of near-anarchy. The fact remains, however, that *Bushidō* continued as an ideal for the warrior, and that its tenets were observed, albeit with occasional modifications, by the *bushi* and their emulators. *Bushidō* can hardly be said to have developed its ethical aspects during these years, but what is more remarkable is that it survived at all.

The increase in power of the provincial *daimyō* during the *Sengoku jidai* was such that they promulgated their own legal codes in their fiefs, which in many cases had taken on an aspect of more or less autonomous states, *bunkoku.* One such legal code was the *Jinkaishū,* promulgated by the *daimyō* of Mutsu, Date Tanemune, in 1536. The disturbed times were clearly reflected in the *Jinkaishū,* which was entirely pragmatic in character. It stated unequivocally that clerics were forbidden to carry a *katana,* long sword, i.e. one that could be used in fighting. This kind of frequently repeated prohibition was much needed and often ignored in the *Sengoku jidai.* As well as armed risings of peasants, *tsuchi-ikki,* and lower samurai and peasants, *kuni-ikki,* the religious risings, *Ikkō-ikki,* presented a grave threat to local *daimyō* and the *Bakufu* alike.

Ikkō-ikki was the name given to armed risings of the followers of the *Ikkō* school, a branch of the *Jōdo Shin-shū,* the True Pure Land school of Amidist Buddhism, which originated in the teachings of the turbulent monk Shinran (1172-1262). For more than a century, from the time of the *Ōnin* War until the frequent campaigns of Oda Nobunaga against the militant Buddhist clergy in the 1570s and 80s, armed monks played an important part in the power struggles of the period. The *Jinkaishū* provides interesting insights into the Japanese application of the law by stating that when a *bushi* committed *seppuku* leaving a written statement explaining his reasons for killing himself and naming an enemy, the latter was to be punished. To cut down a person mistaking him for somebody else was a punishable crime, and when someone was killed on the battlefield by a man from his own side (presumably by mistake in the heat of the fray) the dead *bushi* was to be accorded the same honours as those who had fallen for enemy weapons. Acts of private vengeance were expressly forbidden, and personal slights should be referred to the *daimyō*'s court of appeal. Runaway peasants were to be brought back to their masters forthwith, a necessary measure at a time when the countryside appears to have been swarming with bands of various *ikki.*

Characteristic of Japanese legislation is the prohibition against harbouring the wife, children, other relatives, servants, and even valuables, of a relation convicted of a crime. Harsh measures of this kind effectively prevented the restoration of the family fortunes of the condemned man, and it is not difficult to see how it was possible even for prominent *buke* families to be consigned to oblivion and destitution at one stroke. The idea that the family members of someone who was sentenced for a crime were themselves guilty, or that the professional scribe who was ordered by the forger of a document to copy it out was himself to suffer the same punishment as the forger, permeated the entire legal system, remaining in force until the end of the Tokugawa *Bakufu*.[99]

This particular aspect of Japanese legislation attracted the attention of foreign visitors to the country, and most of the early European missionaries and travellers commented on the exceptional severity of the Japanese criminal law and its effectiveness as a deterrent. The idea of guilt by association did not lose its practical implications until the introduction of a legal system based on judicial principles similar to those applied in Western countries. Certain vestiges remain in the popular conception, however, and the remarkably low crime rate in today's Japan is attributed, at least partly, to the idea that the criminal act reflects negatively on the reputation of the family of the perpetrator. During the Tokugawa *Bakufu* a *daimyō* was held responsible for the actions of his subordinates, and rash acts by loyal retainers could cause the fief to be confiscated by the authorities. The arbitrary manner in which individual cases were judged is illustrated by the Akō affair, discussed below, where inaction on the part of a *daimyō*'s retainers produced the same result.

Oda Nobunaga (1534-1582), Toyotomi Hideyoshi (1537-1598) and Tokugawa Ieyasu (1542-1616), all of them ruthless and despotic even by the standards of the *Sengoku jidai*, demanded, and usually got, absolute loyalty from the *daimyō* who joined them. Their individual characters, as perceived by their contemporaries, are illuminated by a popular parable, in which the three are confronted with a recalcitrant *hototogisu*, a kind of cuckoo, in a cage. Oda Nobunaga declares that unless the bird begins to sing he will kill it, while Toyotomi Hideyoshi says that he will find a means to make the bird sing, and Tokugawa Ieyasu states that he is prepared to wait until the bird sings.[100]

Oda was assassinated by a disgruntled retainer in 1582, before he had been appointed to the office of Shōgun which was within his grasp. From the famous seal inscribed *Tenka fubu* (the whole country under one sword) which he

began to use officially already in 1567, and from his elevation to ever higher court rank, culminating with his appointment to *Daijō daijin* (Great Chancellor), it is clear that
Oda aspired to the highest political power. To accomplish
his objective Oda needed to be able to trust not only his
vassals but also their subordinates. When the old Takeda
fiefs of Kai and Shinano were distributed after the defeat of
Takeda Katsuyori, son and heir of his chief adversary Takeda
Shingen (1521-1573) in 1582, Oda issued regulations to
the effect that loyal *bushi* were to be left undisturbed, while
potential troublemakers were to be expelled or forced to
commit *seppuku*.[101] Oda did not live long enough to develop the full potential of his notions of grandeur, unlike
his successor, Toyotomi Hideyoshi, whose last years were
clouded by his ill-conceived Korean campaign which ended
in ignominious withdrawal after heavy losses.

Unlike Oda and Tokugawa, Toyotomi Hideyoshi was not
of *bushi* stock. What members of the warrior nobility had
learned from childhood he had taught himself, combining
his innate strategic and tactical talents with an uncommon
ability for psychological assessment of his fellow men. He
had the extravagant tastes of the *parvenu*, and appears to
have become obsessed with the idea that his name and line
should be preserved and perpetuated through his son and
heir, Hideyori (1592-1615), as well as by means of grandi-
ose buildings such as the castles at Fushimi and Osaka
and the gigantic Buddha statue at Amida-ga-mine in Kyoto.
He considered himself an instrument of higher powers,
'one who had encountered the will of Heaven', *Tentō ni
aikanau mono ya*, and acted accordingly.

The life-style of Toyotomi was very far removed from the
austere and restrained ideals of the *bushi*. As a passionate
devotee of *chadō* (the Way of Tea), he patronised Sen no
Rikyū, the father of *Cha-no-yu* or the 'Tea-Ceremony', as
we know it. Before their disagreement in 1591, after which
Rikyū was ordered to commit *seppuku*, Hideyoshi had
allowed Rikyū to preside over two famous tea gatherings on
a grand scale, one at Osaka Castle, and the other at Kitano
in Kyoto. The general public was invited to take part in the
latter gathering, which was held in the open, and Hideyoshi
can be credited with having popularised the art of tea.
Despite his love of luxury—he built a tea-room entirely

decorated in gold with tea bowls and utensils of the same material—Hideyoshi, however, showed his appreciation of the refinement of simplicity by also serving tea in a simple grass hut, using plain earthenware utensils. His flamboyant and extravagant attitude concealed a pragmatist who had acquired a shrewd understanding of the *bushi* psyche.

By means of the *katanagari* (Sword Hunt) of 1588 he managed at last to disarm the peasants and curb the *ikki*. Commoners were forbidden to possess all forms of weapons, and the confiscated swords were to be used as nails and bolts in the construction of the huge statue of Amida Buddha, according to the edict. Thus a further incentive for giving up one's arms was added, namely that of a meritorious deed which would ensure a favourable rebirth. By completely separating warriors from peasants, *hei-nō-bunri*, Toyotomi Hideyoshi laid the foundations for the Tokugawa system of four clearly defined social classes, samurai, peasants, artisans and merchants. His cadastral surveys, *kenchi*, rice tax, *kokudaka*, and village organisation, *mura*, effectively put an end to the chaotic social conditions which had made his own rise to power possible, and by destroying some fortified castles, *shirowari*, and transferring certain *daimyō, kunigae*, he got the *buke* under control. He himself never attained the office of Shōgun, although he was the *de facto* ruler of Japan from 1582 to his death in 1598. Officially he was given the title of *Kampaku* (regent) but personally he preferred the title *Taikō* (His Highness) (literally 'Great Palace'), which was used of a retired *kampaku*.

To prevent others from following his own example by changing their social status, whether upwards or downwards, Toyotomi Hideyoshi issued legal decrees prohibiting peasants from engaging in trade and *bushi* from living as peasants. A *bushi* who had left his lord without permission was not to be accepted into the service of another without an investigation of the circumstances. He was liable to be arrested and forcibly returned to his original lord, and violation of these laws was severely dealt with. If *bushi* or peasants who had attempted to change their status were discovered, the entire village or town where they were living would be punished. When a *bushi* had entered the service of a new master without the permission of his former lord, three heads were to be offered to the latter in compensation. If this was not done the new lord was considered to be responsible and duly punished.[102]

The so-called House Laws of Toyotomi Hideyoshi, *Taikō Shikimoku*, are deceptively simple and truistic, indicating down-to-earth common sense combined with a shrewd understanding of the foibles of human nature. 'Rise early', 'Avoid heavy drinking', 'Be on your guard against women', and 'Think of your own future' could be the rules of anyone determined to better his lot and get on in the world. 'Beware of thoughtless people', 'Beware of practical jokes', 'Do not tire of things', 'Set up fences in your hearts against wandering or extravagant thoughts', and 'Hold nobody in contempt' show a firm grasp of the essentials of the *bushi* ethos. The complexity of his character is shown not only by the contrast between his pragmatism and his attempts to become deified as an incarnation of Hachiman under the name of *Toyokuni Daimyōjin* in the Toyokuni Jinja, but also by his rapidly changing moods.

Some of the early Europeans in Japan who met him have reported very favourably on his great charm and courtesy when he personally showed them around Fushimi Castle, then under construction. Not long afterwards, however, he issued an edict, in 1587, expelling all Christian missionaries from the country on pain of death. It is recorded in the annals of Japan that one of his favourite sayings was '*Kubi haneru beshi*', which can be translated as echoing the Queen of Hearts' 'Off with his head!' That he was basically a realist is demonstrated by his famous and often quoted *jisei no ku*, the 'farewell poem' or 'swan song' which he is supposed to have composed on his deathbed, in accordance with the *bushi* tradition of summing up one's life when *in extremis*: 'I came like the dew/I vanish like the dew/My whole life/and Osaka Castle/is a dream within a dream.'[103]

To say that Tokugawa Ieyasu took over a united and pacified Japan after the death Toyotomi Hideyoshi in 1598 would be a gross exaggeration. Nevertheless, the foundations of what was to become the Tokugawa *Bakufu* had been firmly laid, and the social structure organised by Toyotomi Hideyoshi was to remain virtually unaltered for the next three centuries. The transfer of power to Tokugawa Ieyasu did not take place unopposed, however, Firstly, he had sworn allegiance to the house of Toyotomi, promising the dying Hideyoshi to protect the interests of his son and heir, Hideyori, then six years old. Secondly, there were many influential *buke* who were themselves prepared to compete for the political power, as Toyotomi partisans or for their own private ends.

The Battle of Sekigahara in 1600, in which the scales tipped over in favour of Tokugawa Ieyasu, proved decisive, and in 1603 he was appointed Shōgun. It was not until 1615, however, the year before his death, that the opposition was finally suppressed in the Battle of Osaka Castle. This edifice, next to his son the apple of Toyotomi Hideyoshi's eye, was razed to the ground and the Toyotomi clan exterminated. The *Sengoku jidai* had come to an end after a last half-century of exceptional social, intellectual and cultural mobility. Fortunes had been made and lost, families had risen from obscurity while others had sunk into oblivion, and new and hitherto unknown impulses had arrived with the European missionaries and traders.

The first Europeans in Japan were some Portuguese sailors who had been blown off course *en route* to China and landed at Tanegashima in 1543. They were soon followed by the Spanish Jesuit missionary Francisco Xavier in 1549, and from that time a large number of merchants and missionaries of different nationalities, Spanish, Portuguese, Dutch, English and French and religious orders, chiefly Jesuits, Franciscans and Dominicans, established themselves in the country. The Jesuits were particularly successful in their propagation of the Christian faith, and when Xavier returned to Goa after two years in Japan he left behind him a community of about eight hundred Christians. During the next thirty years the number of converts increased rapidly, until there were some 150,000 *Kirishitan*, as the Christians were known, at the time of Toyotomi Hideyoshi's edict of banishment in 1587.

The popularity of the new religion has been explained partly by the fact that the Jesuits used a Buddhist terminology in their teaching of the doctrine, and by the general turbulence of the times, which had created an atmosphere where a faith promising coherence in this life and salvation in the next held great appeal. As had frequently been the case in the evangelisation of Europe, noblemen who became converts were baptised with their entire households. Once a *daimyō* had become a Christian his samurai felt obliged by the laws of loyalty to follow his example, but when the persecutions began in 1597 the numbers of *Kirishitan* dwindled rapidly, as those who had never wholeheartedly embraced the new faith apostatised. With the Shimabara Rebellion, which was quelled in blood in 1637, the so-called 'Christian century' came to a close. During the first fifty years of virtually unhindered European contact with Japan the Dutch and English East India Companies had been established, churches, seminaries and charitable institutions had been built, books had been printed in Latin, and Western art, architecture and culture had left their mark. There was even what can best be described as a goodwill mission from the Christian *daimyō* of Bungo, Omura and Arima to the Pope, Gregory XIII. The *primus motor* behind this venture was the Italian Jesuit Alessandro Valignano, whose journey with four young Japanese boys to Portugal, Spain and Italy lasted from 1582 to 1590. Nearly three centuries were to pass before any of their countrymen were again allowed to visit Europe.

Although the number of converts of *bushi* stock was considerable, and included several *daimyō*, there appear to have been no notable instances of Christian influence on the theory and practice of *Bushidō*. Like firearms, which began to be manufactured at Tanegashima soon after the landing of the Portuguese, Christianity was fashionable in the late *Sengoku jidai*, together with other novelties from the West. Firearms were used in battle until the consolidation of the country under the Tokugawa *Bakufu* effectively put an end to warfare. There was never any question, however, of firearms ever superseding the sword as the chief weapon of the *bushi*. Once the persecutions of Christians had begun in earnest in 1597 the new religion was doomed in Japan, and the Tokugawa *Bakufu* with its almost paranoid fear of secret conspiracies which might lead to political upheaval and insurrection adopted stern measures to extirpate the possibly subversive faith. All *Kirishitan*, including infants and children, who did not apostatise were executed. The proscription of Christianity offered yet another opportunity for controlling the population. All Japanese were required to register at a Buddhist temple near their home, a form of census which proved very effective. The *e-fumi* ceremony took place annually all over Japan, where the inhabitants were assembled village by village, and in the towns and cities ward by ward, and made to tread on plaques representing the crucified Christ or the Virgin and Child, in order to demonstrate that they were not Christians.

PART IV: THE TOKUGAWA BAKUFU AND THE CODIFICATION OF BUSHIDŌ

Tokugawa Ieyasu confirmed the old values anew. One of his most decisive steps was to reestablish shōgunal power along the lines of the early Kamakura *Bakufu*. Like Minamoto Yoritomo he realised the importance of setting up his headquarters on the East coast, at a safe distance from Kyoto and possible political intrigue, and chose the then fairly minor castle town of Edo, present-day Tokyo. In 1611 all the *daimyō* of Japan swore an oath of fealty to Tokugawa Ieyasu, thus becoming his personal vassals. To safeguard their loyalty the *sankin kōtai* system was developed, whereby the *daimyō* were required to spend part of the year in their residences in Edo. When they took up residence in their respective fiefs their families had to remain in Edo, a hostage system which proved most effective.

The laws of the Tokugawa *Bakufu* were considerably more detailed and comprehensive than any previous legislation. The two codes first to be promulgated were the laws for the court nobility, *Kuge Sho-Hatto*, of 1613, and the laws for the military houses, *Buke Sho-Hatto*, of 1615, while Tokugawa Ieyasu was still alive. His successors made various additions and amendments over the years, but these legal codes, regulating the affairs of the court and warrior nobility respectively, remained in force without major changes until the end of the Tokugawa *Bakufu*. Rules and regulations affecting the common people were posted on public notice-boards, *kosatsu*, whenever necessary. Under the eighth Shōgun, Tokugawa Yoshimune (regnavit 1716-1745), a compendium of existing criminal laws was promulgated under the name *Sadamegaki Hyakkajō* (The Edict in One Hundred Articles), for the use of the courts of justice, but again most of these laws were customary, dating from the earliest Tokugawa legislation.

The *Kuge Sho-Hatto* and *Buke Sho-Hatto* devote considerable space to detailed regulations concerning personal apparel and expenditure, and additional or amended sumptuary laws were an ever recurring feature of the

Tokugawa *Bakufu*. The *Buke Sho-Hatto* went into minute detail in its regulations concerning the lives and conditions of the *buke* and *bushi*. The same also applies to the *Shoshi Hatto*, a set of laws for the *hatamoto*, the direct vassals of the Shōgun whose annual income did not exceed 10.000 *koku* per annum. The *Shoshi Hatto* was first promulgated in 1632, but after 1683 it was incorporated in the *Buke Sho-Hatto*. The code clearly states that the distinction between lord and vassal must be plainly indicated by the quality of their garments, and there is a list of garments which the ordinary *bushi* may not wear, e.g. silk with woven patterns, wadded silk coats, *kosode*, and purple or purple-lined silk coats. Damasks and silk brocades are especially mentioned as unsuitable.

The use of palanquins, *kago*, was restricted to *daimyō*, their families and high-ranking retainers. The *kuge* naturally enjoyed the privilege of travelling in a *kago*, and certain other categories were also allowed to use one, e.g. abbots and the higher clergy, medical doctors, and the elderly and infirm. A stern injunction to all *bushi* to avoid ostentation and practice frugality was repeated in every subsequent edition of the *Buke Sho-Hatto*, as were the regulations concerning clothing and personal belongings. Fine and valuable household utensils, such as cups made of lacquer or precious metals were not to be used, except on especially festive occasions such as birthdays, weddings or New Year's Day, or when entertaining a particularly important guest of high rank. The only display of personal luxury a samurai was permitted was in his weapons. Almost the only way of demonstrating individual taste, as well as personal wealth, was in the material and artistic design chosen for the sword furniture and the ornaments on the hilt, *menuki*. These, the pommels, *kashira* and *fuchi*, and the guard, *tsuba*, were often designed by outstanding artists and craftsmen with gold or silver inlays.

In the formal exchange of gifts, always an important part of Japanese social intercourse, the value must not exceed one *Ōgon*, the largest gold coin, which was worth seven and a half *ryō* or *koban*. This was the common price of a horse or a sword, the most suitable gift from one *bushi* to another, although the sum was frequently given in cash. Depending on the rank of the parties the sum could be reduced, 100 copper cash being the lower limit. *Kosode*, wadded silk coats, were also suitable gifts among *daimyō*, ten being the maximum amount. Wine and foodstuffs, 'in moderation' as the code states without specifying the amounts allowed, were common gifts then as they still are today.

Bribery and favouritism were strictly forbidden, and the *daimyō* and *Bakufu* statesmen were repeatedly exhorted to choose their officials on the grounds of ability, merit and character. Nothing resembling the Chinese examination system for government officials ever existed in Japan, however, where heredity and clan membership remained the most common means of attaining office and promotion.

There could be no unauthorised association between the retainers of different *daimyō*, nor were marriages within the fief to be contracted without permission from the superior. The opening sentence of the *Buke Sho-Hatto* stated unequivocally that the two concepts *Bun* and *Bu*, learning and the military arts, were to form the guiding principle in the lives of all samurai. 'Literature first, and arms next to it, was the rule of the ancients. They must be cultivated concurrently. Archery and horsemanship are the most essential for the Military Houses (*Buke*). Weapons of warfare are ill-omened words to utter; the use of them, however, is an unavoidable necessity. In times of peace and good order we must not forget that disturbances may arise. Dare we omit to practise our warlike exercises and drill?'[104]

The *Shoshi Hatto* (Laws for the Knights or Gentry), special laws for the *hatamoto*, became obsolete after 1683, and the *Buke Sho-Hatto* applied to those of *hatamoto* rank as well. While in force, however, between 1632 and 1683, the *Shoshi Hatto* opened with articles very similar to those of the *Buke Sho-Hatto*. 'The Way of a Samurai (military vassal) is to take pleasure in his military service, without negligence. (. . .) Loyalty and filialty must be prized, and the rules of ceremonial decorum correctly carried out, and the attention constantly direction to literary cultivation and military accomplishments. Rectitude of conduct is to be made the first concern, so that there may be no degeneration of morals/among the lower orders under you/.'[105]

Elaborate measures were taken to ensure that the hard-won peaceful conditions were to last. Infringements of the law were punished by banishment, and this applied particularly to *bushi*, as one of the articles states bluntly: 'Fellows of savage disposition (being retainers), are an apt weapon for overthrowing the domain or the family employing them, and a deadly instrument for cutting off the (cultivating common) people. How can such be tolerated?' The *daimyō* were allowed to keep their residential castles in repair, but additional construction work, especially of fortifications, was prohibited, for the reason that 'Crenellated walls and deep moats (of castles) are the causes of anarchy.'[106]

In later versions of the *Buke Sho-Hatto* similar injunctions were regularly repeated and new clauses appeared. 'The scheming of innovations, the forming of parties and the taking of oaths is strictly forbidden,' appeared for the first time in Iemitsu's (regnavit 1622-1651) version of 1635, together with a direct mention of Christianity by name: 'The Christian sect is to be strictly prohibited in all the provinces and in all places.' We may note that this version was promulgated just before the outbreak of the Shimabara Rebellion. The next version, of 1663, under the fourth Shōgun, Ietsuna (regnavit 1651-1680), contained an interesting addition, verbally communicated to the *daimyō* at the same date, namely an official prohibition of the practice of *junshi*. 'That the custom of following a master in death is wrong and unprofitable is a caution which has been at times given of old; but, owing to the fact that it has not actually been prohibited, the number of those who cut their belly to follow their lord on his decease has become very great. For the future, to those retainers who may be animated by such an idea, their respective lords should intimate, constantly and in very strong terms, their disapproval of the custom. If, notwithstanding this warning, any instance of the practice should occur, it will be deemed that the deceased lord was to blame for unreadiness. Henceforward, moreover, his son and successor will be held to be blameworthy for incompetence, as not having prevented the suicides.'[107]

That this expression of supreme *bushi* loyalty should have been denounced in the legal code as a blameworthy act, for which a third party might be punished, demonstrates the *Bakufu*'s panic fear of disturbances of the public order. Contrary to the custom in Europe, where public executions were considered a deterrent from crime, executions in Japan were only attended by officials in the course of their duties, and members of the public were forbidden to assemble on the execution-ground. Those about to be executed were however customarily paraded through the streets before the sentence was carried out, and their heads gibbeted or the entire corpses displayed afterwards, depending on whether they were samurai or commoners.

The fact that the prohibition of *junshi* appeared in 1663 may at least partly have been a result of the *Rōnin* Conspiracy of 1651. This attempt at overthrowing the Tokugawa *Bakufu* failed prematurely when one of the confederates revealed the plan in a feverish delirium, but the *Bakufu* regarded the threat as very serious indeed and increased its vigilance, although the repeated injunctions against *junshi* had little effect.

The anxiety caused by the Akō affair, fifty years after the *Rōnin* Conspiracy, is reflected in the 1710 version of the *Buke Sho-Hatto*, under the sixth *Shōgun*, Ienobu (regnavit 1707-1712). One clause deals with the occurrence of some extraordinary disturbance, in which case everyone, except those immediately concerned, was to remain where he happened to be and not move to the scene of the matter or even attempt to meet friends and discuss it. The prohibition against *junshi* was repeated yet again, with the addition: 'And other things sternly prohibited are, the forming of cliques or parties, the taking of mutual oaths, as such proceedings are a wanton disregard of right principles and tend to result in the infringement of established institutions,' an indication of the *Bakufu*'s alarm over the recent drama of the loyal forty-seven *rōnin* and their private and unauthorised vengeance.[108]

Despite the political and social turmoil and upheaval the country had undergone in the *Sengoku jidai* period very little had changed where the old *bushi* values were concerned. Even during the most tumultuous period observance of the ideals of *Bushidō* was the rule rather than the exception, and there were individuals who displayed remarkable strength of character in the face of adversity. A poignant vignette illustrating this is quoted by Murdoch concerning the execution of Ishida Mitsunari (1560-1600), former governor of Kyoto and vassal of Toyotomi Hideyoshi. Having fought on the losing side at Sekigahara Ishida was being led through Kyoto on his way to the execution-ground when he asked for hot water to quench his thirst. None was available, and he was offered a persimmon instead. Ishida declined, explaining that the fruit was not good for his health, whereupon his guards jeered at him, saying that it was ridiculous for someone about to be beheaded to be concerned about his health. Ishida is said to have replied: 'It is natural that to men like you it should seem ridiculous. But a man who aims at a great thing is ever bent upon accomplishing his objective, even to the very moment when his head is to fall into the blood-pit. It is a case of the proverb "Sparrows cannot understand eagles". '[109]

With the consolidation of the Tokugawa *Bakufu*, and the peaceful conditions brought about by Tokugawa Ieyasu's careful planning and stern measures, the *bushi* gradually became transformed into government officials rather than active warriors. As was explicitly stated in the *Buke Sho-Hatto*, training in the martial arts took precedence in the lives of the *bushi*, in conjunction with letters, i.e. the Chinese Classics. From this time there were, however, few opportunities for samurai to practise their warlike skills in earnest. Although the vendetta, *katakiuchi*, remained a not uncommon way of settling private disputes, permission must be sought from the authorities before carrying it out.

A major problem in the early decades of the Tokugawa *Bakufu* was the question of the *rōnin*. After Sekigahara, and especially after the Battle of Osaka Castle in 1615, vast numbers of samurai had lost their feudal lords and become *rōnin*. As a result of the fall of Osaka Castle and the final defeat of the Toyotomi faction 50,000 *rōnin* are estimated to have roamed about the country in search of re-employment, or, since the chances of finding a new lord were slight indeed, any form of livelihood. Those who possessed sufficient learning might become teachers of Confucianism, *jusha*, or instructors in the art of swordsmanship, and there was also the possibility of taking the tonsure and entering a Zen Buddhist monastery or some other school of Buddhism. Other *rōnin*, however, became outlaws or joined the criminal or half-criminal underworld of the major cities, to some extent merging with groups like the *otokodate*. This large group of well-trained and armed former samurai, who might easily have become soldiers of fortune if the Tokugawa *Bakufu* had not taken legal and practical steps to prevent this, constituted a serious threat to the country's new-found political and social stability.

Out of the chaotic conditions of the *Sengoku jidai* and the enforced inaction during the Tokugawa *Bakufu* which drastically curtailed the freedom of movement of the *bushi* and eroded their *raison d'être* as active warriors came however a need for discussion and definition of *Bushidō*. The codification of the rules of *Bushidō* was undertaken mainly by Confucian scholars of *bushi* stock. Of the so-called 'Three Great *Rōnin*' of the Tokugawa era, one, Yui Shōsetsu, was involved in the *Rōnin* Conspiracy of 1651, and was forced to commit *seppuku* when the plot to overthrow the *Bakufu* came to light. Another, Kumazawa Banzan (1619-1691), became a Neo-Confucian *jusha* and a reformer of the samurai system. The third, Yamaga Sokō (1622-1685), also a *jusha* but more interested in the original ideas of Confucius than in their Neo-Confucian interpretation, is credited with having coined the term *Bushidō*.

Before considering Yamaga Sokō and his contemporaries we must look at some of their precursors. Miyamoto Musashi (1584-1645?) wrote his treatise on swordsmanship, the *Go Rin Shō* (A Book of Five Rings), at the end of his eventful life which had been characterised by an uncommon degree of individualism. He fought in the great battles of his time, at Sekigahara on the losing side and at Osaka and Shimabara on the side of the victor, and spent his entire life perfecting his fighting techniques, never settling down for long in one place. Although his *Go Rin Shō* is primarily a treatise on the philosophy and practice of military strategy and swordsmanship, it also documents the changing times in which Miyamoto lived. His disgust with the lack of understanding of the warrior's *métier* and the opportunism he had seen all around him is reflected in terse statements such as 'There is no warrior in the world today who really understands the Way of strategy', and 'Recently there have been people getting on in the world as strategists, but they are usually just sword-fencers.'[110]

When expounding the techniques, physical as well as

mental, necessary for gaining proficiency in his two-sworded school of fencing, the *Nitō ryū*, Miyamoto listed his basic principles: 'Do not think dishonestly; The Way is in training; Become acquainted with every art; Know the Ways of all professions; Distinguish between gain and loss in worldly matters; Develop intuitive judgement and understanding for everything; Perceive those things which cannot be seen; Pay attention even to trifles; Do nothing which is of no use.'[111] This absolute pragmatism, strongly reminiscent of the sentiments found in the *Imagawa-jō* of Ryōshun as well as in the *Taikō Shikimoku*, the so-called Precepts of Toyotomi Hideyoshi, echoes the *bushi* ideals expressed in the House Laws and in the legal codes from the *Jōei Shikimoku* onwards.

'Generally speaking', wrote Miyamoto Musashi, 'the Way of the warrior is resolute acceptance of death. Although not only warriors but priests, women, peasants and lowlier folk have been known to die readily in the cause of duty or out of shame, this is a different thing. The warrior is different in that studying the Way of strategy is based on overcoming men. By victory gained in crossing swords with individuals, or enjoining battle with large numbers, we can attain power and fame for ourselves or our lord. This is the virtue of strategy.'[112] The emphasis on the *bushi*'s readiness to die for his lord was to become a central theme in the Tokugawa period writings on *Bushidō*, and it is interesting to find it so clearly and unequivocally expressed in Miyamoto's martial arts manual.

One of the foremost Neo-Confucian scholars of the early Tokugawa *Bakufu*, who collaborated closely with Tokugawa Ieyasu in formulating the *Buke Sho-Hatto*, was Hayashi Razan, also called Dōshun (1583-1657). Hayashi was an exponent of the *Shushi-gaku*, the Neo-Confucian school based on the teachings of the Chinese Confucian scholar Chu Hsi (1130-1200). Neo-Confucian ideas had been introduced in Japan with Zen Buddhism, and when the Confucian scholars began to dissociate their teachings from Buddhism in the sixteenth and seventeenth centuries they gained acceptance among the leading statesmen of the period. The other important Neo-Confucian school was the *Ōyōmei-gaku*, the school of Wang Yang-ming (1472-1529). There were also many eminent Confucian scholars who adhered to the traditional teachings of Confucius himself and of Mencius, their school being known as *Ko-gaku* or *Fukko-gaku*. One of the key concepts of the Chu Hsi school was *ri* (Chin. *li*), usually translated as 'principle', whereas the characteristic concept of the Wang Yang-ming school was *shin*, 'mind' or 'intuition'. The Chu Hsi school was rational, founding its philosophy on the Five Relations and on precedents from Chinese history, while the Wang Yang-ming school maintained that moral intuition led to right action. Their ideals were essentially the same, e.g. loyalty, propriety, benevolence and righteousness, although the means of attaining them differed.

In Hayashi Razan's definition of the position of the *bushi* in society, the predilection for the complementary rather than the dualistic which characterises Oriental philosophy and religion is clearly illustrated. 'To have the arts of peace, but not the arts of war, is to lack courage. To have the arts of war, but not the arts of peace, is to lack wisdom. (. . .) A man who is dedicated and has a mission to perform is called a samurai (or *shi*). A man who is of inner worth and upright conduct, who has moral principles and mastery of the arts is also called a samurai. A man who pursues learning, too, is called a samurai. A man who serves/at court/without neglecting the mountains and forests is also called a samurai. The term samurai (or *shi*) is indeed broad.'[113]

Hayashi Razan was appointed official *jusha* to Tokugawa Ieyasu in 1608, and his house at Ueno in Edo, where he kept his vast library, became a seat of Confucian learning. This was given the name *Kobun-in* (Hall of Confucian Learning), under Razan's son Gahō (1618-1680) and became the shōgunal university. Under the fifth Shōgun, Tokugawa Tsunayoshi, Razan's grandson, Hayashi Nobuatsu, also called Hōkō (1644-1732), was given the title *Daigaku-no-kami* (Head of the State University), and the seat of learning was moved to the district of Yushima in Edo in 1691 and given the name of *Shōheikō* (The School of Prosperous Peace). The office of *Daigaku-no-kami* remained hereditary in the Hayashi family throughout the Tokugawa *Bakufu*, and the twelfth in line, Gakusai, lived on well into the Meiji period, dying in 1906.

From the time of Tokugawa Ieyasu the Chu Hsi school

was thus officially recognized and approved. The school of Wang Yang-ming received no official sanction, however, and was at times actively discouraged and indeed banned by the government. The founder of this school in Japan was Nakae Tōju (1608-1648), often called the Sage of Ōmi after his native province. Although he was the son of a farmer Nakae was adopted by his grandfather, a samurai in the service of the *daimyō* of Ōmi, and brought up as a *bushi*. Of all the virtues Nakae valued filial piety the most, and he lived according to his principles by resigning from his post in a feudal domain in order to return to his native village and take care of his mother. Despite the fact that he lived in semi-seclusion many eminent *jusha* sought him out, and his teachings received widespread recognition. His views on the combination of *Bun* and *Bu* echoed those of Hayashi Razan: 'No true learning is without arms and no true arms without learning.'[114]

In his chief work, the *Okina mondō* (Dialogue With an Old Man), Nakae discussed the duties of a *bushi*: 'The samurai must give single-hearted obedience; forsaking self, he must serve his master, he must be well-versed in his duties, must be faithful to friends, careful of his words, seeking to do right in all things, and in time of danger be prepared to do his lord efficient service.' (. . .) 'The duties of the samurai may be summed up in single-hearted loyalty, the sacrifice of self for lord and country. He must serve his lord as he would his parents, for the lord is the nourisher of the body his parents gave. The samurai of rank must counsel his lord, giving good advice even though it prove distasteful, and dissuading from evil even at the sacrifice of life itself.'[115]

When discussing martial accomplishments Nakae held up Minamoto Yoshitsune and Benkei as paragons of *bushi* virtues, claiming that they had surpassed their contemporaries in learning.' The bravery of the wise man consists in obeying the way, being true to principle and desiring nothing else. He is ready to give up life itself in the service of parent or lord. He neither loves life nor fears death, and thus has destroyed the root of cowardice.' (. . .) 'There are three grades of samurai. The first, endowed with great bravery, obedient to virtue, skilled in accomplishments. The second is not so well instructed in the truth, but loyal, unselfish, and skilful; but the third is selfish and full of lusts. As these last are many the lord has need for caution. Further, there are three examinations: in virtue, capacity and accomplishments. Virtue is the union of *jin* and *gi*, learning and arms; capacity, the power to govern with wisdom in all things; accomplishments, skill in law, in service, in overcoming difficulties and in conquering enemies. These are the pillars of the examination, and rank and salary are to be bestowed in accordance therewith.

'The heart of the ruler was the mirror of the law of old. If the mirror were clouded, all examinations must fail; if the lord excelled in virtue, it was impossible to palm off a false skill upon him.' (. . .) 'We must consider virtue, talent, force, and fate. Virtue is this virtue of arms and letters as described above; talent is the power of moving men at will— wisdom in war, prescience of enemies' plans, knowledge of the forces of heaven and earth; force is preponderance of strength; fate is our natural destiny. Virtue conquers talent, talent overcomes force, and force is superior to fate. If virtue and talent balance, fate wins; then, too, in the last extremity, as the destruction of a nation, fate conquers in spite of virtue and talents.' (. . .)

'The sage excels all men in all things and is divine; the superior man is one degree below the sage and does not attain to the divine; the hero in other things is one degree below superior man, but in war is his equal; the adventurer has the military talents of the hero but lacks his virtues. Sage, superior man and hero bless the land in war or peace; the adventurer is useful only in war and often brings evil on the land. He is to be employed for his talent's sake, but cautiously, and is not to be entrusted with too much power or given too high rank. Following duty, though a man be slain there is not a wound upon him; but wanting virtue, though he live to be fourscore and die in peace he is disgraced as the wretch who is beheaded or sawn asunder.' (. . .) 'Wise men do not desire the name without the virtue: they value it only as a reflection of truth; they are not indignant though their good deeds be unobserved.'[116]

The writings of Nakae Tōju contain the essentials of the *bushi* ethic: loyalty, self-sacrifice and filial piety, the latter directed towards the feudal lord in equal measure. He emphasised duty, the fact that the samurai in a responsible position was obliged to tender advice which would further the cause of his lord and the domain while disregarding his private affairs and possibly jeopardising his own career or even his life. Nakae's views on fame echo those of the Chinese literati, namely that virtue is its own reward. This sober philosophy, far removed from the flamboyant exuberance of the *Heike* and *Hōgen Monogatari*, is characteristic of the distaste for individual exploits, particularly of a warlike nature, which was fostered under the Tokugawa *Bakufu*.

It was an exponent of *Ko-gaku*, the original Confucianism, Yamaga Sokō (1622-1685), however, who wrote the first treatises actually analysing the concept of *Bushidō* while at the same time coining the term itself. As a young man Yamaga had studied under Hayashi Razan, and between 1652 and 1660 he was in the employ of the *daimyō* of Akō, Asano Naganao, as military instructor. He left his position in order to open a school in Edo where he taught the Confucian Classics and all aspects of military science, including strategy, tactics, intelligence, and the use of arms. In 1665 he fell foul of the authorities when he openly criticised Neo-Confucianism as a corruption of the original teachings of Confucius, and from 1666 to 1675 he lived in exile in Akō.

In his earliest work on *Bushidō*, *Bukyō Shogaku* (Introduction to the Warrior's Creed), written in 1656, he gave an outline of the duty of the *bushi*. 'The way of the samurai is placing himself under the control of his lord, to follow absolutely unto death. (. . .) If he cannot give up treasures and finds pleasure in material possessions, then he is necessarily deficient as regards weapons and arms. In time of stress he will be almost unable to forget his home.'[117] In Yamaga's view the *bushi* was an upholder of the social order, who by his example kept the fabric of society intact. 'For a samurai nothing is more important than duty,' he wrote in his treatise on 'The Way of the Samurai', *Shidō*. The concept of *gi* 'duty' or 'righteousness' is the key word in Yamaga's writings on *Bushidō*. By acting righteously and fulfilling his duty in the microcosm of his own station in life the *bushi* set an example for the common people, thus influencing favourably the macrocosm of the domain and the country at large.

In his *Shidō* Yamaga discussed the reasons for the seemingly unproductive life of the *bushi*. This was a question of
particular importance under the Tokugawa *Bakufu*, which
effectively relieved the warrior of most of his warlike functions, reducing him to a local administrator and civil servant with sentry duties in a closed totalitarian state. 'Generation after generation men have taken their livelihood
from tilling the soil, or devised and manufactured tools, or
produced profit from mutual trade, so that peoples' needs
were satisfied. Thus the occupations of farmer, artisan, and
merchant necessarily grew up as complementary to one
another. However, the samurai eats food without growing
it, uses utensils without manufacturing them, and profits
without buying or selling. What is the justification for this?
When I reflect today on my pursuit in life/I realize that/I
was born into a family whose ancestors for generations
have been warriors, and whose pursuit is service at court.
The samurai is one who does not cultivate, does not manufacture, and does not engage in trade, but it cannot be that
he has no function at all as a samurai. He who satisfied his
needs without performing any function at all would more
properly be called an idler. Therefore one must devote all
one's mind to the detailed examination of one's calling.'[118]
    Reflecting on this question Yamaga reaches the conclu-
sion that the *bushi* has two interconnected functions: to
lead a life in which even the most insignificant gesture is
dictated by his sense of righteousness and justice, and
thus to constitute, in his person, a model of morally correct
behaviour for the common people. 'The business of the
samurai consists in reflecting on his own station in life, in
discharging loyal service to his master if he has one, in
deepening his fidelity in associations with friends, and with
due consideration of his own position, in devoting himself
to duty above all.' (. . .) 'The samurai dispenses with the
business of the farmer, artisan and merchant and confines
himself to practising this Way; should there be someone in
the three classes of the common people who transgresses
against these moral principles, the samurai summarily
punishes him and thus upholds proper moral principles in
the land. It would not do for the samurai to know the
martial and civil virtues without manifesting them. Since
this is the case, outwardly he stands in physical readiness

for any call to service and inwardly he strives to fulfil the Way of the lord and subject, friend and friend, father and son, older and younger brother, and husband and wife.

'Within his heart he keeps to the ways of peace, but without he keeps his weapons ready for use. The three classes of the common people make him their teacher and respect him. By following his teachings, they are enabled to understand what is fundamental and what is secondary. Herein lies the Way of the samurai, the means by which he earns his clothing, food and shelter; and by which his heart is put at ease, and he is enabled to pay back at length his obligation to his lord and the kindness of his parents. Were there no such duty, it would be as though one were to steal the kindness of one's parents, greedily devour the income of one's master, and make one's whole life a career of robbery and brigandage. This would be very grievous. Thus I say that one must first study in detail the duties of one's own station in life. Those who have no such understanding should immediately join one of the three classes of the common people.' (. . .) 'But if perchance one should wish public service and desire to remain a samurai, he should sustain his life by performing menial functions, he should accept a small income, he should limit his obligation to his master, and he should do easy tasks/such as/gate-keeping and night-watch duty.' (. . .) 'The man who takes or seeks the pay of a samurai and is covetous of salary without in the slightest degree comprehending his function must feel shame in his heart. Therefore I say that that which the samurai should take as his fundamental aim is to know his own functions.'[119]

While under a cloud for his criticism of Neo-Confucianism Yamaga Sokō wrote the *Haisho zampitsu* (An Autobiography in Exile), where he compared his own country with China and concluded that Japan rather than China deserved the appellation Middle Kingdom. Pointing out that Japan had never been conquered he extolled his country's military valour. In his view, however, Japan was equally the abode of great sages. By going straight to the writings of Confucius himself he had come to understand the meaning of the philosophy of the sages. 'To me, therefore, the guiding path to the teaching of the Sages is that which involves personal cultivation, the guidance of others, the maintaining of peace and order in the world, and the winning of honour and fame. I come from a samurai family and have the five obligations of human relationship which attach to my person and station. My own thought and conduct, as well as my five obligations in relations with others, are what I as a samurai must give first attention to. In addition, however, there are both major and minor matters to which the samurai must give his attention. In minor matters, such as dress, food, dwelling, and all implements and their uses, he must live up to the best samurai traditions of good form. This is particularly true in connection with training in the arts of war and with the manufacture and use of armour and horse trappings.

'Among major matters there are the maintenance of peace and order in the world; rites and festivals; the control of feudal states and districts; mountains and forests, seas and rivers, farms and rice fields, temples and shrines; and the disposition of suits and appeals among the four classes of people. In addition, there is military command and organisation, strategy in war and tactics in battle, the quartering and provisioning of troops, and the building of fortifications—all those preparations for war which are the daily concern of generals and officers. No matter how much training he undergoes, if the studies pursued by a samurai do not enable him to get results in all these fields, then they serve no useful purpose and fail to follow the guiding principle of the sages' teaching.' (. . .) 'If one follows this approach to learning, intelligence will renew itself, and virtue will of itself be heightened; humanity will be deepened and courage strengthened. Finally, one will attain to a state of mind in which success and fame are of no account, in which unselfishness and self-forgetfulness will be the rule.'[120]

The nationalistic fervour of Yamaga Sokō is echoed in a famous anecdote concerning another *jusha*, Yamazaki Ansai (1618-1682), an exponent of the Chu Hsi school. He once asked his students what they were to do if a Chinese army under the command of Confucius and Mencius were to attack Japan. When they were unable to provide an answer be declared: 'I would put on armour and take up a spear to fight and capture them alive in the service of my country. That is what Confucius and Mencius teach us to do.'[121]

Despite the strenuous efforts of the *jusha* to establish and maintain a national Japanese learning, inspired by, yet independent of and preferably surpassing, Chinese Confucianism, their writings contain a strong undercurrent of the ingrained sense of inferiority vis-à-vis China.

Kumazawa Banzan (1619-1691), a pupil of Nakae Tōju, was interested in contemporary Japanese conditions and appears to have been an eminently practical man. It is not difficult to see why the pragmatic Wang Yang-ming school held a greater attraction for him than the more theoretical Chu Hsi school. Kumazawa Banzan had a distinguished although rather brief career as Chief Minister to the *daimyō* of Okayama, Ikeda. Born into a *bushi* family in straitened circumstances, Kumazawa had had the good fortune to escape *rōnin* status when he served Ikeda as a samurai in his youth. From his memoirs it is clear that Kumazawa left nothing to chance, and his pragmatism is evident in the rigorous training he subjected himself to. 'When I was on the night watch at my master's residence in Edo, I kept a wooden sword and a pair of straw sandals in my bamboo hamper, and with these I used to put myself through military drill in the darkened court after everyone was asleep. I also practised running about over the roofs of the out-buildings far removed from the sleeping rooms. This I did so as to be able to handle myself nimbly if a fire should break out. There were a few who noticed me at these exercises and they were reported to have said that I was probably possessed by a hobgoblin (i.e. a *tengu*). This was before I was twenty years old. After that I hardened myself by going into the fields on hot summer days and shooting skylarks with a gun, since I did not own a falcon for hawking. In the winter months I often spent several days in the mountains taking no night clothes or bed quilt with me, and wearing only a lined jacket of cotton over a thin cotton shirt.' (. . .) 'In such a way I disciplined myself until I was thirty-seven or -eight years old and avoided becoming fleshy. I was fully aware of my want of talent and believed I could never hope to be of any great service to my country, so I was all the more resolved to do my best as a common *samurai*.'[122]

This, then, was the ideal single-minded discipline with which a *bushi* tempered himself to become a weapon for the use of his lord. The majority never attained to such a state of perfection, and not everyone tried, but the image of the true samurai who resembled a well-honed blade resting in its scabbard always ready for use persisted until the end of the Tokugawa *Bakufu*, providing inspiration for *bushi* and commoners alike.

The pragmatism of Kumazawa Banzan meant that he wanted to see results, and his career ended after less than a decade when his ideas for reform met with opposition from a clique of fief officials who were alarmed by the proposed innovations. The latter half of his life was spent in retirement, although his writings remained influential. A reform plan which he presented to the Shōgun only a few years before his death was considered so potentially subversive that his movements were restricted and closely watched until his dying day. The *rōnin* problem was one which concerned Kumazawa Banzan deeply. Having himself experienced the conditions common to most *rōnin* in his youth he was anxious to improve their lot and at the same time get them to contribute actively to the national economy. To save the *rōnin* from dire poverty and starvation Kumazawa advocated a return to old values, harking back to the Heian period and the origins of the *bushi*. 'When the samurai become farmer-soldiers, the martial spirit of the nation will be greatly strengthened and it will deserve to be called a martial country. Ever since the samurai and farmers became separate classes, the samurai have become sickly and their hands and feet have grown weak.' (. . .) 'On the whole, a noble and lasting social order can only be built on a farmer-soldier basis. Now is the time to restore the farmer-soldier of olden times.'[123] It is easy to see why this call for economic independence on the part of the *bushi* should have alarmed the authorities representing a system based on strictly regulated interdependence, and Kumazawa did not improve matters by stating that none of the shōguns since Kamakura times had governed in accordance with the principles of the sage-kings, i.e. the culture heroes who figure as the first rulers in the mythology of China, and under whose benevolent rule the country and people were said to have flourished.

The ideas prevailing during the first century of Tokugawa rule are reflected not only in the writings of the Confucian scholars, but also in the fiction of the period, that is the literature written for the entertainment of the increasingly prosperous townsmen, *chōnin*. Ihara Saikaku (1642-1693), the leading popular author of the period, who wrote as an outsider congratulating himself on not being obliged by an accident of birth to lead the severely restricted life of a *bushi*, regarded the code of behaviour enforced by *Bushidō* with a certain amount of awe, however. Best known for his risqué tales of contemporary life in the major cities, such as *Kōshoku Ichidai Otoko* (The Life of an Amorous Man), 1682, *Kōshoku Gonin Onna* (Five Women Who Chose Love), 1686, and *Kōshoku Ichidai Onna* (The Life of an Amorous Woman), 1686, Saikaku also published several collections of tales where *bushi* were the chief protagonists or figured prominently. The first of these, *Nanshoku Ōkagami* (The Great Mirror of Manly Love), 1687, dealt exclusively with male homosexuality, a subject which naturally had to include samurai. Other works, such as *Budō Denrai Ki* (The Transmission of the Martial Arts), 1687, and the *Buke Giri Monogatari* (Tales of Samurai Honour), 1688, depicted various aspects of samurai life, with some emphasis on the more spectacular, i.e. sword-fights, especially vendettas, *katakiuchi*.

Ihara Saikaku is famous for his light and humorous vein, although he never attempted to conceal the tragedy of a *curriculum vitae* like that in 'The Life of an Amorous Woman', which began frivolously enough and ended in degradation. His works on the lives of the samurai express mingled admiration and commiseration, and it is clear that he, a merchant's son, able to indulge his interest in writing and lead the life of a *flâneur* observing human foibles, had difficulties in understanding the rules of *Bushidō*, spoken as well as unspoken. The uncompromising rigidity with which the *bushi* upheld his ethical code, regardless of the cost in suffering or indeed lives, seems to have struck Ihara as faintly ridiculous—another case of sparrows and eagles, perhaps—although one detects in his writings a slightly grudging admiration for those who possessed the self-discipline to stick to their principles unconditionally.

PART V: THE AKŌ AFFAIR

P robably the best example of the theory and practice of
Bushidō under the Tokugawa *Bakufu*, and how it was
judged, officially as well as by public opinion, is furnished
by the so-called Akō Affair. This series of events, which
occurred between 1701 and 1703, is perhaps better known
as the story of the 'Loyal Forty-seven *Rōnin*', or *Chūshingura*,
'The Treasury of Loyal Retainers', often called *Genroku
Chūshingura*, after the period (1688-1704) in which it took
place.

These events have furnished material for scores of novels, stories, dramas, works of art, and in recent times films,
and over the centuries they have been constantly embellished, romanticised and embroidered upon. In brief outline the actual historical events were as follows: in 1701
the *daimyō* of Akō, Asano Takumi-no-kami Naganori, attacked the Master of Ceremonies at the shōgunal court,
Kira Kōzuke-no-suke Yoshinaka, with drawn sword in one
of the corridors of Edo Castle, residence of Tsunayoshi, the
fifth Tokugawa Shōgun. The exact circumstances leading
to Asano's action have never been known, but Asano claimed
to have been insulted by Kira. An explanation agreed upon
by most commentators of the affair is that Kira, who was
well known to exact bribes, had been expecting a *douceur*
from Asano, and that he deliberately gave false or mislead-
ing instructions concerning a ceremony over which Asano
had to preside when this was not forthcoming.

Kira received two cuts, neither of them fatal, and Asano
was arrested, sentenced to death through *seppuku*, and
carried out his sentence on the day of the attack. When the
news reached the fief of Akō Asano's retainers discussed
what action to take. The *Bakufu* requested the immediate
surrender of the fief, and some of the retainers wished to
oppose this by barricading themselves in Akō Castle, an
action known as *rōjō*, while others wanted to follow their
lord in death by means of *junshi*, this action being called
oibara. They were shocked and angered by the fact that
Kira was not only still alive but also not punished.

One man, Ōishi Kura-no-suke Yoshio, took a leading

role from the beginning. He was in favour of *oibara*, but first sent a petition to the *Bakufu*, requesting that the fief be transferred to Asano's younger brother, Daigaku. Before this petition reached the authorities, however, *Bakufu* officials arrived at Akō and the fief was surrendered. Ōishi repeated his request for the appointment of Asano Daigaku as the new *daimyō* of Akō, and while the *Bakufu* deliberated the Akō samurai could take no action for fear of compromising Asano Daigaku. After more than a year the *Bakufu* decided to confiscate the fief, a move which formally reduced the Akō retainers to the status of *rōnin*. Ōishi and the men who had previously joined in his *oibara* plan now decided to avenge their dead lord by killing Kira. Since they anticipated that a formal request to the authorities would be refused, they planned their act of vengeance in the utmost secrecy, sworn confederacies being prohibited by law. The number of conspirators was forty-seven, including Ōishi and his son, Ōishi Chikara.

Having travelled to Edo clandestinely and separately, they mounted a nocturnal attack on Kira's residence in the last month of 1702. Kira's guards were taken by surprise, and the *rōnin* informed his neighbours that this was a case of private vengeance, asking them not to interfere. We may note that the version of the *Buke Sho-Hatto* in force at the time strictly forbade interference in private disputes, and none of Kira's neighbours came to his assistance. Kira was found and beheaded, and the *rōnin* immediately carried his head to the Buddhist temple of Sengakuji, where Asano was buried. They had all survived the skirmish, and one man, an *ashigaru*, was sent to Asano's widow and brother with news of the successful outcome of their venture. Thus only forty-six *rōnin* reached the Sengakuji, where they washed Kira's head and placed it on the tomb of their lord as an offering to appease his soul. Two of the *rōnin* brought the authorities a written account of the affair during the day following the attack, and later that day they were all interrogated by *Bakufu* officials and delivered into the custody of four *daimyō*, to be held there until they could be sentenced. Ōishi and sixteen of the *rōnin* were held by the wealthy and influential *daimyō* of Higo, Hosokawa, who is said to have received his prisoners in person to express his approval of their action.

The killing of Kira Yoshinaka by the Akō *rōnin* aroused public interest to an extraordinary degree, broadsheet accounts of the affair being hawked in the streets of Edo only two days after the event. The general public was virtually unanimously in favour of the forty-seven, whereas the *Bakufu* officials and Confucian scholars who were obliged to consider the matter from a legal point of view were divided in their opinions. After lengthy deliberations, in which the most eminent *jusha* of the time took active, and sometimes impassioned, part, the *Hyōjōshō*, Supreme Court of the *Bakufu*, sentenced the Akō *rōnin* to death by *seppuku*. This was a lenient form of punishment under the circumstances, allowing the *rōnin* to die with honour like samurai, a privilege they were not strictly legally entitled to, having lost their feudal lord. When Ōishi received his sentence he was at the same time told privately by the *Bakufu* official who brought it that the estate of Kira Sahyōe, son and heir of Kira Yoshinaka, had been confiscated by the authorities that very day.

The Akō *rōnin* committed *seppuku* on the same day, in the *daimyō yashiki* where they had been held in custody, and were buried together near the tomb of Asano Naganori in the grounds of the Sengakuji. The forty-seventh man, who had been dispatched to Akō with news of the death of Kira came forward in 1704 and gave himself up to the authorities. The *Bakufu* however allowed the matter to drop, and he lived out his life in Edo, dying at the age of eighty-two. People from all walks of life demonstrated their reverence and admiration by visiting the graves of the Akō *rōnin*, and it was not unusual for samurai and *rōnin* to commit *seppuku* in their vicinity. A.B. Mitford, the British diplomat who served in Japan in the 1860s, mentions a case of *seppuku* carried out by a *rōnin* in front of the tomb of Ōishi Chikara in 1868.[124]

From the point of view of the existing legal code, i.e. the revised version of the *Buke Sho-Hatto* promulgated in 1683 by the fifth Shōgun, Tokugawa Tsunayoshi (1646-1709, in office 1680-1709), the case might appear to be open and shut. The Akō *rōnin* had committed a number of criminal offences. They had joined in a confederacy with the purpose of avenging their dead lord, and they had carried out an act of private vengeance without seeking permission from, or indeed even notifying, the authorities. The *Buke Sho-Hatto* stated unequivocally that 'It is forbidden to devise innovations, to form cliques, or to enter into sworn confederacies', and that 'Private disputes are absolutely forbidden. In case the circumstances are such as to render a dispute unavoidable, application must be made to the Magistrate and his opinion taken. Under no circumstances is it permissible for other persons to take sides as partisans in a dispute; any person doing so will be held more culpable than the principals in the quarrel.'[125]

Furthermore, the Akō *rōnin* had resolved to commit *junshi* together if their mission to kill Kira Yoshinaka were to fail, and thus seriously contemplated yet another infringement of the *Buke Sho-Hatto*, which stated: 'Following a lord in death is to be more than ever discouraged.'[126] A violation of the prohibition against *junshi* resulted in the successor of the deceased lord being considered incompetent, and could lead to the confiscation of his fief. The *rōnin* had thus committed two criminal offences and planned a third. In their own eyes, however, they had acted strictly in accordance with the principles of *Bushidō*. By avenging the death of their lord, a death which they regarded as unjust, they had upheld the Confucian precept concerning filial piety which stated that no man could live under the same heaven as his father's murderer. As we have seen above, the rules of filial piety applied equally to one's father and feudal lord.

The crux of the matter was, however, that although the great majority of *jusha* who commented on the case agreed that the Akō *rōnin* had acted according to the principle of *gi* 'righteousness' or 'duty', they also had to admit that this action had been in defiance of the existing laws. The animated discussion which took place among the leading *jusha* of the time thus focused on one important point, namely whether the principles of *Bushidō* should be allowed to override the laws of the *Bakufu*. In the end a form of compromise was reached, whereby the *rōnin* were sentenced to death, although they were permitted to die honourably as samurai by their own hands. The discussion of the case had been fraught with emotion, and the question was one which concerned the very foundations of the Tokugawa *Bakufu*. In view of this, the government's decision to take no action when the forty-seventh *rōnin* reappeared a year later is all the more understandable. The conflict lay between private and public observation of *Bushidō*, and in order to preserve its own existence the *Bakufu* must uphold the legal system, discouraging individual initiative.

One of the leading Confucian scholars of the period was Ogyū Sorai (1666-1728), a traditionalist who opposed the teachings of the Chu Hsi school. He was employed as *jusha* by the very influential *daimyō* Yanagisawa Yoshiyasu, who occupied a post in the *Bakufu* equivalent to that of Prime Minister. When Yanagisawa was asked by the *Shōgun*, Tsunayoshi, for his opinion of the Akō affair he consulted his two *jusha*, one of whom was Ogyū. The authorities, in an effort to get away from the really burning issue of loyalty to the principle of *Bushidō*, were inclined to treat the affair as a case of common burglary, on the pretext that the Akō *rōnin* had indeed broken into Kira's residence. The punishment for this crime was decapitation by the public headsman.

Ogyū's opinion is recorded in the *Yanagisawa-ke hizō jikki* (A Treasured Record of the Yanagisawa House). 'Now, because one has in truth turned to minute circumstances in the various deliberations, I think that one has not paid attention to the essential part of the matter. Generally, the teachings of the Sages say that, in regard to any matter, one concerns oneself with the central part; one does not concern oneself with the minute details. Since at the present time those on high consider loyalty and filial piety the first virtues of government, it would be lacking in compassion to judge this case in which the plotter acted in accordance with these virtues, as a case of burglary. If cases in which people have loyalty and filial piety in mind and act accordingly, are considered as burglary, how then shall cases be judged which are committed with disloyal and unfilial intentions? Therefore, leaving Chinese matters aside, if the decision orders that *seppuku* be carried out on the basis of precedents of our present rule, it would also be in accordance with the wishes of those plotters, and how would it not set an example for the world?'[127]

Ogyū Sorai then received a request directly from the *Bakufu* to give his opinion of the affair, and his reply is recorded in the *Sorai giritsusho* (Sorai's Application of the Law). 'Righteousness is the way to make oneself pure, while the laws constitute the rules of the world. With rites we control our minds while with righteousness we control our acts. The fact that the forty-six samurai have now taken revenge for their lord means that these samurai know their shame. Although that act was righteous since it was/in accordance with/the way of making oneself pure, it was in the last analysis an act based on private and selfish considerations, because it concerned a matter that was limited to that faction. Although the original reason was that Naganori broke the etiquette of the castle and was/for that reason/ condemned/to commit *seppuku/*, still revenge was taken through Lord Kira. To plot a disturbance without official permission is not allowed by the law. In judging the crime and/fixing the/punishment of the forty-six samurai, Lord Uesugi's wish will also be fulfilled if they are sentenced to commit *seppuku* in accordance with the samurai ritual. The reason why we must say that they took their loyalty lightly is because of public considerations. If we let public considerations be hurt by private considera-tions, it will later be impossible to set up laws for the world.'[128]

It seems probable that Ogyū Sorai may be credited with having found the honourable and satisfactory solution to an almost impossible situation. His personal admiration for the Akō *rōnin* is rather thinly veiled, but in his capacity as adviser to a government official he had to further the interests of the *Bakufu*. The firmness with which he presented his diplomatic solution may well have been the decisive factor in convincing the *Bakufu* to abandon the accusation of burglary and allow the *rōnin* to commit *seppuku*, thus saving them from dying ignominiously like common criminals. What Ogyū disapproved of was not the action of the *rōnin* as such, but the illegal manner in which it was carried out and the fact that their lord, Asano Naganori, had indeed been guilty of an armed assault in the Shōgunal residence. The drawing of a sword in the Shogun's palace was a capital offence. The *rōnin* regarded their revenge as justified, however, since they considered that Asano had been unjustly treated and provoked by Kira, a view which was shared by the majority of the commentators of the case.

Dazai Shundai (1680-1747). Ogyū Sorai's pupil, differed
markedly from his teacher in that he was completely nega-
tive. He put much of the blame on Yamaga Sokō, who had
been dead for seventeen years when the Akō affair occurred, but whom Dazai considered quilty by his association with the Asano family. As we have seen, Yamaga Sokō
had been military instructor in the service of Asano
Naganori's great-grandfather during the years 1652-1660,
and had also spent his exile at Akō from 1666 to 1675.
Many have wished to see a connection between Yamaga
Sokō and Ōishi Kuranosuke or some of the other *rōnin* of
Akō, but despite a persistent tradition there is no proof that
any of the forty-seven *rōnin* were ever taught by Yamaga
Sokō in person. Dazai Shundai, however, was emphatic in
his condemnation of the Akō *rōnin*. In his opinion they had
acted contrary to the concept of *gi*, since Kira had not killed
their lord, and when they gave up Akō Castle to the authorities without struggle and without committing *seppuku*
they had acted against the precepts of *Bushidō*. Dazai
Shundai went one step further, arguing that if the Akō
rōnin regarded Asano's death sentence as unjust they
should have sent in a formal complaint to the *Bakufu*,
directing their vengeful feelings against the government, an
exceptionally revolutionary idea.[129]

Muro Kyūsō (1658-1734), an exponent of the Chu Hsi
school, wrote a laudatory work, the *Akō gijin roku* (A
Record of the Righteous Men of Akō) immediately after the
events of the Akō affair, characterising the *rōnin* as *gishi*
(righteous retainers). In his writings Muro Kyūsō was a
staunch upholder of *Bushidō* and traditional samurai values. His famous work *Shundai zatsuwa* (Conversations at
Suruga-dai) contains many examples of proper and fitting
behaviour for a *bushi*, expressing a great deal of nostalgia
for the 'good old days'. 'Nothing is more important to the
samurai than duty. Second in importance comes life, and
then money.' (. . .) 'When faced with however unpleasant a
duty, the way of the samurai consists in regarding his own
wishes—even his life itself—as of less values than rubbish.
How much less should he value money?' (. . .) 'In ancient
Japan, in keeping with its name of "the country of the
sages", manners were pure and simple, and not prevented
by/consideration for/prices and profits. Even where duty

was not rigorously defended, there was an inbred sense of honour which had not entirely disappeared. Though manners changed greatly with the coming of military government, the samurai still knew nothing at all of money matters, and they were frugal and direct, and not the slightest bit given to extravagance. This was true until recent times . . .' (. . .) 'Thus have social standards changed since fifty or sixty years ago. At about that time there was a samurai in Kaga named Aochi Uneme. His son, named Kurando (Aochi Saiken), was a friend of mine. Uneme said to his sons and disciples:" Though the attainment of prosperity by exchanging goods with others is practised freely in the world, you should have nothing to do with it. In buying at a loss, it is all right for the gain to be on the other side. However, winning in trade differs from winning at chess, for when one buys at a profit and the gain is to oneself, there is no satisfaction, but on the contrary the heart becomes spiteful. To rejoice when one makes a profitable transaction or buys valuable merchandise cheaply is part of the merchant's trade, but it is unpardonable in a samurai." [130]

Like many of his contemporaries Muro was disgusted by the changing attitudes of the times. To him the Akō affair must have been a cheering sign that all was not yet lost when there were still men who were willing to forfeit their lives while upholding the old virtues. On *Bushidō* he wrote: 'To the samurai, righteousness comes always first, as the matter of the greatest importance. Then comes life, and after that money. Always do what is right, even though the doing of it cost you your life.' [131]

An impassioned eulogy was composed by Hayashi Nobuatsu, also called Hōkō (1644-1732). He had been consulted by the *Bakufu* in his official capacity as *Daigaku-no-kami*, head of the Confucian State University, and had pleaded for the lives of the Akō *rōnin*. When the *Bakufu's* sentence was contrary to his recommendation Hayashi wrote a poem alluding to a number of famous episodes from Chinese history: 'They charged through the gates, scorning Ching K'o (who had failed to assassinate the emperor of ancient Ch'in, Shih Huang). The cold wind at I Shui (where Ching K'o parted with his friends) is like the spirit of the valiant warriors. Like Yu Jang (of ancient Chin who drank lye to become a mute, and painted his body with lacquer to become leprous while biding his time to avenge his master's death) they drank lye and allowed their bodies to waste away. The elegy that mourns T'ien Heng's death (the ruler of Ch'i upon whose death 500 loyal followers committed suicide) draws copious tears. Sincerity pierces the sun. Why should they hesitate to die? The spirit of justice pierces the mountains. Life is indeed of little value. All forty-six men will fall to the sword. Heaven shown no signs of saving these loyal and righteous men.'[132]

Hayashi's unreserved praise for the *rōnin* attracted a great deal of attention and comment. In his official writings on the affair, however, Hayashi expressed his views with more circumspection. 'If we consider this matter in accordance with the spirit of the Classics, we are forced to conclude that *on the basis of their motives*, it was proper for them to sleep on rush mats, use their swords as pillows, and take revenge upon their sworn enemy, who could not be permitted to remain under the same sky as theirs. It violates the way of the samurai to cling to life and endure shame. *But from the standpoint of the law*, those who behave as opponents of the law must be executed. Although they acted to fulfil the wishes of their dead lord, they broke the law of the land. In this respect, their behaviour was wanton and disobedient. Hence it became necessary to arrest and execute them, and to make them an example to the nation and to future generations. In this way we can uphold and clarify the law of the land. *The two/* the motivational approach and the legal approach/*may seem to differ but in fact they can co-exist and do not contradict one another*. At the top of society there must be a benevolent prince and wise officials who clarify the law and issue decrees. Below, there must be loyal subjects and righteous samurai who give free play to their feelings, fulfil their wishes, and willingly accept punishment for the sake of the law. How could they have any regrets as a result?'[133]

Although he clearly shows himself to be a staunch defender of law and order, Hayashi at the same time maintains that society needs those who, like the Akō *rōnin*, put the rules of *Bushidō* first, act accordingly, and accept the consequences. Hayashi's opinion that the wisely governed state must to some extent tolerate dissidents who chose to act in defiance of the existing laws, was quite as revolutionary in Tokugawa Japan as Dazai Shundai's oblique criticism of the *Bakufu*.

Each individual *jusha* had his own interpretation of *Bushidō*, and although there was a common consensus concerning the key elements of the warrior ethic, opinions differed widely when it came to practical application of the principles. The Confucianists with their training in pragmatism recognised the incontrovertible fact that theory is one thing and practice quite another, and that not everyone can at all times live up to his ideals. This apparent truism is something which even latter-day commentators have to keep constantly in mind.

In the eyes of the general public the Akō *rōnin* were paragons of samurai virtue, and the leading playwrights of the time transformed the actual events into plays which gained immense popularity. The famous Chikamatsu Monzaemon (1653-1724) wrote a play for the *Bunraku*, puppet play, stage in 1706, the *Goban Taiheiki* (A Chronicle of Great Peace Played on a Chessboard), which evaded censorship by means of its fourteenth-century setting. In 1748 three playwrights, Takeda Izumo (1691-1756), Miyoshi Shōraku (1696-1772) and Namiki Senryū (1695-1751) wrote the play entitled *Chūshingura* (The Treasury of Loyal Retainers), which to this day is regularly performed on the *Kabuki* stage, usually around 14 December, the anniversary of the attack on Kira by the Akō *rōnin*.[134]

PART VI: THE TOKUGAWA PEACE AND THE INTRUSION OF THE WESTERN WORLD

The *Nabeshima Rongo* (Analects of the Nabeshima Clan), better known as *Hagakure* (Hidden Among Leaves), emanates from the same period as the Akō affair. This combined clan history and discourse on *Bushidō* was written down some time between 1701 and 1716 from the dictation of Yamamoto Tsunetomo (1659-1719) who had taken the tonsure under the name Jōchō. After the Meiji Restoration it gained widespread recognition far outside the domain for which it was intended. The core of the *Hagakure* is to be found in the famous dictum '*Bushidō to wa shinu koto to mitsuketari*' ('*Bushidō* consists in dying— that is the conclusion I have reached').

The *Hagakure*'s interpretation of *Bushidō* is at times impassioned, with a strong note a religious fervour. 'One can never be called a good vassal unless he dedicates himself to his lord, making it his sole object worth living and dying for, to consolidate the dominion of his lord by bravely dying to all other mundane desires and making himself a ghostly being who keeps worrying over his master's affairs around the clock and who stints no labour in putting them in order.' (. . .) 'Though Śākyamuni or Confucius were here in person to preach what we have never heard of before, we should not be a bit shaken in our conviction. Let them cast us into hell and eternal damnation: the one thing needful for us is loyalty to our liege lord.' (. . .) 'I am only a vassal of my lord. Let him be kind to me or cruel as he will; let him not know me at all; it is all the same to me. For my part, not a moment passes without my heart being filled even to overflowing with the bliss of having him for my lord whom I hold dear with my eyes swimming in tears, being penetrated with an exulting sense of thankfulness.' (. . .) 'Whenever one is taken into service to the lord, he should serve the lord without any consideration of his own self. Even if one is dismissed or is ordered to commit harakiri, one should accept the action as one of the services to the lord, and should be sincerely concerned with the destiny of the lord's house wherever one may be. Such should be the fundamental spirit of the Nabeshima samurai. As far as I am concerned, I have never thought of attaining buddhahood, which would not fit me at all, but I am completely prepared to be born seven times as a Nabeshima samurai in order to work for the cause of the domain.'[135]

The loyalty to the feudal lord is seen here as the all-encompassing concern of the *bushi*. It should take precedence over every aspect of his private life, dominating his thoughts to the exclusion of even the traditional religions. By obeying the rules of *Bushidō* the samurai enters the path to damnation with open eyes, since he who has taken life will be condemned to one of the Buddhist hells. The author of the *Hagakure* even states boldly that he is prepared to serve his lord not only through the customary three existences, but through seven rebirths.

The dictum '*Bushidō* consists in dying—that is the conclusion I have reached' is far from being a laconic statement of an unavoidable fact. Instead, it exhorts the *bushi* to constant awareness of his duties. 'When one eternally repeats his vow to die at any moment at the call of his duty every morning, and every evening, one can act freely in *Bushidō* at a moment's notice, thus fulfilling his duties as a feudal vassal without a flaw, even to the very last moment of his life.'[136] The true *bushi*, according to the *Hagakure*, should concentrate on one objective only, i.e. his loyal service to his lord, and by keeping his mind totally void of all other considerations he will be able to act with the unconscious ease advocated by the great masters of swordsmanship, who in their treatises frequently used the imagery of Zen Buddhism, likening the ideal mind to an unclouded mirror or a surface of still water. This permanent state of mental alertness would thus enable the *bushi* to act spontaneously, at a moment's notice, and the *Hagakure* clearly favours the unpremeditated form of attack. 'The right way of avenging is to strike at an enemy without delay or hesitation, even in the danger of being killed by him. In this case, it is no disgrace at all to be killed by the object of one's vengeance.'[137]

The meticulously planned vendetta of the Akō *rōnin* was

therefore totally out of line with the views of the *Hagakure*, which favoured the headlong approach, regardless of the consequences. The great risk in the Akō affair was that Kira, who was in his sixties, might have died before the planned attack on him took place, in which case the Akō *rōnin* would have failed utterly to live up to the precepts of *Bushidō*. Regarded in this light, Asano's sudden attack on Kira in the shōgunal palace, whatever the reason for it, was completely consistent with *Bushidō* as defined by the *Hagakure*. The conclusion that '*Bushidō* consists in dying' in fact echoes Nakae Tōju's characterisation of the bravery of the wise man, who, because he neither loves life nor fears death, has destroyed the root of cowardice.

If the tone of the *Hagakure* at times appears emotional, the writings of the traditional Confucian scholar Daidōji Yūzan Shigesuke (1639-1731) presented his views on the significance of *Bushidō* in practical, matter-of-fact terms. Daidōji Yūzan came from a distinguished family, which was descended from the Taira and related to the Hōjō, and his father and grandfather had been Tokugawa vassals. He studied under Yamaga Sokō and later served as military instructor in the households of the Matsudaira *daimyō* of Aizu and Echizen who were related to the Tokugawa clan. Because of his unusual longevity his life spanned the rules of six Shōguns, from Iemitsu to Yoshimune. His work *Budō Shoshinshū* (The Beginner's Book of *Bushidō*), contains practical advice rather than philosophical speculation or attempts at justifying the existence of the *bushi*. 'But if he determines simply to live for today and take no thought for the morrow, so that when he stands before his lord to receive his commands he thinks of it as his last appearance, and when he looks on the faces of his relatives he feels that he will never see them again, then will his duty and regard for both of them be completely sincere and his mind be in accord with the path of loyalty and filial duty.'

Sincerity and the performance of his duties alone did not make a man a true samurai in the eyes of Yūzan: 'But in Bushidō, however loyal and filial a man may be in his heart, if he is lacking in the correct etiquette and manners by which respect is shown to lord or parent, he cannot be regarded as living in proper conformity with it.' (. . .) 'Wherever he may be lying down or sleeping, his feet must never for an instant be pointing in the direction of his lord's presence. If he sets up a straw bale for archery practice anywhere, the arrows must never fall towards the place where his lord is. Similarly, when he puts down his spear or halberd their points must never be in the direction either. And should he hear any talk about his lord or should anything about him escape his own lips if he is lying down he must spring up, and if he is sitting at ease he must straighten himself up, for that is the Way of the Samurai.' A crested garment presented to a samurai by his lord should never be worn on its own: 'For if he wears a garment with the lord's crest only it might look as though he were a relative, and that would be impolite. And when these garments with the lord's crest become too old to be worn any longer, the crests should be cut off them and burnt, so that they may not be soiled and treated with disrespect.'

In presenting his views on proper conduct for a *bushi*, Yūzan displayed a rare consideration for women. 'Much less is it fitting for such a one (a samurai) to lay his hand on his sword or menace his wife with his clenched fist, an outrageous thing that only a cowardly samurai would think of doing. For a girl born in a warrior house and of age to be married would never, if she were a man, for a moment tolerate being threatened by the fist of anyone. It is only because she is unfortunately born a woman that she has to shed tears and put up with it.' Since his loyalty should at all times be to his lord, Yūzan warned that a *bushi* ought never to make intimate friends. The son of an elder brother should be treated with the deference due to an heir-presumptive, whereas relations with a sister's son should be neutral and distant. A samurai must always keep the impermanence of his existence and fortune in mind. 'Realising all this, even in this present peaceful age a samurai who wishes to keep his *Bushidō* unsullied will certainly not think of his house as a permanent residence or lavish any care on any elaborate decoration.'

The *bushi* ought to study the records of old battles in order to strengthen his character and learn how to die honourably in battle if called upon to do so: 'As he has to die, the aim of a samurai should be to fall performing some great deed of valour that will astonish both friend and foe

alike and make his death regretted by his lord and commander and so leave behind a great name to the generations to come.' (. . .) 'And if unfortunately he gets the worst
of it and he and his head have to part company, when his
opponent asks for his name he must declare it at once
loudly and clearly and yield up his head with a smile on his
lips and without the slightest sign of fear.' (. . .) 'And in the
words of the Sage (Confucius), too, it is written that when
a man is about to die his words should be such as appear
right.'

When a samurai wanted to accomplish some spectacular
feat which would make him famous, Daidōji Yūzan considered that some action which brought about a positive
result was preferable to the act of *junshi*. He advocated the
killing of a corrupt councillor who was poisoning his lord's
mind. According to Yūzan every high-ranking family was
plagued by an evil spirit which would cause untimely
deaths among promising family members and which might
appear in the shape of a malevolent clan elder. 'Therefore
it is best to seize this great rascal of a councillor who is the
evil spirit of the house, and either stab him through or cut
off his head, whichever you prefer, and so put an end to
him and his corrupt practices. And then you must straight-
way commit seppuku yourself. Thus there will be no open
breach or lawsuit or sentence and your lord's person will
not be attainted, so that the whole clan will continue to live
in security and there will be no open trouble in the Empire.
And one who acts thus is a model samurai who does a deed
a hundredfold better than *junshi*, for he has the three
qualities of loyalty and faithfulness and valour, and will
hand down a glorious name to posterity.'[138] This direct and
radical method of dealing with undesirable members of the
fief council recommended by Daidōji Yūzan bears a close
resemblance to the precipitate approach favoured by the
Hagakure.

The writings of Arai Hakuseki (1657-1725) are evidence
of a stoical temperament not unlike that of the ideal Roman
patrician. The parallel from the classical world can indeed
be taken somewhat further, since Arai Hakuseki, as an
ardent Japanese nationalist, opposed the teachings of the
strongly pro-Chinese Ogyū Sorai. The situation with regard
to Chinese learning and statecraft was in fact not dissimi-

lar to that of classical Rome, where the extent and importance of Greek influence was debated by the philosophers
and scholars. Arai Hakuseki, who was a Neo-Confucianist
of the Chu Hsi school, occupied the very influential post of
adviser to the sixth Shōgun, Tokugawa Ienobu (1662-1712,
regnavit 1707-1712) and his young successor, the seventh
Tokugawa Shōgun, Ietsugu (1709-1716, regnavit 1712-1716).

During his time in office Arai even eclipsed Hayashi
Nobuatsu, who otherwise, as *Daigaku no Kami*, had the
final say concerning official Confucian policies. In his autobiographical work *Oritaku Shiba no Ki* (Told Round a
Brushwood Fire), Arai frequently referred to the shortcom-
ings of Hayashi Nobuatsu. By quoting Tokugawa Ienobu
himself, Arai was even able to state obliquely that Hayashi
had not grasped the meaning and significance of *Bushidō*.
Hayashi had recorded in a historical chronicle an incident
in which Tokugawa Hirotada (1526-1549), the father of
Tokugawa Ieyasu, was wounded by a man who was then
pursued and killed by others. By failing to mention that
Hirotada had been incapacitated by a thigh wound and was
thus unable himself to run after his enemy, Hayashi
Nobuatsu had displayed his own ignorance and exposed
Hirotada to the unfounded suspicion of cowardice, an
outrageous mistake in the eyes of Arai.

While every inch a statesman, devoting himself with
imagination and foresight to the promotion of Tokugawa
rule, Arai Hakuseki took great pride in the warlike qualities
of his ancestors. He was constantly aware of the demands
of *Bushidō*, and, as we have already seen, when he was
given a sum of money by his lord the first thing he did was
to buy himself a suit of armour, the better to be able to
serve him should the need arise. From childhood Arai had
been interested in martial pursuits, demanding at the age
of eleven to be taught how to wield his sword, and in his
writings the lowered standards of his own times were frequently criticised. The early years of his father, Arai Masanari
(1601-1682), appear to have corresponded to Arai's warrior
ideal when he compared them to the present degenerate
age. 'Not long after the civil wars, when my father was still
young, men were chivalrous and were accustomed to setting a high value on nobility of spirit, in contrast to the
situation today.'[139]

Arai's grandfather, Arai Kageyu, had died in 1609, when his son was still a child, and the few recollections of him which Arai's father was able to transmit were cherished by Arai Hakuseki, who opened his autobiography with them. His father's most vivid memory provides an eloquent testimony to the *bushi* spirit. 'Whenever grandfather ate, he always took his chopsticks from a black lacquered box, decorated in gold with irises, and when he had finished eating, he put them back in the box and placed it by his side. When father asked his old nurse about it, she told him that once, after grandfather had taken a good head in a battle, the general said to him when he presented himself: "You must be weary with fighting. Eat this." He pushed forward his dinner-tray and gave it to grandfather with the chopsticks. This became a famous incident at the time, and so grandfather would never let them leave his side.'[140]

Thus, to Arai's grandfather, the chopsticks served as a constant reminder both of his own feat of taking the head of an important enemy, and of the extraordinary attention and honour shown him in public by his commander. His father's unvaried habit appears to have made an indelible impression on Arai's father, who in this way received an early and wordless lesson in *bushi* fidelity and pride, remembering to his dying day the colour and decoration of the lacquer box. Arai's admiration for his father was great, and he portrayed him in *Oritaku Shiba no Ki* as a model *bushi* of the old school, endowed with all the virtues and character traits associated with a thorough training in the precepts of *Bushidō*. He lead an austere and regular life, rose early, dressed simply and ate frugally. When appearing in public, however, he was careful always to dress well in accordance with his rank. 'He would not use any fan that was not executed by masters of the first rank, and he was even more particular about weapons, like his two swords.'[141]

He appears to have possessed great psychological insight and courage. Once, as a fairly junior samurai, he was put in charge of three prisoners, low-ranking samurai accused of burglary. He ordered that the men's swords be returned to them, and then stayed day and night with them during the period of investigation, telling them plainly that he was well aware of the fact that they could kill him if they wanted to escape. They were proved innocent, but were nevertheless dismissed from their service. Before leaving they came to thank him for his trust in them, and for the fact that they had been allowed to keep their swords and were thus able to seek other employment. Their gratitude for this outweighed the resentment they felt for having been unfairly accused and dismissed. Long after his father's death Arai learned from an abbot how his father, who had taken the tonsure in his old age, had disarmed a drunken man who was threatening people with a sword in the temple where he lived. Arai's father, who was then past eighty, had calmly approached the man, grasped hold of his sword-arm and thrown him to the ground, wrenched the sword from him, thrown it outside into a ditch, and quietly returned to his cell.

It is characteristic of the historical watershed in which he lived that Arai's father told him of several chance encounters with acquaintances who had become *rōnin* and fallen on hard times. One of them, who in youthful exuberance had trespassed on another domain, had been caught, and later had cut down three samurai in revenge, had taken refuge in a village in his ancestral fief, living as one of the villagers. Another man, who lived with his aged father in a rustic cottage and earned their living as a woodcutter, still retained his two swords, his last valuable possessions and the insignia of his rank. Arai's father told him how the man took them out of the bamboo poles where they were kept hidden. 'With his back to the fire-light, he drew the two swords from their scabbards and laid them before me. Both the blades shone like ice.'[142]

The scene seems to have etched itself into the memory of Arai's father, and from him it was transmitted to his son, who was sufficiently impressed by this vivid and dramatic illustration of the uncertainty of a *bushi*'s existence to include it in his memoirs. The reason given by the man for having withdrawn from active service was that his stipend as a samurai was insufficient for him to be able to support his father. In this particular case of filial piety the man considered his obligation towards his father to be more important than that which he owed his feudal lord, and both the Arais apparently approved.

The father of Arai Hakuseki seems to have been a taciturn man who lived up to the old ideal of speaking only

when one has necessary information to impart. His remarks on various episodes from his life, which his son
recorded in his autobiographical work, took the form of
rather terse maxims concerning *bushi* honour and proper
conduct. From his own father he had learned never to
speak disparagingly about others, or indeed himself, and
he also advised his son to be circumspect in his speech and
refrain from taking the names of *kami* and buddhas in vain.
Mention of the superior quality of one's sword was a serious breach of etiquette—it was improper for a *bushi* to
boast in any way, and for him to have worn an inferior
blade, or to have admitted as much in public, would have
been absurd. He was careful to preserve his dignity, and
explained to his son that in order to avoid the debilitating
effects of old age he had trained himself to concentrate on
a few things and master them thoroughly, and in his daily
life he had established an unvarying routine which enabled
him to manage on his own without assistance.

Two things which he told his son made an especially
strong impression. One was to practise endurance of what
seemed particularly hard to endure, the other was to dis-
miss from his mind the two emotions most likely to breed
hatred among men, namely greed and lust. It was a characteristic of the *bushi* to keep their emotions under strict
control, and Arai's father appears to have excelled in this
respect, according to the reminiscences of his son: 'He was
not a man who showed his feelings, and I never remember
him laughing loudly, much less did I ever hear him scold-
ing people roughly. When he spoke, he used as few words
as possible; his manners were imposing, and I never saw
him surprised, perturbed, or lacking in self-control.' (. . .)
'When he had leisure, he swept clean the room he regularly
used, hung an old painting on the wall, placed a few
seasonal flowers in a vase and spent the day in silent
contemplation before them. He also painted but did not like
the use of colours. Except when he was ill, he did not have
servants to wait on him but did everything for himself.'[143]
Arai's literary portrait of his father showed him to have
been a true Confucian scholar-gentleman, with the calm
fatalism of the Buddhist and the *bushi*'s ingrained superiority which made him aware of being an example to his
inferiors at all times.

The historical writings of Arai Hakuseki are evidence of an incisive and independent mind. Always loyal to the Tokugawa *Bakufu*, Arai was far from advocating fundamental changes to the basic system, but he did suggest and work for a number of innovations, for example the use of the title *Ō* 'King' or 'Prince' for the Shōgun. This usage, which was of short duration, defined the Shōgun as an independent ruler under the sovereignty of the Emperor and simplified his dealings with foreign envoys. In the *Tokushi Yoron* (Essays on Political History), Arai departed sharply from the traditional historical chronicles, providing a critical analysis of the events recorded. Preconceived notions and prejudices held little appeal for Arai. Of Kiso Yoshinaka, who was invariably described in the *Heike Monogatari* and other contemporary chronicles as rustic and uncouth, Arai made the poignant remark: '. . . how does Yoshinaka's being a rustic, untrained in etiquette, detract from his meritorious deeds?'[144]

It is obvious that Arai was no great admirer of Minamoto Yoritomo, and the success of the Genji in the *Gempei* War he ascribed in very large measure to the efforts of Kiso Yoshinaka and Minamoto Yoshitsune. The latter was mentioned in laudatory tones: 'Yoshitsune never harboured any feeling of disloyalty toward Yoritomo. He was merely unaware of Yoritomo's evil intentions', an elegant way of blaming Minamoto Yoritomo for Yoshitsune's disgrace and death.[145] *Buke* rule was the only conceivable form of government in Japan, according to Arai's blunt and withering analysis in the *Tokushi Yoron*. 'Ever since the Middle Ages, in times of conflict it was only the warriors who strove to be faithful and considered what was right, and exerted their strength and sacrificed their lives. When things became even slightly peaceful, however, it was the court nobles and the priests who enjoyed high positions and fat salaries and treated the warriors like servants. But when disturbances arose they saved their necks and scuttled away like mice, and not a single one risked his life to do his duty. Indeed, this kind of rabble must be called the bane of Japan. So, since it is only right that those who have taken it upon themselves to do what is honourable should be rewarded, it was not without reason that thereafter the military houses gained control of Japan.'[146]

With an expanding bureaucracy and strict measures circumscribing individual freedom of movement and thought, the Tokugawa *Bakufu* gradually took on the aspect of a police state. The *bushi*, although largely reduced to civil servants, guarded their privileges jealously, and were apt to resort to their swords when a dispute arose or when a commoner was considered disrespectful. Despite the emergence of an increasingly wealthy bourgeoisie of merchants and artisans, the *bushi*, rich or poor, dominated society politically as well as ideologically. The *bushi* lifestyle, of which *Bushidō* was the chief component, was the norm and ideal, even to those of the bourgeoisie who like Ihara Saikaku were fairly comfortably off and from time to time permitted themselves to look at the samurai with a certain cynical amusement.

The purely warlike side of *Bushidō* was almost entirely reduced to theory under the Tokugawa *Bakufu*, and kept alive through training in the martial arts and the strategy of warfare. There were those, however, also among the Neo-Confucian scholars, whose pragmatism forced them to express their views on *Bushidō* in action. The nineteenth century was a period of fundamental change in Japan, and the turbulent decades from the arrival of Commodore Perry in 1853, and the restoration to power of Emperor Meiji in 1868, to the defeat of the rebellious troops of Saigō Takamori in 1877, saw many examples of individual interpretations of the spirit of *Bushidō*.

Yoshida Shōin (1830-1859) was brought up in the tradition of the teachings of Yamaga Sokō, and succeeded his adoptive father as military instructor. Like his teacher, Sakuma Shōzan (1811-1864), Yoshida adhered to the *Sonnō Jōi* (Revere the Emperor—expel the barbarians), school of thought. Sakuma came to realise that it was necessary for Japan to adopt Western science and learning and give up its seclusion in order to defend its sovereignty, but Yoshida did not live long enough to gain this insight. He was impetuous, and seems to have preferred the headlong approach advocated in the *Hagakure*. In 1854 Yoshida was discovered as he tried to stow away on board of one of Commodore Perry's ships. Attempting to leave Japan was a capital offence under the Tokugawa *Bakufu*, but through the intercession of influential benefactors Yoshida got off with a short prison sentence followed by confinement in his native fief of Chōshū, where he was even allowed to continue his teaching.

In permitting the so-called 'black ships' of Commodore Perry to approach the Japanese coast unopposed the Shōgun had revealed his incompetence as a ruler in the eyes of Yoshida Shōin, who began to advocate an uprising of commoners. He wanted the hard-working and faithful provincial peasants to overthrow the *buke*, whom he considered self-seeking, lax and cowardly. Yoshida's conception of *Bushidō* is apparent in his writings. 'Once the will is resolved, one's spirit is strengthened. Even a peasant's will is hard to deny, but a samurai of resolute will can sway ten thousand men.' (. . .) 'Life and death, union and separation, follow hard upon one another. Nothing is steadfast but the will, nothing endures but one's achievements. These alone count in life.' (. . .) 'Those who take up the science of war must not fail to master the/Confucian/ Classics. The reason is that arms are dangerous instruments and not necessarily forces for good. How can we safely entrust them to any but those who have schooled themselves in the precepts of the Classics and can use these weapons for the realization of Humanity and Righteousness? To quell violence and disorder, to repulse barbarians and brigands, to rescue living souls from agony and torture, to save the nation from imminent downfall— these are the true ends of Humanity and Righteousness.' (. . .)

'From the beginning of the year to the end, day and night, morning and evening, in action and repose, in speech and silence, the warrior must keep death constantly before him and have ever in mind that the one death/which he has to give/should not be suffered in vain. In other words/ he must have perfect control over his own death/just as if he were holding an intemperate steed in rein. Only he who truly keeps death in mind this way can understand what is meant by/Yamaga Sokō's maxim of/'preparedness'.'[147]

True to his penchant for direct action, Yoshida decided to assassinate the shōgunal emissary who was to obtain the Emperor's formal approval of a treaty with the United States of America. His plans were discovered, Yoshida was condemned to death and decapitated in 1859. When he was being taken to Edo as a prisoner he wrote in a letter to his sisters: 'Always keep in mind, you who are to become mothers, that it is the usual thing for a samurai to die.'[148] Among his last poems, written in prison before his execution, was the following: 'That such an act/Would have such a result/I knew well enough./What made me do it anyhow/Was the spirit of Yamato.'[149] *Yamato damashii* (the spirit of Yamato), was considered to be the expression of the characteristic valour of ancient Japan which was recorded in the *Kojiki* and the *Nihongi*. This concept came into more common use from the time of the Meiji Restoration, and was later used to bolster the Japanese claims to uniqueness.

The Meiji Restoration of 1868 put an end to nearly seven centuries of *bushi* dominance. With the fall of the Tokugawa *Bakufu* the work to abolish the privileges of the *samurai* had begun. In 1871 the wearing of the two swords was decreed to be no longer obligatory, and the same applied to the characteristic hairstyle of the *bushi*. Peasants were allowed to ride on horseback in public roads, and were no longer required to dismount when encountering a *samurai*, and the latter lost his legal right to cut down on the spot any commoner who behaved rudely. In 1876 the wearing of swords was prohibited, and the *samurai* class irrevocably abolished. The process was by no means painless, and there were many who preferred to die sword in hand rather than relinquish their status and privileges without any struggle.

Saigō Takamori (1827-1877), a statesman and military leader from the influential and warlike fief of Satsuma in Kyushu, was disgruntled by the government's cautious policies after the Restoration, and began a rebellion which might easily have resulted in civil war if his *bushi* troops had not been defeated in 1877 by the government's conscript army. Saigō's adherence to the principles of *Bushidō* is apparent from one of his recorded sayings: 'One who wants neither life, nor name, nor rank, nor money, is hardly to be controlled. It is only such indomitable men who can carry great affairs of state through adversities to completion.'[150]

The feelings of the *bushi* when confronted with the radical changes proposed by the new imperial government were mixed indeed. From the partial opening of the country which followed the treaty of 1854 there had been attacks on foreigners who came to Japan in the diplomatic service or to engage in trade. Hotheaded young samurai from the provinces joined the *Sonnō Jōi* movement, and on a number of occasions took action by cutting down foreigners upon slight, if any, provocation, their mere presence in Japan often being considered provocation enough.

The new Imperial Parliament, which was a result of the Restoration and opened in the spring of 1869, debated, among many questions, issues relating to the privileges and lifestyle of the *bushi*. The British diplomat Algernon Bertram Mitford, 1st Baron Redesdale (1837-1917), who was posted to the British Embassy in Japan in 1866, quoted from the parliamentary debates held in 1869 in his *Recollections*. The proposal to prohibit *seppuku* gave rise to a number of impassioned speeches defending this custom, which was seen by an overwhelming majority of the members as 'the embodiment in practice of devotion to principle', to quote one speaker. Others expressed their views on the subject in similar terms. 'It is an ornament of our country, and is one reason of its superiority over the countries beyond the seas', 'We ought to maintain a custom which fosters a sense of shame in the military caste and in the existence of which doubtless consists the superiority of Japan over other countries.' ; 'Why should this custom be prohibited in imitation of the effeminacy of foreign nations?' ; 'In this Country of the Gods it is not necessary to discuss such a law.' ; 'The *seppuku* has its origin in the vital energy of this divine country and is the shrine of the *Yamato Damashii*. Its practice should be extended.'

In the ensuing vote there were three ayes, two hundred noes, and six abstentions. Mitford commented that there was a widely circulated rumour, the truth of which he was unable to ascertain, that one of those who had voted for the prohibition of *seppuku* was subsequently murdered as a direct result of his position concerning this issue. A proposal to make the wearing of two swords optional instead of compulsory was unanimously voted down. Mitford quoted one of the speakers in the debate, who echoed the Neo-Confucian scholars in their definitions of *Bushidō*: 'It is a good maxim for the soldier in peace-time never to forget war. What shall we say of a measure that asks us, even in the midst of civil disorder, to forget the existence of civil disorder? What, I ask, is the character of the times in which we live? The object of the soldier caste wearing two swords is that they may suppress war by war; but as the chief glory of the sword consists in its resting quietly in its sheath, it follows that a natural stimulus is given to letters.'[151] In a few years the compulsory wearing of swords was neverthe-less abolished, the first step towards the dissolution of the *samurai* system.

Over the centuries, and especially during the Tokugawa *Bakufu*, the common people had attempted to emulate part of the ethical system of the leading élite, i.e. the *buke*. With the Meiji Restoration this became actively encouraged, and the loyalty which had formerly been directed towards the feudal lord was now transferred to the Emperor. The entire population, high and low alike, were taught to regard the Emperor as their liege lord, whose august and benevolent rule they were to requite with gratitude and obedience. The many stories of rural headmasters who perished in the flames in an attempt to save the burning school's most valuable possession, the portrait of the Emperor, are by no means apocryphal. The popular devotion to Emperor Meiji received its most dramatic expression in the suicide of one of his mot illustrious subjects, General Nogi Maresuke, hero of the Russo-Japanese War, who committed *junshi* to follow his lord in death in the traditional *bushi* manner. Especially among military men of *bushi* stock the custom of *seppuku* lingered on well into this century. Many of the conspirators behind the attempted military coup of 1936 killed themselves in this manner when the coup failed.

The *Kokutai no Hongi* (Fundamentals of Our National Polity), which was published by the Ministry of Education in 1937, was intended as an ideological and ethical manual which was to inculcate the desired nationalistic emotions. Referring to its historical past Japan was depicted as the repository of unique qualities which were to be integrated with such elements of Western culture and learning as might prove useful. Loyalty and filial piety were fundamen-tal concepts: 'Loyalty means to reverence the emperor as/our/pivot and to follow him implicitly.' (. . .) 'Hence, offering our lives for the sake of the emperor does not mean so-called self-sacrifice, but the casting aside of our little selves to live under his august grace and the enhancing of the genuine life of the people of a State.' (. . .) 'In our country filial piety is a Way of the highest importance.' (. . .) 'Our country is a great family nation, and the Imperial Household is the head family of the subjects and the nucleus of national life. . .' (. . .) 'The spirit of harmony is built on the concord of all things.' (. . .) 'A pure, cloudless heart is a heart which, dying to one's ego and one's own ends, finds life in fundamentals and the true Way. That means, it is a heart that lives in the Way of unity between the Sovereign and his subjects, a Way that has come down to us ever since the founding of the empire.'

The blind and unquestioning obedience requested of the people paved the way for subsequent excesses. The spirit of *Bushidō* was evoked in the *Kokutai no Hongi*, but this concept was presented in a manner which bore little relation to the pragmatism of the early Neo-Confucians, although their names were invoked in an effort to lend legitimacy to the changeling. '*Bushidō* may be cited as showing an outstanding characteristic of our national morality. In the world of warriors one sees inherited the totalitarian structure and spirit of the ancient clans peculiar to our nation. Hence, though the teachings of Confucianism and Buddhism have been followed, these have been transcended. That is to say, though a sense of obligation binds master and servant, this has developed into a spirit of self-effacement and of meeting death with perfect calmness.' (. . .) 'It is this same *bushidō* that shed itself of an outdated feudalism at the time of the Meiji Restoration, increased in splendour, became the Way of loyalty and patriotism, and has evolved before us as the spirit of the imperial forces.'[152]

The dismissal here of Buddhism and Confucianism was entirely in line with the establishment of Shinto as the state religion which followed the Meiji Restoration, and a conscious effort to emphasise the indigenous and play down foreign influence. It is also interesting to note that the description of the relationship of superior and subordinate as being based on self-effacement on the part of the subordinate hardly tallies with the conception of the *bushi* ethic prior to the establishment of the Tokugawa *Bakufu*.

The individual warrior may have been expected to serve his lord with no consideration for his own private affairs or condition, but he was proud of his personal achievements in that they served to enhance the glory of his lord. Self-sacrifice was the norm, but self-effacement was not encouraged. We may recall for a moment the father and grandfather of Arai Hakuseki, the latter preserving throughout his life the token of his lord's esteem when he had been singled out for praise after performing a deed of valour, the former taking meticulous care to appear in public with swords, accessories and garments befitting his status so as not to disgrace his clan. Each *bushi*, whether of high or low rank, was supposed to know his place in the *Bakufu* machinery, and strive to perform his duty to the utmost of his ability. Self-effacement had of old been forced upon the commoners, and when this trait, which had been necessary for survival under *buke* rule, was elevated to a principle, the mindless conformism which it engendered eventually led to disaster and defeat.

In 1970 the author Mishima Yukio (1925-1970) added herostratic notoriety to his literary fame by an ill-conceived para-military coup attempt which ended with his committing *seppuku*. From his early youth Mishima had been fascinated by the *Hagakure*, which he, with his schooling in Western thought and philosophy, interpreted as an expression of nihilism. In a commentary on the work, entitled *Hagakure Nyūmon*, 'Introduction to *Hagakure*', written in 1967, Mishima made an impassioned plea for a return to the *bushi* values of the past. The final words form a *cri de coeur* which in retrospect seems like an attempted justification of his own end: 'We tend to suffer from the illusion that we are capable of dying for a belief or theory. What *Hagakure* is insisting is that even a merciless death, a futile death that bears neither flower nor fruit, has dignity as the death of a human being. If we value so highly the dignity of life, how can we not also value the dignity of death? No death may be called futile.'[153]

5

Bushi Influence on Culture and the Arts

Z en Buddhism, which was brought to Japan from China about the time of the founding of the Kamakura *Bakufu*, proved a powerful source of inspiration for a number of art forms associated with the *bushi*. Calligraphy, *shōdō*, in the form of poems and letters, mostly *billets-doux*, written in the many cursive scripts which developed in the Heian period, had been an important minor art form in that era. Love affairs as well as life-long attachments often began with the glimpse of a specimen of a particularly elegant handwriting, and if the script was flawless and aesthetically appealing this fact could outweigh a lack of originality in the text itself. In the secluded world of the Heian court circles calligraphy was one of the accomplishments necessary for acceptance into polite society, together with the ability to compose letters and poems suitable for the occasion, the mood and the season. Another form of calligraphy had existed since the introduction of Buddhism in Japan, namely the copying of Buddhist sutras in the Chinese script and to some extent in the original Sanskrit. As with religious texts in Europe this work was usually

194

done by monks and priests, but there were laymen who undertook this labour in order to acquire merit or as a deed of expiation. The *Hōgen Monogatari*, in a passage already quoted above, relates how the Emperor Sutoku personally copied the sutras in order to present them to a temple, and how terrifying the expression of his fury became when the gift was rejected.

With the arrival of Zen Buddhism from China a new art form was introduced. In a culture which employs a pictographic script, the borderline between calligraphy and painting is vague indeed. The same implements, a brush and a cake of black ink rubbed on an inkstone and diluted with water, are used, and we may note that the Japanese verb '*kaku*' may refer to the writing of a letter as well as the drawing or painting of a picture. The scriptureless teachings of Zen were transmitted intuitively, and the master's insight into the faith could be put on paper in the form of a still life or the picture of an animal, or of one or more characters expressing a key concept. Famous examples of the Zen style are the paintings by the Chinese master Much'i, known as Mokkei in Japanese, who flourished in the latter half of the thirteenth century. His best known work is perhaps the picture, kept in the Daitokuji in Kyoto, of six persimmons, an ink painting which epitomises this simple and expressive style. Different shades are used with a subtlety which brings the fruits to life, demonstrating that in the hands of a master artist the medium of black ink on paper offers limitless possibilities.

Zen calligraphy is always vigorous and forceful, the characters being expressive by the style of their execution as well as through their intrinsic meaning. Abstraction, i.e. the absence of superfluous detail and ornamentation, is characteristic of Zen. Among later Zen artists, the eighteenth century Sengai is outstanding, his most famous work being a sheet of paper on which he has drawn a triangle, a square and a circle.

The art of poetry has ancient traditions in Japan, and it flourished in the elegant love poems exchanged by the Heian courtiers and their ladies. The short, poignant *tanka*, expressive of a mood, continued to be popular in the Kamakura period, when it was taken up by the *buke*. Under the influence of Zen Buddhism the *tanka* developed from being predominantly love poetry into expressing the evanescence of life in general. *Renga*, linked verses, became popular under the Muromachi *Bakufu*. These poems were often composed in convivial circumstances by an entire party, each person contributing one verse on a chosen theme. There was also a humorous style of *renga*, known as *haikai*.

Another art form patronised by the *buke* was the *Nō* drama, a combination of poetry, dance and music, which was developed during the early Muromachi *Bakufu* by the Kanze family, notably Kan'ami (1333-1384) and his son Zeami (1363-1443). Its origins are to be sought in the ceremonial dances and processions which were performed at the Imperial court on religious feast days and on the occasion of births, deaths, marriages and enthronements. Masked plays and dances were an important feature of religious as well as secular life in oriental and classical antiquity. The phenomenon was widespread throughout Asia, and played an important part in the Hindu and Buddhist cult of India and Tibet, spreading eastwards with Buddhism.

In the Nara period in Japan *Gigaku* masked plays with humorous and grotesque elements were popular. *Bugaku* masked dance and *Gagaku* music were adopted by the Imperial court at Nara in imitation of the Imperial court of T'ang China, remaining largely unchanged to this day in Japan while they have long since disappeared in China. The *Nō* theatre has retained many ancient elements. The lyrics of the *Nō* drama, *utai*, are recited in a sort of chant by the masked actors who are accompanied by musicians and a chorus. The plots of *Nō* plays are usually strongly Buddhist in flavour, a common theme being the appearance of a ghost who tells the story of its wanton or misguided life, and who is eventually reconciled and finds peace and salvation, sometimes through the ministrations of a priest. The lyrics are full of symbolism and hidden meaning, with allusions to much that is left unsaid, the movements of the actors are restrained, there is no *décor*, and the impression is one of hieratic calm and simplicity. This was in absolute harmony with the *bushi* ethos, the life of a samurai swinging like a pendulum between sudden and violent action and quiet, contemplative repose.

Like he drama of classical Greece the aim of a *Nō* play is to bring about a state of catharsis in the mind of the spectator, temporarily clearing his mind of everyday concerns. The *Nō* masks and costumes were of exquisite craftsmanship and sumptuous materials, and the *métier* of actor became hereditary, like most Japanese crafts. A *Nō* performance would usually comprise several plays, and there were comic interludes, *kyōgen*, with unmasked actors performing in simple costumes. A common theme of the *kyōgen* plays was that of a rich but stupid man fooled by a clever servant, and even the haughty samurai would be shown to be outwitted by crafty and disrespectful commoners.

The practice of tea drinking began in earnest in Japan with the arrival of Zen Buddhism. Zen monks used green tea as a stimulant in order to stay awake during long hours of meditation, and tea was also considered to have general medicinal properties. The serving and drinking of tea gradually developed into a ceremony which attracted the attention and interest of the *bushi* and which became known as *cha-no-yu*, literally 'tea and hot water'. This 'secular' tea-ceremony, if we use the term to distinguish it from the Buddhist offering of tea to the Buddha or the spirits of the dead, developed its own rules and etiquette over the years. The *Shōgun* Ashikaga Yoshimasa (1436-1490, regnavit 1443-1473) retired to his Higashiyama villa in Kyoto in 1477 to spend his remaining years there. Of the buildings at Higashiyama, the *Ginkakuji* (Silver Pavilion) is perhaps the most famous, but its rank is disputed by a small adjacent building which houses the earliest tea room in Japan. In this small room, the size of four and a half *tatami* mats, Ashikaga Yoshimasa used to serve tea to a circle of intimates.

Cha-no-yu as we know it today, however, developed later, during the turbulent last quarter of the sixteenth century. The Azuchi period, also known as Momoyama, 'Peach Hill', (1575-1600) saw the violent culmination of the civil wars of the so-called *Sengoku jidai*, and at the same time a remarkable flourishing of the arts. Under the enthusiastic patronage of Toyotomi Hideyoshi, the tea master Sen no Rikyū (1521-1591) revised already existing rules and created new ones. The Zen Buddhist influence was strong. Everything connected with *cha-no-yu* was of the utmost simplicity, from the decoration of the tea room to the kettle, water jar, tea caddy, bamboo spoon, and earthenware cups. Tranquillity was the key word, and on no account should the ceremony be disturbed by talk of everyday matters. The tea room became a haven where the *bushi* could withdraw from the turmoil around him and experience a few fleeting moments of peace in congenial company. That the tea room was exceptional is shown by the fact that swords were customarily left outside, although in a far from perfect world no place was completely safe, and there were instances of assassinations even in tea rooms.

Toyotomi Hideyoshi, who was nothing if not a realist and a born strategist, however, never allowed his relaxations to banish all thoughts of military matters. Once, during a campaign in which he had lost three generals, he ordered Sen no Rikyū to perform *cha-no-yu* while they were resting during a retreat form the battlefield. While the ceremony was still in progress a messenger arrived with good news from the front. Hideyoshi asked for a second cup of tea, after which be marched his troops back, intercepting and routing the enemy.

The utter simplicity which was originally the signum of *cha-no-yu* gradually gave way to luxury and ostentation. Some of this was of the inverted kind, so that a plain bamboo spoon fashioned by the hands of a master like Sen no Rikyū became a priceless heirloom, or a broken and mended tea caddy might change hands for a fabulous sum. There was also more blatant ostentation, encouraged by the example of Toyotomi Hideyoshi who had all the *parvenu*'s love of the glitter of precious metals. No expense was spared in the construction of his legendary Fushimi Castle, which apparently had been so imbued with his forceful personality that it had to be razed to the ground by the Tokugawas, who wished to have as few tangible memories of him as possible. Only fragments remain, such as the *Daishoin* Hall and a gate, *Karamon*, in the so-called 'Chinese' style at the Nishi-Honganji temple in Kyoto. *Cha-no-yu* was one of Toyotomi Hideyoshi's great interests, and in order to celebrate it in what he considered to be a suitable manner, he had a tea room constructed in which every architectural detail was gilt, gold lacquer or solid gold, and where all the utensils were made of gold, except the bamboo ladle and tea whisk and the *tatami* mats. This was far from the ideals of *cha-no-yu*, but Sen no Rikyū was obliged to perform the ceremony when his despotic ruler asked him to do so. In 1592 he was ordered to commit *seppuku*, probably as a result of one of the sudden whims which became more frequent towards the end of Toyotomi Hideyoshi's life.

A simple flower arrangement reflecting the mood of the season and the atmosphere which the host wished to instil among his guests was an important feature of the tea room, where it was displayed in the alcove, *tokonoma*, which was the focal point of the room. The art of flower arrangement, *ikebana*, also became popular with the *bushi*. Like *cha-no-yu* it was originally a pastime for men, but later it became practised by both sexes. To this day it is one of the accomplishments which enhance a young woman's value on the marriage market, rather like the ability to play the piano and do needlework in nineteenth-century Europe.

The Momoyama period was also the heyday of Western influence prior to the Meiji Restoration. Many European arts and fashions were adopted by the *bushi*, and the reports of the Catholic missionaries and the European merchants in Japan contain innumerable references to the absorbing interest with which technical novelties as well as works or art and items of clothing were received. Much was immediately adopted, such as the art of painting on a gold background, which was taken over from European religious works of art. This technique was used for the *byōbu*, large folding screens, which are such a necessary element in Japanese traditional interior decoration. A late flourishing of the ornate style typical of Momoyama art is to be found in the architecture and decoration of the Tōshōgu, the funerary temple of Tokugawa Ieyasu, which was constructed at Nikkō in the 1630s as a syncretistic amalgamation of a Shinto shrine and a Buddhist temple. Woodcarvings and painted decorations cover every inch of the famous Yōmeimon gate, leading to the inner part of the building complex, and the result is very far removed from the effect produced by Zen Buddhist or traditional Shinto art. The funerary temples dedicated to Tokugawa Ieyasu's immediate successors are already considerably less ornate and elaborate.

After the excesses of the *Sengoku jidai*, the Tokugawa *Bakufu* strove to enforce strict control over every aspect of society. We have seen above that the promulgation of detailed sumptuary laws as well as the atmosphere generated by the *Bakufu* of the early Tokugawa period, encouraged a reversal to the old *bushi* ideals. As time went by, however, and many *bushi* families found their circumstances increasingly straitened, merchants and artisans became ever wealthier. With more leisure and the means to pay for their entertainments this growing bourgeoisie came to support a number of new arts which developed out of traditional forms. *Kabuki* theatre, colourful and boisterous, in vivid contrast to the restrained and understated *Nō*, gained immense popularity, as did the *Bunraku* puppet play. The plots were often based on recent events, frequently of a romantic nature, e.g. the not infrequent *shinjū*, "love suicides", of unhappy couples not permitted to marry because of social conventions or other adverse circumstances. As we have seen in the case of the Akō affair dramatic events also found their way, sometimes virtually immediately and thinly disguised so as not to incur censorship, onto both the *Kabuki* and *Bunraku* stages.

A popular prose literature, based on the lives of the townsmen, *chōnin*, themselves, flourished under the Tokugawa *Bakufu*, the greatest author being the aforementioned Ihara Saikaku. In the field of poetry the seventeen-syllable *haiku* was perfected into a distinct genre of its own by Matsuo Bashō (1644-1694), a vagabond and free spirit of *bushi* stock. The popular art forms attracted many *bushi*, although they were theoretically prohibited from attending performances of *Kabuki* and *Bunraku*, which the older generation regarded as vulgar and unsuitable for warriors who ought to maintain their distance and refrain from mingling with the populace. Intermarriage between the daughters of wealthy *chōnin* and the sons of impoverished *bushi* did not diminish the reverence and awe with which the samurai were regarded by commoners, since the woman in Japan traditionally marries away from her own family, severing her links with her background and adopting the customs and values of her husband's family as well as its social status.

Despite the official Tokugawa policy of *Sakoku* (closed

country) which strictly regulated the numbers, activities
and movements of foreigners in Japan and prohibited the
Japanese from travelling abroad, a certain amount of Western learning seeped through. *Rangaku*, literally 'Dutch
learning', as it was known, especially Western medicine,
interested Japanese scholars, many of them Neo-Confu-
cianists and medical doctors of *bushi* stock. Their studies
had to be carried out clandestinely, against immense lin-
guistic difficulties. Apart from a small group of interpreters
attached to Deshima at Nagasaki who knew Dutch, no
Japanese had any knowledge of a European language. The
early *Rangakusha*, who were lucky enough to obtain a
Dutch seventeenth-century work on medicine, were obliged
to teach themselves Dutch as they laboriously worked their
way through the book in order to translate it into Japanese,
in a manner reminiscent of people trying to interpret a
message written in cipher. By the end of the eighteenth
century there were several among the physicians at the
Shōgunal court in Edo who were proficient enough in
Dutch to be able to discuss professional matters with a
European colleague. When Carl Peter Thunberg visited the
Shōgunal court in the spring of 1776, he met two of the
leading *Rangakusha*, Nakagawa Jun'an and Katsuragawa
Hoshū, and held long conversations with them almost
daily during the three weeks of his visit. He lectured to
them on physics, botany, medicine and surgery, and was
impressed by their insatiable thirst for learning and the
diligence and energy with which they tried to master an
alien science.

The Western world was an unknown entity to the vast
majority of Japanese during the Tokugawa *Bakufu*. Through
the *Rangakusha* and the people living in Nagasaki or along
the *Tōkaidō* (Eastern Sea) route which the annual embassies followed to and from Edo, however, some vague ideas
of the *Namban* (Southern Barbarians) were in circulation.
When the Meiji Restoration opened the doors of Japan to
foreign diplomats and merchants the effect was similar to
the breaking of a dam. Suddenly Japan was flooded with
foreign impulses, ideas and goods. Foreign experts and
specialists were called in to develop Japanese industry,
administration and education along Western lines. Japanese officials travelled abroad on fact-finding missions, the

first of these embassies being the so-called Iwakura mission of 1871. Prince Iwakura Tomomi (1825-1883) was himself a *kuge*, as were many of the Meiji statesmen, but the majority of the reformers, thinkers and statesmen who formed Meiji Japan were *bushi*, from high-ranking scions of *daimyō* families to ordinary *samurai*. The first decades of the Meiji period were a time a flux, politically as well as culturally. New values were introduced, old traditions, such as the *chonmage*, the male hairstyle with shaven forehead and the long remaining hair gathered in a queue and tied up on the top of the head, as well as the *samurai* privilege of wearing two swords, were abolished, and society kept changing at a furious pace.

The adoption of foreign manners and costume became a way of demonstrating that one was progressive and fashionable, and when the Empress appeared in public in 1873 with her teeth in their natural state and not painted black, her example was quickly followed by other high-born ladies of fashion and gradually spread downwards. The virtually unquestioning admiration for anything Western, which was automatically regarded as superior and which lent a certain status to its wearer, meant that many incongruous combinations of Western and Japanese traditions and fashions occurred. A bowler hat worn with kimono and *geta*, the high wooden clogs, was only one of the more immediately conspicuous clashes of two different cultures.

In the realm of ideas there were greater and more significant changes. As we have seen concerning *Bushidō*, the old *samurai* ideals became adulterated by being taught to school-children in a vulgar and simplified version, where the former obligation to the feudal lord had been replaced by unquestioning loyalty to the Emperor. This mindless devotion and blind obedience to authority, in emulation of alleged *bushi* ethics, eventually brought disaster to the country and gave *Bushidō* the bad reputation, especially in the West, from which it is only now beginning to recover.

Despite the upheavals and general turmoil of the last century, however, many of the good qualities, especially from the ethical side of *Bushidō*, have quietly persisted as part of the national consciousness. Loyalty, one of the key factors in the concept of *Bushidō*, remains the prop and mainstay of Japanese society. Although there are some signs of change, it is still extremely rare for people to change their occupation or employer. Constancy is expected of the employees, who for their part have been able to enjoy the security of life-long employment. The mutual obligations between employer and employee have worked to great advantage for both parties where the stability of the workforce is concerned. When, as often happens, the stability turns into rigidity, there are however obvious disadvantages to the system, and there are now not a few disgruntled employees who discover themselves to be in a dead end, with no chance of further promotion in the company and no possibility to resign and seek new opportunities elsewhere. Part of this loyalty is based on the Confucian system of the Five Relations, and in a family context the younger generation still generally looks after its elders when they become old and infirm.

A major factor in private as well as public life is the *senpai-kōhai* relationship. An interaction and interdependence between senior and junior occurs in all contexts and on all levels of society, from kindergarten to the Diet. Seniority in any form, even if it only means that one student is in his second year and another in his first year at the same university, inspires, and indeed demands, deferential behaviour. The legacy from *Bushidō* is especially clearly discernible in the case of university students engaged in *budō* sports, i.e. martial arts such as *judō, kendō* and archery, *kyūdō*. The *kōhai* usually act as pages to their *senpai*, fetching and carrying in a manner reminiscent of the system of 'fagging' in some British public schools. Ideally, the *senpai* are expected to treat their *kōhai* with consideration, acting as their mentors, but arrogance and arbitrary corporal punishment is far from unusual.

Another *bushi* legacy which is still flourishing is the rigid self-discipline which demands that private feelings of grief, resentment, anger, and even joy, be hidden from view and never displayed in public, nor in private for that matter, to any but the most intimate friends. The masking of one's feelings behind a bland and neutral exterior was a necessary precaution in an age when one could never be certain of who was friend or foe, and when semi-communal living behind paper walls made restraint and discretion imperative. It was also a result of the fatalistic nature of the

Buddhist faith, which taught a stoical acceptance of the unavoidable.

The *bushi* cultivated an attitude of unconcerned nonchalance under all circumstances, and the starving man would take out and use his toothpick in an effort to keep up appearances. Carl Peter Thunberg, a perceptive man of strong opinions, noted this characteristic with some dismay, as other Westerners had done before him and were to do long after him. 'Never have I seen a people less moved by violent emotions that this. One may scold and revile them, or question their honour as much as one pleases, while they never reply with a word. Only with a slow "oo" do they as it were express great astonishment, and silently conceive the bitterest hatred for their enemy. This can henceforth never be eradicated, whether through apologies, the passing of time, or a change in circumstances. Thus they do not like to treat their enemy discourteously by word or gesture, but often deceive him as well as others by feigning friendship until the occasion sooner or later presents itself to inflict some major damage or misfortune on him.'[154]

The modern Japanese attitude towards suicide as an honourable solution to an insurmountable problem is yet another reminiscence of the ethical code of *Bushidō*. No social stigma is attached to it, and there are no religious prohibitions. With the Buddhist belief in a perpetual cycle of births, deaths and rebirths governed by the sum total of one's actions, *karma*, acquired during previous existences as well as the present one, the individual may always hope for a more propitious rebirth. The method of committing suicide by means of *seppuku*, however, is no longer practised, except by occasional fanatics like Mishima Yukio. Nowadays people throw themselves out of the windows of tall buildings, in front of railway trains, or use poisons or sleeping pills. Mountains, the craters of volcanoes and steep cliffs overhanging the sea are popular suicide spots of a more traditional nature, linked to the Shinto belief in sacred mountains as the abode of *kami* as well as dead ancestors.

The aesthetic and artistic ideals of the *bushi* have remained the traditional lodestar, although sometimes in theory only. Highly skilled craftsmen working in natural materials such as wood, bamboo, straw and clay, and refined ones like paper, cotton, hemp, silk and lacquer, still produce objects whose utter simplicity of shape in conjunction with a restrained use of decoration makes them aesthetically pleasing even if the primary intention was not to create a work of art but a utilitarian object. Garish colours, elaborate patterns and overdecoration hold great appeal for popular tastes, however, and contemporary Japan displays some sharp contrasts and variations in aesthetic perception. Western impulses and imports, as well as modern synthetic materials, have made most of the traditional crafts obsolete. One may hope, however, that there will be an aesthetic reawakening in Japan which will bring about a renaissance for traditional arts and crafts and a renewed appreciation of their purely artistic values. In the West this has gradually begun, no doubt partly as a result of the new interest in so-called 'ethnic' art.

The shadow of the adulterated version of *Bushidō* is looming on the political horizon again. The *Yasukuni Jinja*, has begun to receive official recognition. This has caused a great deal of controversy, and several groups, religious and political as well as independent, strongly oppose this, which is seen as the first step towards a reestablishment of militarism.

Another attempted step in the same direction might be the expurgation of recent history books for use in schools. Historical facts, such as the Japanese annexation of Manchuria, have been omitted or extensively rewritten in a more favourable light, a practice which appears to have caused considerably greater indignation abroad, particularly in China, than at home.

On the level of mass communication, even the most casual observer cannot help noticing the tremendous popularity of television series dealing with the more colourful and swashbuckling aspects of the lives of the *bushi*. The same is true of the cinema, and there is also a literary genre devoted to the heroic adventures of samurai heroes, often set in a *Sengoku jidai* context. The 'samurai genre' appears to enjoy the same vogue in Japan as the so-called 'Westerns' did in the United States and Europe a couple of decades ago. In the world of advertising it is notable that samurai in full armour have become quite frequent in advertisements, e.g. for Japanese cars or electronic equipment. The warrior image, which was severely damaged and sullied during the last war, is once again regarded in a favourable light. Apparently the warrior is seen to project qualities such as resolution, steadfastness and strength, and the awesome helmeted samurai brandishing his sword is beginning to supersede the cherry blossoms and *geisha* in advertisements directed towards the foreign market.

Thus the idea of the valiant *bushi* of the *Gunki Monogatari* lives on in the consciousness of the general public in Japan today. The popular image of the samurai, however, has been changed almost beyond recognition, and turned into a one-dimensional stereotype. The question is not only how far removed this idealised samurai has become from his flesh and blood ancestors, but also to what extent present-day notions of *Bushidō* are detached from the original concept, as it was perceived by those who practised it. Yamaga Sokō and his contemporaries had codified a *bushi* ethos which still retained its vitality. This was true even at the time of the Akō affair, but under the rigid rule of the Tokugawa *Bakufu Bushidō* gradually lost momentum and became ossified, until it could be used by the Meiji government to inculcate feelings of loyalty towards the Emperor in the population at large.

The many dimensions of the original *bushi* ethic, religion, customs, beliefs and character run a serious risk of being obscured by the more facile image of the samurai as a romantic hero pure and simple. From time to time we may therefore need to remind ourselves that the *bushi* were not only warriors, but also complex human beings, subject to the ideas, conventions and customs of their times. Although in theory they all obeyed the same set of rules, they were individuals, viewing the practice of *Bushidō* pragmatically and from different angles according to the circumstances in which they found themselves.

The notion of *Bushidō*, as it was codified by the Neo-Confucian *jusha*, has come to constitute a basis, an integral part of Japanese culture distilled through centuries of theory and practice. It is the origin of a great many ethical values in modern Japan, which cannot be fully understood unless the creative and dynamic diversity of the original *bushi* tradition is taken into account.

Footnotes

CHAPTER 1

1. For descriptions and illustrations of *haniwa* see Kidder, J.E. Jr., *Japan Before Buddhism*, London, 1966, pp. 192-201.
————, *Ancient Japan*, Oxford, 1977

Elisseeff, Vadime, *The Ancient Civilization of Japan*, London, 1974

2. Haguenauer, Charles, *Résultat des travaux japonais* (1955-1956) touchant l'histoire du Japon, 1ère partie: Revue historique, CCXX, Presses Universitaires de France, Paris, octobre-décembre 1958, p. 338.

3. Joüon des Longrais, Frédéric, *L'Est et l'Ouest*, Institutions du Japon et de l'Occident comparées, Maison Franco-Japonaise, Tokyo, 1958, pp. 182-183.

4. Hall, J.W., *Government and Local Power in Japan 500 to 1700, A Study Based on Bizen Province*, Princeton University Press, 1966, pp. 34-40.

5. Snellen, J.B., '*Shoku Nihongi, Chronicles of Japan, continued, from 697-791 A.D.*, translated and annotated by J.B. Snellen', Transactions of the Asiatic Society of Japan, Second Series, Vol. XI, December 1934, Tokyo, p. 180 and p. 215.

6. The full text of this code is to be found in the Kokushi Taikei editions. The articles by G.B. Sansom entitled 'Early Japanese Law and Administration', Part I and II, in the Transactions of the Asiatic Society of Japan, Second Series, Vol. IX, Tokyo, December 1932, and Vol. XI, December 1934, however give an annotated paraphrase of the *Ryō no Gige*, a largely unchanged edition of the *Yōrō Ryō* brought out in 833. See especially Part I, pp. 88-90, 89-99.

7. Snellen, J.B., *Op. cit.*, p. 225.

8. Joüon des Longrais, F., *Op. cit.*, p. 198.

9. *Ibid.*, pp. 199-200.

10. Haguenauer, C., *Origines de la civilisation japonaise, Introduction à l'étude de la préhistoire du Japon, Première Partie*, Paris, 1956, p. 404. See also Haguenauer, Revue historique, CCXX, Presses Universitaires de France, Paris, octobre-décembre 1958, p. 338, and Revue historique, CCXXII, octobre-décembre, 1959, p. 350.

11. Joüon des Longrais, F., *Op. cit.*, pp. 202-203.

12. The *Heike Monogatari* was written in the early Kamakura period. The date of the *Hōgen Monogatari* is uncertain, and it may be late Kamakura or even later. Quotations in the text are from two translations into English: *The Tale of the Heike*, transl. by Kitagawa Hiroshi and Bruce T. Tsuchida, University of Tokyo Press, 1981, and Kellogg, E.R., Hōgen Monogatari, Transactions of the Asiatic Society of Japan, Vol. XLV, Part I, Tokyo, 1917.

13. *The Tale of the Heike*, transl. by Kitagawa Hiroshi and Bruce T. Tsuchida, University of Tokyo Press, 1981, p. 330.

14. Sato, Shinichi and Ikeuchi, Yoshisuke, *Chūsei Hōrei Shiryō Shū*, Vol. 1, Tokyo, 1955, pp. 3-36. A partial translation of the *Goseibai Shikimoku* into English can be found in an article by John Carey Hall entitled 'Japanese Feudal Law: The Institutes of Judicature: Being a Translation of 'Go Seibai Shikimoku'; The Magisterial Code of the Hojo Power-Holders (A.D. 1232)' in the Transactions of the Asiatic Society of Japan, Vol. XXXIV, Part I, Yokohama, 1906.

CHAPTER 2

15. The Chinese Classics are known in Japan as the *Gokyō* (Five Classics), and the Shishō, 'Four Books'. The former consist of the *Eki-kyō* (I Ching, the Book of Changes), *Sho-kyō* (Shu Ching, the Annals), *Shi-kyō* (the Book of Odes), *Shunjū-saden* (Ch'un-Ch'iu, the Spring and Autumn Annals) and *Raiki* (Li Chi, the Book of Rites). The Four Confucian Books comprise the *Daigaku* (Ta Hsüeh, the Great Learning), *Chū-yō* (Chung-yung, the Doctrine of the Mean), *Rongo* (Lun yü, the Analects) and *Mōshi* (Meng Tze, Mencius).

16. Jean Herbert, in his *Shintō, At the Fountainhead of Japan*, London, 1967, quotes the head of the research division at the Jinja-honchō, Okada Yoneo, on this subject, p. 426.

17. Casal, U.A., *Hachiman, Der Kriegsgott Japans*, Mitteilungen der Deutschen Gesellschaft für Natur- und Völkerkunde Ostasiens, Tokyo, 1962, p. 5.

18. de Visser, M.W., *Ancient Buddhism in Japan, Sutras and Ceremonies in Use in the Seventh and Eighth Centuries A.D. and Their History in Later Times*, Vol. I, Leiden, 1935, p. 213.

de Visser also suggests that the number eight in connection with Hachiman may be a Chinese influence which has to do with the concept of the eight quarters of the world.

19. The *Jinnō Shōtōki* has been translated as *A Chronicle of Gods and Sovereigns* by H. Paul Varley, Columbia University Press, New York, 1980, p. 106.

20. de Visser, M.W., *Op. cit.*, pp. 229-230.

21. *The Tale of the Heike, Op. cit.*, p. 333.

22. Hori, Kyotsu, 'The Economic and Political Effects of the Mongol Wars',

in Hall, J.W. and Mass, J.P., eds., *Medieval Japan, Essays In Institutional History*, Yale University Press, New Haven and London, 1974, p. 186.

23. de Visser, M.W., *Op. cit.*, pp. 155-156.

24. These are Daikoku (Sanskr. *Mahākāla*), Benten (Sanskr. *Sarasvatī*), Bishamon (Sanskr. *Vaiśravana*), Jurōjin, Fukurokuju, Ebisu and Hotei.

25. This ceremony still takes place occasionally among the adherents of *Shugendō*. The sect was proscribed during the Meiji period, but survived, and a small number of *yamabushi* are still to be found in Japan. A most interesting eye-witness account of a contemporary *hi-watari* is given by the eminent scholar of Japanese folk religion Dr Carmen Blacker in her book *The Catalpa Bow*, London, Allen and Unwin, 1976, pp. 250-251.

26. Lowell, Percival, *Occult Japan, or The Way of the Gods. An Esoteric Study of Japanese Personality and Possession*, Boston, 1895, pp. 62-88.

27. This episode was immortalised in the *Nō* play *Kanjinchō*, "The Subscription-list'. A modern cinematic version made by Kurosawa Akira in 1948 under the title *Tora no o fumu otokotachi*, 'The Men Who Trod on the Tiger's Tail', is particularly interesting and masterfully directed and acted.

28. The *tengu* have been analysed by many Western scholars, e.g. M.W. de Visser, 'The Tengu', Transactions of the Asiatic Society of Japan, Vol. XXXVI, Pt.II, Tokyo, 1908; Volker, T., T., The Animal in Far Eastern Art, and Especially in the Art of the Japanese Netsuke, With Reference to Chinese Origins, Traditions, Legends and Art, Leiden, E.J. Brill, 1975; Rotermund, H.O., Die Yamabushi, Aspekte ihres Glaubens, Lebens und ihrer sozialen Funktion in japanischen Mittelalter, Hamburg, Monographien zur Völkerkunde V, 1967.

29. The quotation is taken from E.R. Kellogg's translation of the *Hōgen Monogatari*, Transactions of the Asiatic Society of Japan, Vol. XLV, Pt. I, 1917, pp. 106-107.

30. Kitagawa, H. and B.T. Tsuchida, transl., *The Tale of the Heike*, University of Tokyo Press, 1975, p. 324.

31. Girard, Frédéric, 'Les enseignements du maitre Myōe de Toga-no-o'/ Toga-no-o Myōe Shōnin Yuikun/, *in* Mélanges offerts a M. Charles Haguenauer en l'honneur de son quatre-vingtième anniversaire, Collège de France, Bibliothèque de l'Institut des Hautes Etudes Japonaises, Paris, 1980, p. 508.

CHAPTER 3

32. The tiny minority of Christian peasants (known as the 'Urakami Christians' from the place where they lived and made their reappearance after the Meiji Restoration) who managed to practise their faith in secret were an isolated group and had no influence on their fellow countrymen.

3. Joly, H.L. and Inada, H., Arai Hakuseki—*The Sword Book in Honchō Gunkikō and the Book of Samé, Ko Hi Sei Gi of Inaba Tsūrio*, London, 1913.

34. Aston, W.G., Nihongi, Chronicles of Japan from the Earliest Times to A.D. 697. Transactions and Proceedings of the Japan Society, London, Supplement I, London, 1896, pp. 183-184.

35. Cooper, Michael, S.J., transl. and ed., This Island of Japon, João Rodrigues' Account of 16th-century Japan, Kodansha, Tokyo, 1973, pp. 69-70.

36. Willman, Olof Eriksson, Een kort Beskriffning På een Resa till Ostindien och förbeskreffne Japan Then een Swänsk Mann och Skeps Capiteen Oloff Erichsson Willman benembdh giordt hafwer. Tryckt på Wijsingsborgh Åff Johan Kankel, åhr effter Christi Bördh MDCLXVII, p. 221 Translation by the present author.

37. Kitagawa, H. and B.T. Tsuchida, transl., The Tale of the Heike, University of Tokyo Press, 1975, pp. 280-281.

38. Ackroyd, Joyce, transl., Told Round a Brushwood Fire, The Autobiography of Arai Hakuseki, Univesity of Tokyo Press, 1979, pp. 37, 44-45, 77.

39. Kellogg, E.R. transl., Hōgen Monogatari, Transactions of the Asiatic Society of Japan, Vol. XLV, Pt. I, 1917, p. 48.

40. Haguenauer, Charles, 'La danse rituelle dans la cérémonie du chinkonsai', Journal Asiatique, avril-juin 1930, pp. 324-350. Reprinted in Etudes choisies de Charles Haguenauer, Vol. II, Japon, Etudes de religion, d'histoire et de littérature, Leiden, 1977.

41. Kitagawa, H. and B.T. Tsuchida, transl., The Tale of the Heike, University of Tokyo Press, 1975, p. 689.

42. Brown, D.M. and I. Ishida, transl. and ed., The Future and the Past, a translation and study of the Gukanshō, an interpretative history of Japan written in 1219, University of California Press, 1979, p. 143.

43. Ibid., p. 144. The term jiun, 'time fate' or 'destiny of the times', is a Buddhist concept which goes back to the idea of cyclical time. Thus the present era is Mappō, the time of the 'decline of the Law'.

44. Ibid., p. 414. The 'Land Stewards' mentioned in the text were the jitō, local representatives of the Kamakura Bakufu.

45. Miyamoto Musashi, A Book of Five Rings, transl. by Victor Harris, London, 1974, p. 95.

46. Leggett, Trevor, Zen and the Ways, London, 1978, pp. 158-160.

47. Ibid., pp. 161-163.

48. Ibid., pp. 191.

49. The Tale of the Heike, op. cit., pp. 271-272.

50. Mitford's Japan, The Memoirs and Recollections 1866-1906 of the first Lord Redesdale, ed. by Hugh Cortazzi, London, 1985, pp. 84-89.

51. Ibid., pp. 159-160.

52. Pigeot, Jacqueline, 'Les suicides de femmes par noyade dans la littérature narrative du Japon ancien', Mélanges offerts a M. Charles Haguenauer, en l'honneur de son quatre-vingtième anniversaire, Collège de France,

Bibliothèque de l'Institut des Hautes Etudes Japonaises, Paris, 1980, pp. 255-258.

53. *Ibid.*, pp. 266-67.

54. Kitagawa, H. and B.T. Tsuchida, transl., *The Tale of the Heike*, University of Tokyo Press, 1975, p. 701.

55. Wilson, William Ritchie, The Way of Bow and Arrow. The Japanese Warrior in *Konjaku Monogatari*, Monumenta Nipponica, Vol. XXVIII, No. 2, Summer 1973, pp. 177-233. The tales show strong Chinese influence, and as well as opening with a fixed formula they end with a concluding moral.

56. *The Tale of the Heike, op. cit.*, pp. 579-580.

57. *Ibid.*, p. 369.

58. Chamberlain, B.H., 'A Short Memoir From the Seventeenth Century', Transactions of the Asiatic Society of Japan, Vol. VIII, Yokohama, 1880, p. 139.

59. *The Tale of the Heike*, op. cit., pp. 522-523.

60. Brown, D.M. and I. Ishida, transl. and ed., *The Future and the Past, a translation and study of the Gukanshō, an interpretative history of Japan written in 1219*, University of California Press, 1979, p. 138.

61. *The Tale of the Heike*, op. cit., p. 513.

62. *Ibid.*, p. 732.

63. *Ibid.*, pp. 557-558.

64. Ackroyd, Joyce, transl., *Lessons from History, The Tokushi Yoron by Arai Hakuseki*, University of Queensland Press, 1982, p. 247.

65. Joüon des Longrais, Frédéric, *L'Est et L'Ouest, Institutions du Japon et de l'Occident comparées*, Maison Franco-Japonaise, Tokyo, 1958, pp. 117-166.

66. *The Tale of the Heike*, op. cit., p. 175.

67. Joüon des Longrais, F., op. cit., p. 146.

68. de Bary, Wm. Theodore, ed., *Sources of Japanese Tradition*, New York and London, 1964, Vol. I, p. 205.

69. For a discussion of the *ikki* movement vide Davis, D.L., 'Ikki in Late Medieval Japan', in Hall, J.W. and Mass, J.P., eds., *Medieval Japan, Essays in Institutional History*, Yale University Press, New Haven and London, 1974, pp. 221-247.

70. Thunberg, Carl Peter, Resa uti Europa, Africa, Asia, förrättad åren 1770-1779, Upsala, 1791, Fjerde delen, p. 62. Translation by the present author.

71. For a discussion of the practice and significance of tattooing in Japan vide Van Gulik, W.R., *Irezumi, The Pattern of Dermatography in Japan*, Leiden, 1982.

CHAPTER 4

72.. Chamberlain, B.H., transl., *Kojiki, or 'Records of Ancient Matters'*, Transactions of the Asiatic Society of Japan, Supplement to Vol. X, Yokohama, 1883, pp. 60-63; Facsimile ed., Asiatic Society of Japan, Tokyo, 1973, pp. 72-76.

73. *Ibid.*, pp. 203-209; 1973 ed., pp. 248-253.

74. Kellogg, E.R. transl., *Hōgen Monogatari*, Transactions of the Asiatic Society of Japan, Vol. XLV, Pt. I, 1917, p. 39. Rokuson-Ō, 894-961, also called Tsunemoto, was the first to carry the family name Minamoto. Sutoku-In was the retired Emperor Sutoku, while the Emperor referred to in the text was Go-Shirakawa. The Sadaijin, or Minister of the Left, was Yorinaga.

75. *The Tale of the Heike*, op. cit., p. 269. The imperial prince referred to was Mochihito (1150-1180), son of Go-Shirakawa by a Fujiwara lady, who had taken sides with the Minamoto against the Taira.

76. *Ibid.*, p. 520. Yoshinaka was Minamoto Yoritomo's cousin, who had gone over to the Taira side after a quarrel.

77. *Ibid.*, p. 663.

78. *Ibid.*, pp. 559-560.

79. *Ibid.*, pp. 554-556.

80. *Ibid.*, pp. 561-563.

81. *Ibid.*, p. 657. This battle took place in 1185, shortly before the Battle of Dan-no-Ura.

82. Hall, John Carey, 'The Hojo Code of Judicature', Transactions of the Asiatic Society of Japan, Vol. XXXIV, Pt. I, Yokohama, 1906, pp. 1-48.

83. An English translation of the *Kemmu* Code is to be found under the title 'Japanese Feudal Laws II—The Ashikaga Code', by John Carey Hall, Transactions of the Asiatic Society of Japan, Vol. XXXVI, Pt. II, Yokohama, 1908, pp. 1-23.

84. Sansom, George B., 'The Tsuredzure Gusa of Yoshida no Kaneyoshi, Being the Meditations of a Recluse in the 14th Century', Transactions of the Asiatic Society of Japan, Vol. XXXIX, Yokohama, 1911, pp. 56 and 73-74.

85. The Book of the Order of Chivalry by Raymond Lull, *in* Herlihy, David, *The History of Feudalism*, London, 1970, p. 309.

86. *Ibid.*, p. 313.

87. *Ibid.*, pp. 314-315.

88. *Ibid.*, pp. 316-317.

89. Renondeau, G., Histoire des moines guerriers du Japon, Mélanges publiés par L'Institut des Hautes Etudes Chinoises, Tôme premier, Paris, 1957, p. 173.

90. *Ibid.*, pp. 265-266. The Miidera had been burned down by Taira

Kiyomori. A *dōju* was an armed temple servant, although the border-line between laymen and monks who carried arms appears to have been rather vague.

91. For an analysis of the Buddhist attitude to war, see Paul Demiéville, Le Bouddhisme et la Guerre, Post-scriptum à l"Histoire des moines guerriers du Japon" de G. Renondeau, op. cit.

92. Herlihy, David, *The History of Feudalism*, London, 1970, pp. 289-292.

93. *Ibid.*, pp. 294-296.

94. Cooper, Michael, S.J., transl. and ed., *This Island of Japon, João Rodrigues' Account of 16th Century Japan*, Tokyo and New York, 1973, p. 127.

95. Mc Cullough, Helen Craig, transl. and ed., 'A Tale of Mutsu', Harvard Journal of Asiatic Studies, Vol. 25, 1964-65, p. 192.

96. *Ibid.*, p. 192.

97. *Ibid.*, p. 203.

98. The *Imagawa-jō* has been translated by Carl Steenstrup, 'The Imagawa Letter. A Muromachi Warrior's Code of Conduct Which Became a Tokugawa Schoolbook', Monumenta Nipponica, Vol. XXVIII, No. 3, 1973, pp. 295-316.

99. For a translation of the *Jinkaishū*, see Röhl, Wilhelm, 'Jinkaishū, Ein Beitrag zum mittelalterlichen japanischen Recht', Mitteilungen der Deutschen Gesellschaft für Natur- und Völkerkunde Ostasiens, Tokyo, 1960.

100. Oda: 'Nakaneba korosu, hototogisu'. Toyotomi: 'Nakashite miyō, hototogisu.' Tokugawa: 'Nakumade matō, hototogisu',

101. Hall, J.W., Nagahara, K., and Yamamura, K., eds., *Japan Before Tokugawa, Political Consolidation and Economic Growth, 1500 to 1650*, Princeton University Press, 1981. 'The Political Posture of Oda Nobunaga', by Fujiki Hisashi and George Elison, p. 189.

102. De Bary, W.T., ed., *Sources of Japanese Tradition*, Vol. I, pp. 320-321.

103. 'Tsuyu to oki/Tsuyu to kienan/Waga mi kana/Naniwa no koto wa/ Yume no mata yume.'

104. Hall, John Carey, 'Japanese Feudal Laws III. The Tokugawa Legislation, Part I', Transactions of the Asiatic Society of Japan, Vol. XXXVIII, Part IV, Tokyo, 1911, p. 288. Parenthesis by the present author.

105. *Ibid.*, p. 309; p. 311.

106. *Ibid.*, pp. 288-289.

107. *Ibid.*, p. 294; p. 297; p. 298.

108. *Ibid.*, p. 307.

109. Murdoch, J. and I. Yamagata, *A History of Japan*, Vol. II, London, 1925, p. 435.

110. Miyamoto Musashi, *A Book of Five Rings*, transl. by Victor Harris, London, 1974, pp. 37 and 40.

111. *Ibid.*, p. 49.

112. *Ibid.*, p. 38.

113. de Bary, W.T., ed., *Sources of Japanese Tradition*, Columbia University Press, New York and London, 1958, Vol. I, p. 347. The term *shi* (Chin. *shih*) can be translated as 'knight' or 'gentleman' and refers to the scholar-bureaucrat of the Chinese Confucian system of government.

114. Fisher, Galen M., 'Nakae Tōju, The Sage of Ōmi', Transactions of the Asiatic Society of Japan, Vol. XXXVI, Part I, Yokohama, 1908, p. 71.

115. *Ibid.*, pp. 72-73.

116. *Ibid.*, pp. 80-84.

117. Earl, David M., *Emperor and Nation in Japan—Political Thinkers of the Tokugawa Period*, Seattle, 1964, p. 40.

118. de Bary, W.T., ed., *Sources of Japanese Tradition*, Columbia University Press, New York and London, 1958, Vol. I, p. 389.

119. *Ibid.*, pp. 390-391.

120. *Ibid.*, pp. 400-401.

121. *Ibid.*, pp. 360-361.

122. *Ibid.*, pp. 378-379. The present author's remark in parenthesis.

123. *Ibid.*, pp. 382-383.

124. Mitford, A.B., *Tales of Old Japan*, Vol. I, London, 1871, pp. 33-34.

125. Hall, John Carey, 'Japanese Feudal Laws III. The Tokugawa Legislation, Part I', Transactions of the Asiatic Society of Japan, Vol. XXXVIII, Part IV, 1911, p. 299

126. *Ibid.*, p. 301.

127. Lidin, Olof G., The Life of Ogyū Sorai. A Tokugawa Confucian Philosopher, Lund, 1973, pp. 48-49.

128. *Ibid.*, p. 49. Uesugi was the son of Kira Yoshinaka and lord of Yonesawa.

129. Nagashima, Yoichi, 'Akō-affaeren, Bushidō og Yamaga Sokō', Copenhagen 1976,. p. 12. Unpublished paper, privately communicated.

130. de Bary, W.T., ed., *Sources of Japanese Tradition*, Vol. I, Columbia University Press, New York, and London, 1965, pp. 428-430.

131. Lloyd, A., 'Historical Development of the Shushi Philosophy in Japan', Transactions of the Asiatic Society of Japan, Vol. XXXIV, Part IV, Yokohama, 1907, p. 17.

132. Maruyama, M., *Studies in the Intellectual History of Tokugawa Japan*, transl. by Mikiso Hane, Princeton University Press, University of Tokyo Press, 1974, pp. 72-73. Maruyama's parentheses.

133. *Ibid.*, p. 73. Maruyama's italics and brackets.

134. For a detailed analysis of the above events, see my *Samurai Religion II. The Akō Affair: A Practical Example of Bushidō*, Upsala, 1977.

135. Furukawa Tesshi, 'The Individual in Japanese Ethics', *in* Moore, C.A., ed., *The Japanese Mind. Essentials of Japanese Philosophy and Culture, East-West Centre Press,* University of Hawaii Press, Honolulu, 1967, pp. 232-233.

136. *Ibid.,* p. 230.

137. *Ibid.,* p. 229.

138. Sadler A.L., *The Beginner's Book of Bushidō. Being a Translation of Daidōji Yūzan's Budō Shosinshū,* KBS 2600 Anniversary Essay Series, Tokyo, Kokusai Bunka Shinkokai/The Society for International Cultural Relations/, 1941, pp. 3-79.

139. Ackroyd, Joyce, transl., *Told Round a Brushwood Fire, The Autobiography of Arai Hakuseki,* University of Tokyo Press, Tokyo, 1979, p. 39.

140. *Ibid.,* p. 37.

141. *Ibid.,* p. 47.

142. *Ibid.,* p. 52.

143. *Ibid.,* pp. 46-47.

144. Ackroyd, Joyce, transl., *Lessons from History, The Tokushi Yoron by Arai Hakuseki,* University of Queensland Press, 1982, p. 65.

145. *Ibid.,* p. 72.

146. *Ibid.,* pp. 236-237.

147. de Bary, W.T., ed., *Sources of Japanese Tradition,* Columbia University Press, New York and London, 1965, Vol. II, pp. 111-114.

148. Coleman, H.E., 'The Life of Shōin Yoshida', Transactions of the Asiatic Society of Japan, Vol. XLV, Part I, 1917, p. 188.

149. de Bary, op. cit., p. 111. "Kaku sureba/Kaku naru mono to/Shiri nagara/Yamu ni yamarenu/Yamato damashii."

150. Leggett, T.P., The Tiger's Cave, Translations of Japanese Zen Texts, London, 1977, p. 173.

151. *Mitford's Japan. The Memoirs and Recollections, 1866-1906, of Algernon Bertram Mitford, the first Lord Redesdale,* ed. by Hugh Cortazzi, London, The Athlone Press, 1985, p. 160.

152. de Bary, W.T., ed., *Sources of Japanese Tradition,* Columbia University Press, New York and London, 1965, Part II, pp. 280-285.

153. *Yukio Mishima on Hagakure, The Samurai Ethic and Modern Japan,* transl. by Kathryn Sparling, Penguin Books, 1979, p. 94.

CHAPTER 5

154. Thunberg, Carl Peter, Tal om Japanska Nationen, hållet för Kongl. Vetensk. Akademien, vid Praesidii Nedläggande den 3 Novemb. 1784 af Carl Peter Thunberg, Med. och Botan. Professor, Stockholm, år 1784. Tryckt hos Johan Georg Lange, p. 13. English translation by the present author.

Bibliography

Ackroyd, Joyce, transl., *Told Round a Brushwood Fire, The Autobiography of Arai Hakuseki*, University of Tokyo Press, Tokyo, 1979.

——, transl., *Lessons From History, The Tokushi Yoron by Arai Hakuseki*, University of Queensland Press, 1982.

Aston, W.G., transl., *Nihongi, Chronicles of Japan from the Earliest Times to A.D. 697*, Transactions and Proceedings of the Japan Society, Supplement I, London, 1896. Reprinted, London, 1956.

de Bary, Wm. T., R. Tsunoda, D. Keene, eds., *Sources of Japanese Tradition*, Vol. I-II, Columbia University Press, New York and London, 1965.

Blacker, Carmen, *The Catalpa Bow*, Allen and Unwin, London, 1976.

Blomberg, D. Catharina M., *Samurai Religion I, Some Aspects of Warrior Manners and Customs in Feudal Japan Samurai Religion II, the Akō Affair, A Practical Example of Bushidō*, Upsala, 1976-77.

——, 'Carl Peter Thunberg, A Swedish Scholar in Tokugawa Japan', in Nish, Ian, ed., *Contemporary European Writing on Japan, Scholarly Views From Eastern and Western Europe*, Paul Norbury Publications, 1988.

——, 'The Vicissitudes of Bushidō', in Boscaro, A., Gatti, F., Raveri, M., eds., *Rethinking Japan*, Vol. 2, Social Sciences, Ideology and Thought, Paul Norbury Publications, 1989.

——' "A Strange White Smile": A Survey of Tooth-blackening and other Dental Practices in Japan', *Japan Forum*, Vol.2, No.2, Oxford University Press, October 1990.

Brown, D.M. and I. Ishida, transl. and ed., *The Future and the Past, a Translation and Study of the Gukanshō, an Interpretative History of Japan Written in 1219*, University of California Press, 1979.

Casal, U.A., 'Hachiman, Der Kriegsgott Japans', Mitteilungen der Deutschen Gesellschaft für Natur- und Völkerkunde Ostasiens, Tokyo, 1962.

Chamberlain, B.H., 'A Short Memoir From the Seventeenth Century', Transactions of the Asiatic Society of Japan, Vol. VIII, Yokohama, 1880.

——, transl., *Kojiki, or 'Records of Ancient Matters'*, Transactions of the Asiatic Society of Japan, Supplement to Vol. X, Yokohama, 1883.

Facsimile edition, Asiatic Society of Japan, Tokyo, 1973.

Coleman, H.E., 'The Life of Shōin Yoshida', Transactions of the Asiatic Society of Japan, Vol. XLV, Part I, 1917.

Cooper, Michael, S.J., transl. and ed., *This Island of Japon, João Rodrigues' Account of 16th Century Japan*, Kodansha, Tokyo and New York, 1973.

Davis, D.L., 'Ikki in Late Medieval Japan', *in* Hall, J.W. and J.P. Mass, eds., *Medieval Japan, Essays in Institutional History*, Yale University Press, New Haven and London, 1974.

Demiéville, Paul, 'Le Bouddhisme et la guerre', Post-scriptum à l'"Histoire des moines guerriers du Japon" de G. Renondeau, Mélanges publiés par l'Institut des Hautes Etudes Chinoises, Tôme premier, Paris, 1957.

Earl, D.M., *Emperor and Nation in Japan—Political Thinkers of the Tokugawa Period*, Seattle, 1964.

Eliot, Sir Charles, *Japanese Buddhism*, Routledge and Kegan Paul, London, 1935. Reprinted 1969.

Elison, G. and D.L. Smith, eds., *Warlords, Artists and Commoners, Japan in the Sixteenth Century*, University of Hawaii Press, 1981.

Elisséeff, Vadime, *The Ancient Civilization of Japan*, London, 1974.

Fisher, Galen M., 'Nakae Tōju, The Sage of Ōmi', Transactions of the Asiatic Society of Japan, Vol. XXXVI, Part I, Yokohama, 1908.

Frank, Bernard, 'Kata-imi et Kata-tagae, Etude sur les inter-dits de direction à l' époque Heian', Bulletin de la Maison Franco-Japonaise, Nouvelle Série, Tôme V, No.2-4, Tokyo, 1958.

Fujiki, H. and G. Elison, 'The Political Posture of Oda Nobunaga', *in* Hall, J.W., Nagahara K. and Yamamura, K., eds., *Japan Before Tokugawa, Political Consolidations and Economic Growth, 1500 to 1650*, Princeton University Press, 1981.

Furukawa, Tesshi, 'The Individual in Japanese Ethics', *in* Moore, C.A., ed., *The Japanese Mind, Essentials of Japanese Philosophy and Culture*, East-West Centre Press, University of Hawaii Press, Honolulu, 1967.

Girard, Frédéric, 'Les enseignements du maitre Myōe de Toga-no-o/Togano-o Myōe Shōnin Yuikun/*in* Melanges offerts a M. Charles Haguenauer en l'honneur de son quatre-vingtième anniversaire, Collège de France, Bibliothèque de l'Institut des Hautes Etudes Japonaises, Paris, 1980.

Haguenauer, Charles, 'La danse rituelle dans la cérémonie du chinkonsai', Journal Asiatique, avril-juin 1930. Reprinted in Etudes choisies de Charles Haguenauer, Vol. II, Japon, Etudes de religion, d'histoire et de littérature, Leiden, 1977.

———, Origines de la civilisation japonaise, Introduction à l'étude de la préhistoire du Japon, Première partie, Paris, 1956.

———, Résultat des travaux japonais (1955-1956) touchant l'histoire du Japon, 1ère partie, Revue Historique, CCXX, Presses universitaires de

France, Paris, octobre-décembre 1958; Ibid., CCXXII, octobre-décembre, 1959.

Hall, J.C., 'Japanese Feudal Laws, I. The Hōjō Code of Judicature', Transactions of the Asiatic Society of Japan, Vol. XXXIV, Part I, Yokohama, 1906.

———, 'Japanese Feudal Laws, II. The Ashikaga Code', TASJ, Vol. XXXVI, Part II, Yokohama, 1908.

———, 'Japanese Feudal Laws, III. The Tokugawa Legislation, Part I-III.', TASJ, Vol. XXXVIII, Part IV, Yokohama, 1911.

Hall, J.C., 'Japanese Feudal Laws, III. The Tokugawa Legislation, Part IV', TASJ, Vol. XXXXI, Part V, Yokohama, 1913.

Hall, J.W., Government and Local Power in Japan 500 to 1700. A Study Based on Bizen Province, Princeton University Press, 1966.

Hall, J.W. and J.P. Mass, eds., Medieval Japan, Essays in Institutional History, Yale University Press, New Haven and London, 1974.

Hall, J.W., and Toyoda, T., eds., Japan in the Muromachi Age, University of California Press, Berkeley and London, 1977.

Hall, J.W., Nagahara, K. and Yamamura, K., eds., Japan Before Tokugawa, Political Consolidation and Economic Growth, 1500 to 1650, Princeton University Press, 1981.

Hall, R.K., ed., Kokutai no Hongi, Cardinal Principles of the National Entity of Japan, transl. by J.O. Gauntlett, Cambridge, Mass., 1949.

Herlihy, David, The History of Feudalism, London, 1970.

Hibino, Y., Nippon Shindo Ron or the National Ideals of the Japanese People, Cambridge, 1928.

Hori, Kyotsu, 'The Economic and Political Effects of the Mongol Wars', in Hall, J.W. and J.P. Mass, eds., Medieval Japan, Essays in Institutional History, Yale University Press, New Haven and London, 1974.

Joly, H.L. and H. Inada, Arai Hakuseki—The Sword Book in Honchō Gunkikō and the Book of Samé, Ko Hi Sei Gi of Inaba Tsūrio, London, 1913.

Joüon des Longrais, Frédéric, L'Est et l'Ouest, Institutions du Japon et de l'occident comparées, Maison Franco-Japonaise, Tokyo, 1958.

Kellogg, E.R., 'Hōgen Monogatari', Transactions of the Asiatic Society of Japan, Vol. XLV, Part I, Tokyo, 1917.

Kidder, J.E. Jr., Japan Before Buddhism, London, 1966.

———, Ancient Japan, Oxford, 1977.

Kitagawa, Hiroshi and Bruce T. Tsuchida, transl., The Tale of the Heike, University of Tokyo Press, 1981.

Leggett, Trevor, The Tiger's Cave, Translations of Japanese Zen Texts,

London, 1977.

———, *Zen and the Ways*, London, 1978.

Lidin, Olof G., *The Life of Ogyū Sorai, A Tokugawa Confucian Philosopher*, Lund, 1973.

Lloyd, A., 'Historical Development of the Shushi Philosophy in Japan', Transactions of the Asiatic Society of Japan, Vol. XXXIV, Part IV, Yokohama, 1907.

Lowell, Percival, *Occult Japan, or the Way of the Gods. An Esoteric Study of Japanese Personality and Possession*, Boston, 1895.

Maruyama, M., *Studies in the Intellectual History of Tokugawa Japan.*, transl. by Mikiso Hane, Princeton University Press, University of Tokyo Press, 1974.

Mass, J.P., *Warrior Government in Early Medieval Japan, A Study of the Kamakura Bakufu, Shugo and Jitō*, Yale University Press, New Haven and London, 1974.

———, *The Kamakura Bakufu, A Study in Documents*, Stanford University Press, Stanford, 1976.

———, *The Development of Kamakura Rule, 1180-1250, A History with Documents*, Stanford University Press, Stanford, 1979.

———, ed., *Court and Bakufu in Japan, Essays in Kamakura History*, Yale University Press, New Haven and London, 1982.

Mc Cullough, Helen Craig, transl. and ed., 'A Tale of Mutsu', Harvard Journal of Asiatic Studies, Vol. 25, 1964-65.

Mishima,Yukio, *On Hagakure, The Samurai Ethic and Modern Japan*, transl. by Kathryn Sparling, Penguin Books, 1979.

Mitford, A.B., *Tales of Old Japan*, Vol. I-II, London, 1871.

Mitford's Japan. The Memoirs and Recollections, 1866-1906, of Algernon Bertram Mitford, the first Lord Redesdale, ed. by Hugh Cortazzi, The Athlone Press, London, 1985.

Miyamoto Musashi, *A Book of Five Rings*, transl. by Victor Harris, London, 1974.

Morris, I., *The World of the Shining Prince, Court Life in Ancient Japan*, London, 1964.

Murdoch, J., *A History of Japan*, Vol. I, Tokyo, 1910. Vol. II with I. Yamagata, London, 1925. Vol. III, rev. and ed. by J.H. Longford, London, 1926.

Pigeot, Jacqueline, 'Les suicides de femmes par noyade dans la littérature narrative du Japon ancien', Mélanges offerts à M. Charles Haguenauer, en l'honneur de son quatre-vingtième anniversaire, Collège de France, Bibliothèque de l'Institut des Hautes Etudes Japonaises, Paris, 1980.

Renondeau, Gaston, *Histoire des moines guerriers du Japon*, Mélanges publiés par l'Institut des Hautes Etudes Chinoises, Tôme premier, Paris, 1957.

Rotermund, H.O., *Die Yamabushi. Aspekte ihres Glaubens. Lebens und ihrer sozialen Funktion in japanischen Mittelalter*, Monographien zur Völkerkunde V, Hamburg, 1967.

Röhl, Wilhelm, 'Jinkaishū, Ein Beitrag zum mittelalterlichen japanischen Recht', Mitteilungen der Deutschen Gesellschaft für Natur- und Völkerkunde Ostasiens, Tokyo, 1960.

Sadler, A.L., *The Beginner's Book of Bushidō, Being a Translation of Daidōji Yūzan's Budō Shoshinshū*, Kokusai Bunka Shinkokai, Tokyo, 1941.

Sansom, G.B., 'The Tsuredzure Gusa of Yoshida no Kaneyoshi, Being the Meditations of a Recluse in the 14th Century', Transactions of the Asiatic Society of Japan, Vol. XXXIX, Yokohama, 1911.

——, 'Early Japanese Law and Administration', Part I, Transactions of the Asiatic Society of Japan, Second Series, Vol. IX, Tokyo, 1932; Part II, TASJ, Second Series, Vol. XI, Tokyo, 1934.

Shinoda, M., *The Founding of the Kamakura Shōgunate, 1180-1185*, New York, 1960.

Snellen, J.B., 'Shoku Nihongi, Chronicles of Japan, Continued, From 697-791 A.D., translated and annotated by J.B. Snellen', Transactions of the Asiatic Society of Japan, Second Series, Vol. XI, Tokyo, 1934.

Steenstrup, Carl, 'The Imagawa Letter. A Muromachi Warrior's Code of Conduct Which Became a Tokugawa Schoolbook', Monumenta Nipponica, Vol. XXVIII, No. 3, Tokyo, 1973.

Suzuki, D.T., Zen and Japanese Culture, Bollingen Series LXIV, Princeton University Press, 1971.

Thunberg, Carl Peter, Tal om Japanska Nationen, hållet för Kongl. Vetensk. Akademien, vid Praesidii Nedläggande den 3 Novemb. 1784 af Carl Peter Thunberg, Med. och Botan. Professor, Stockholm, År 1784.

Thunberg, Carl Peter, Resa uti Europa, Africa, Asia, förrättad åren 1770-1779, Vol. I-IV, Upsala, 1791.

Van Gulik, W.R., *Irezumi, The Pattern of Dermatography in Japan*, E.J. Brill, Leiden, 1982.

de Visser, M.W., 'The Tengu', Transactions of the Asiatic Society of Japan, Vol. XXXVI, Pt. II, Yokohama, 1908.

——, Ancient Buddhism in Japan, Sutras and Ceremonies in Use in the Seventh and Eighth Centuries A.D. and Their History in Later Times, Vol. I, Leiden, 1935.

Volker, T., The Animal in Far Eastern Art, and Especially in the Art of the Japanese Netsuke, With Reference to Chinese Origins, Traditions, Legends and Art, E.J. Brill, Leiden, 1975.

Willman, Olof Eriksson, Een kort Beskriffning På een Resa till Ostindien och förbeskreffne Japan Then een Swänsk Mann och Skeps Capiteen Oloff Erichsson Willman benembdh giordt hafwer. Tryckt på Wijsingsborgh aff Johan Kankel, åhr effter Christi Bördh MDCLXVII.

Wilson, W.R., 'The Way of Bow and Arrow. The Japanese Warrior in Konjaku Monogatari', Monumenta Nipponica, Vol. XXVIII, No. 2, Summer, 1973.

Index

Ainu, viii, 10-11, 15, 81
Akō, 74, 83, 96, 142, 160, 167-179, 200, 206
Amaterasu Ō-Mikami, 27-28, 63-66, 105
Amida Buddha, 19, 28-29, 49, 54-55, 80, 89, 94, 99, 123, 125, 130-131, 141, 143-144
Antoku, Emperor, vii, 40, 64-66, 80, 82, 138
Arai Hakuseki, 51, 59, 181-186, 193
Asano Naganori, 167-176, 180
Ashigaru, 44, 168
Ashikaga Bakufu, 17, 44-45, 48, 73, 91, 98-99, 119, 125, 131, 139-140; Tadayoshi, 119; Takauji, 42, 119, 121; Yoshimasa, 89, 197; Yoshimitsu, 138; Yoshiuji, 44
Asuka, viii, 5, 51
Asura, 40, 123
Azuma Kagami, 29, 81

Bakufu, viii, 15-16, 44-45, 50-51, 76, 122, 124, 137, 139, 141, 151-152, 155, 167-176, 193, 196, 200
Be, 6, 9, 52; Ekakibe, 6; Imbe (Imibe), 6; Kurabe, 6; Mononobe, 6; Nuribe, 6; Ō-Tokibe, 6; Urabe, 124
Benkei, 34, 36, 39, 158
Bernard of Clairvaux, 132-133
Bishamon (Tamon), one of the Shi-Tennō, q.v., 31, 56
Biwa-hōshi, ix, 39
Bonji, 55-56
Buddhism, x, 9, 13-14, 18-19, 21-23, 25, 28, 30-32, 37-38, 40, 47, 49, 53-55, 75, 83, 86, 92-93, 97, 99, 115-116, 123, 128-131, 133, 139, 141, 146-147, 154, 156, 185, 199, 204
Buke, 11, 20-21, 38, 42-43, 45-48, 51, 81, 97-98, 106, 108, 116, 119, 122, 124-125, 134, 140-141, 144, 146, 150-151, 166, 186, 188, 191, 193, 195-196
Buke Sho-Hatto, 17, 78, 96, 100, 149-154, 156, 168-170
Bun-Bu, 123, 151, 158
Bunraku, 176, 200
Bushidō, ix-xii, 22, 105-192, 202-206

Ch'an school of Buddhism, see Zen Buddhism
Cha-no-yu, 143, 197-199
Chikamatsu Monzaemon, 176
Chinkonsai, 64
Chōnin, 166, 200
Christianity, 19, 22, 50-51, 100, 126, 128, 130-133, 145-148, 152, 199
Chu Hsi school of Neo-Confucianism (Shushi-gaku), 156-157, 163-164, 171, 173, 182
Chūshingura, 167, 176
Confucianism, x-xii, 10, 19-20, 22, 46, 80, 91-92, 106,118, 121, 123, 126, 128, 135, 137, 139, 154, 156, 160, 164, 166, 170, 175-176, 182, 185, 188, 192, 205, 208; Confucius, 155, 157, 162-164, 177, 181

Daibutsu, 25, 28, 49, 143-144
Daidōji Yūzan Shigesuke, 179-181
Daigaku-no-kami, 157, 174, 182
Daijō-Daijin, 12, 58, 143
Daimyō, 21, 44, 46-48, 51, 59, 77-79, 91, 95, 99, 105, 139-142, 144, 147, 149-152, 158, 160, 164, 167-169, 171, 179, 202
Dan-no-Ura, 39-40, 64-65, 80, 111, 116
Dazai Shundai, 173, 176

Eboshi, 46, 97-98
Edo, 42, 57, 95, 149, 157, 160, 164, 167-169, 189, 201
E-fumi, 50, 148
Engishiki, 8
Esotericism, 23-24, 30-31, 54, 67, 70, 209
Exorcism, 32, 34

Five Relations of Confucianism, 20, 80, 91, 106, 118, 157, 162-163, 203
Folklore and folk religion, 26, 34-35, 37, 60, 80, 97
Fudō Myō-ō, 30-32, 34, 54-55, 90
Fujiwara, clan, 12, 24; Shigetamaro, 81; Sumitomo, 81
Fuke school of Zen Buddhism, 101-103, 125

Gempei War, vii-ix, 12, 14-15, 25-26, 36, 64, 73, 76, 81, 84, 86, 91, 108, 110, 116, 129, 135, 186
Genbuku, 9, 15, 45, 97-98, 126
Genji, see Minamoto
Gi, 126, 135, 160, 170, 173
Giri, 135, 166
Go-Daigō, Emperor, 42, 119-120
Gohei, 25, 79
Go-Kenin, 15, 93, 95
Go-seibai shikimoku, see Jōei Code
Go-Shirakawa, Emperor, 45, 82-83, 86, 124, 212
Go-Toba, Emperor, 53, 124
Go-Uda, Emperor, 27, 124
Gukanshō, 12, 65, 81, 111, 124
Gunki Monogatari, vii, 13, 43, 51, 79-81, 84-85, 87, 90, 105, 108-109, 111, 123, 125, 128, 135, 137, 206

Hachiman, 15, 23-29, 32-33, 49, 58, 66, 87, 90, 93, 120, 136, 145
Hagakure, 128, 177-179, 181, 187, 193
Haniwa, 1-4, 207
Hatamoto, 93, 101, 150
Hayashi Nobuatsu (Hōkō), 157, 174-176, 182; Razan (Dōshun), 156-158, 160
Heads, the taking of, 29, 59, 61, 73-74, 80-89, 110, 113-114, 144, 168, 182, 184
Heian period, viii, 8, 10-12, 16, 19-20, 22, 24, 28-29, 32, 37, 42-43, 45, 49, 51, 73, 81, 105, 107-108, 165, 196
Heiji no Ran, 12, 82
Heike, see Taira
Heike Monogatari, ix, 13, 26, 38, 43, 58, 64-65, 72, 75, 80, 82-89, 94, 108, 112-113, 115, 129-130, 160, 186

Hiei, Mount, 22, 35, 49, 87, 129
Hito-bashira, 77-78
Hi-watari, 32-34, 209
Hōgen Monogatari, ix, 13, 40, 43, 160, 195
Hōgen no Ran, 11-12, 72, 82
Hōjō, clan, 13, 16, 42-43, 84, 119, 125, 131, 133, 138, 170; Masako, 15, 26, 42-43, 108, 117; Tokimasa, 117; Tokiyori, 44; Yasutoki, 47, 117
Hokuchō (Northern Dynasty), 119, 139
Homosexuality, 98, 166
Honami, 55
Honchō Gunkikō, 51
Hōnen, 115
House Laws, 16, 68, 105, 138, 145, 156

Ichijō, Emperor, 54, 57
Ichi-no-Tani, 82-83
Ihara Saikaku, 166, 187, 200
Ikebana, 199
Iki-ryō, 37-38
Ikki, 46, 49-50, 98-100, 129, 139, 141, 144, 211
Ikkō school of Jōdō Shinshū Buddhism, 99-100, 129, 141
Imagawa-jō, 138-139, 156
Inari, 32, 53-54
In, Insei, 16, 27, 45-46
Ise Jingū, 57, 64
Iwashimizu Hachiman Daibosatsu-gū, 25, 27
Izumo Shrine, 54

Jien, 12, 65, 67, 111, 124
Jinkaishū, 140-141
Jinnō Shōtoki, 24
Jisei no ku, 72-73, 77, 145
Jisha-bugyō, 102
Jitō, 27, 67, 210
Jiun, 66, 210
Jizō Bodhisattva, 31, 55
Jōdō school of Buddhism, 19, 21, 28, 72; Jōdō Shinshū school of Buddhism, 19, 99, 141
Jōei Code (Go-seibai shikimoku), 16, 43, 117-120, 138, 156, 208
Jōgan Shiki, 8
Jōmon, 2, 64
Junshi, 72, 77-80, 95, 152, 167, 170, 181, 191
Jusha, 22, 66, 105, 154, 157-158,

163-164, 169-171, 176, 179, 206
Jūshichijō no kenpō, 119

Kabane, 5-6
Kabuki theatre, 103-104, 177, 200
Kamakura, 15-16, 25-26, 28, 44,
46, 95, 117, 119-120, 122
Kamakura *Bakufu,* vii, 11-12, 16-
17, 21, 26-27, 29, 42-43, 68, 81,
84, 91, 93, 105, 108, 111, 116,
119-120, 122-124, 129, 131, 149,
165, 194, 196
Kami, 18-19, 23-24, 27, 37, 66, 185,
204
Kamikaze, 27, 120
Kannon Bodhisattva, 21, 29, 32, 37,
54-55
Kansai (Western provinces), 49, 116-
118
Kanto (Eastern provinces), 10-11,
13, 25, 42, 108, 117
Karma, 38, 131, 135, 204
Katakiuchi, 96, 154, 166
Katanagari, 48-50, 144
Katana-watari, 32-34
Kebiishi Chō, 10, 44
Kegon school of Buddhism, 19, 47
Kemmu Episode, 42
Kemmu shikimoku, 17, 119-122,
138-139
Keppan, 94
Kiai, 70-71
Kin-gin-gumi, 103
Kira Yoshinaka, 167-176, 179
Kishōmon, 93-94
Kiso (Minamoto) Yoshinaka, 75, 85-
87, 110, 186, 212
Kitabatake Chikafusa, 24
Kofun, 1, 5, 51, 90
Kojiki, ix, 4, 20, 23-24, 27, 63, 67,
79-80, 106-107, 180
Kōken, Empress, 25 see also Em-
press Shōtoku
Koku, 25, 84, 95, 150
Kokutai no Hongi, 191-192
Komusō, 101-104, 125
Konjaku Monogatari, 81
Kōya, Mount, 94
Kublai Khan, 120
Kuge, vii, 9-13, 37-38, 42-46, 84-
85, 97-98, 107-108, 116, 122, 124-
125, 134, 136, 150, 202
Kuge Sho-Hatto, 45, 149
Kumazawa Banzan, 155, 164-165

Kunaishō, 7
Kun I, 8
Kyōgen play, xiii, 197
Kyoto, 5, 28, 35-37, 39, 42, 49, 54,
88-89, 116-117, 124, 139, 143,
149, 154, 195, 197-198
Kyushu, 10, 23, 95, 189

Lull, Raymond, 125-128

Mandokoro, 15
Manyōshū, 79
Masamune, 52, 58
Matsuo, Bashō, 200
Meiji, Emperor, xii, 79, 157, 187,
191, 206
Meiji Restoration, 17, 21, 41, 75,
103, 118, 138, 177, 187, 189-
192, 199, 201-202
Mencius, 157, 163-164
Miko, 32
Minamoto, clan, 11-12, 14-15, 25,
39, 46, 58, 60, 67, 72, 82-84, 86,
89, 108, 111-114, 117, 129, 187;
Mitsunaka, 53; Noriyori, 82-83;
Sanetomo, 16, 26, 42, 116-117;
Tametomo, 72, 112; Tameyoshi,
82; Tsunemoto (Rokuson-ō) 14,
109, 212; Yoriie, 16; Yorimasa,
58, 72-73, 80, 86, 110; Yoritomo,
vii, x, 13-15, 25-26, 29, 36-39,
42-46, 53, 75, 83-84, 87, 93, 95,
105, 110, 115-117, 122, 124, 137-
139, 149, 186; Yoritsune, 67;
Yoriyoshi, 25, 135-137;
Yoshichika, 82; Yoshiie (Hachiman
Taro) 15, 25, 136; Yoshimoto, 82;
Yoshitomo, 13, 36, 82; Yoshitsune,
13, 34, 36, 39-40, 54, 70, 80, 82-
83, 87, 111-112, 115, 128, 137-
138, 158, 186; Yukiie, 40, 138
Miroku Buddha, 28, 55
Mishima Yukio, 75, 193, 204
Mitford, Algernon Bertram, Lord
Redesdale, 75-76, 169, 190
Miyamoto Musashi, 36, 68-70, 155-
156
Mochihito, Prince, 86, 212
Momoyama (Azuchi), 116, 197, 199
Monju Bodhisattva, 29-30, 54-55,
132
Muramasa, 58
Murdoch, James, 139, 153
Muro Kyūsō, 173-174

Muromachi, 89, 140, 196
Mutsu Waki, 135-136
Myō-ō, 30, 55, 132; Dai-Itoku, 30-31;
    Fudō, 30-32, 34, 54-55, 90;
    Gosanze, 30-31; Gundari, 30;
    Kongō Yasha, 30

Naginata, 50, 123
Nakae Tōju, 158-159, 164, 179
Namban, 201
Nanchō (Southern Dynasty), 119, 139
Nara, 5, 25, 28, 49, 51, 130, 196
Nengo, 119
Neo-Confucianism, x, 51, 105, 155-
    157, 160-162, 182, 187, 190, 192,
    201, 206
Netsuke, 35
Nihongi, ix, 3-5, 20, 23-24, 27, 52,
    63, 67, 79-80, 106, 189
Nihon Shoki, 6, 11, 31, 80
Ninja, 71
Niō-ō, 31, 54, 132
Nitta Yoshisada, 26
Nō play, xiii, 196-197, 200, 209
Nogi Maresuke, 79, 191
Norito, 18
Nyōrai, Buddhas of healing, 55, 177

Oda Nobunaga, 20, 49, 75, 95, 100,
    131, 141-143
Ogasawara-ryū, 138
Ogyū Sorai, 171-173, 181
Ō-harai, 67
Oibara, 167-168
Ōishi Kuranosuke Yoshio, 167-176
Ōjin, Emperor (also Emperor Honda),
    23-24
Onin War, 48, 139, 141
Osaka, 100, 143, 145-146, 154-155
Otokodate, 47, 100-101, 103-104, 155
Ōyōmei-gaku, see Wang Yang-ming
    school of Neo-Confucianism

Poetry: Haikai, 196; Haiku, 200;
    Renga, 196; Tanka, 195
Pollution, 18, 22, 37, 40, 81, 125
Prajña, 30, 54
Purification, 18, 22, 33-34, 52-53, 60,
    67

Rangaku, 201
Ri, 157
Rodrigues, João, S.J., 57, 135
Rōnin, 47, 68, 74, 83, 96, 100-102,

104, 154-155, 164-165, 167-
176, 178-179, 184

Sabi, 79
Sadaijin, 58, 109
Sadamegaki Hyakkajō, 149
Saigō Takamori, 187, 189
Sake, 44, 83-84, 93, 106
Sakoku, 200
Samurai Dokoro, 15
Sankin-kōtai, 51, 94, 149
Sei Shōnagon, 9
Seiwa, Emperor, 14, 25, 109
Sekigahara, 48, 68, 94, 100, 102,
    146, 154-155
Sengakuji Temple, 168-169
Sengoku jidai, x, 20, 26, 42, 45,
    48, 68, 81, 84-85, 91-93, 98,
    129, 131, 139-142, 146-147,
    153, 155, 197, 199, 205
Sen no Rikyū, 143, 197-199
Seppuku (vulg. harakiri), 63, 72-
    79, 86, 95-96, 137, 141, 143,
    155, 167, 169, 171-173, 177,
    181, 190-191, 193, 199, 204
Seven Gods of Luck, 31, 56, 209
Shikken, 16, 42, 44, 47, 84, 117,
    119, 131, 133
Shimabara Rebellion, 50, 100, 147,
    152, 155
Shimenawa, 52, 79
Shin, 157
Shingon school of Buddhism, 19,
    21, 30, 32, 47, 55
Shinjū, 200
Shinran, 99, 141
Shinto, x, 9, 15, 18-23, 28, 32, 34,
    37, 40, 52-54, 60, 67, 79, 133,
    200, 205
Shi-Tennō, 31, 56, 132
Shōen, 99
Shōgun, x, 11, 14-17, 26-27, 37,
    45, 51, 79, 89, 93-94, 96, 116-
    117, 119, 122, 131, 142, 144,
    146, 150, 152-153, 165, 167,
    169, 171-172, 179, 182, 186,
    188, 197, 201
Shōheikō, 157
Shoku Nihongi, 8
Shokyu Insurrection, 117, 120
Shōmu, Emperor, 25, 28
Shoshi Hatto, 150-151
Shotoku, Empress, 23 see also Em-
    press Kōken

Shotoku Taishi, 19, 31, 120
Shugendō, 32, 34, 209
Shugo, 139
Shushi-gaku, see Chu Hsi school of Neo-Confucianism
Sōhei, 32, 128-131
Sonnō-Jōi, 187, 190
Sugawara Michizane (Tenjin), 37
Suinin, Emperor, 3, 52
Sumptuary laws, 121, 133, 149, 201
Susanoo no Mikoto, 4, 27-28, 63-65, 105
Sutoku, Emperor, 40-41, 94, 109, 195, 212
Swords, 29-30, 32-33, 36, 48, 51-70, 72, 77, 102, 141, 150, 155, 164, 167, 183, 185, 189, 192, 199, 203

Taihō Ritsuryō, 7, 8, 207
Taika Reform, 3-6, 18, 52, 80
Taikō Shikimoku, 145, 156
Taira, clan, 12-15, 26, 39-40, 46, 57, 64, 66, 80, 82-84, 86, 89, 110-116, 137, 179; Atsumori, 84, 114-115; Kiyomori, vii, 12-13, 36, 38, 40, 64, 66, 80, 83, 94, 128; Koremori, 13; Munemori, 80; Tadamori, 89, 115; Yoshimune, 80
Takakura, Emperor, 66, 82
Takeda Katsuyori, 143; Shingen, 87, 143
Tameshigiri, 56
Tanegashima, 50, 146-147
Tang Dynasty, China, 4, 8, 196
Tantrism, see Esotericism
Taoism, 32
Tattooing, 103-104, 211
Tendai school of Buddhism, 19, 21
Tengu, x, 35-37, 41, 70, 164, 209
Thunberg, Carl Peter, 101, 201, 204
Tōdaiji Temple, 25, 28, 49
Tōkaidō Road, 57, 201
Tokiwa, Gōzen, 36
Tokonoma, 199
Tokugawa Bakufu, x, 11, 22, 45, 47, 49-51, 55, 57, 68, 73, 77-79, 81, 91, 93, 96, 100-102, 105-106, 121, 123, 134, 138, 142, 144-145, 147, 149-150, 153-157, 160-161, 165-167, 170, 176-177, 179, 186-187, 190, 191-192, 198, 200-201, 206; Hirotada, 182; Iemitsu, 152, 179; Iemochi, 37; Ienobu, 51, 59, 153, 182; Ietsugu, 51, 183; Ietsuna,

78, 152; Ieyasu, 17, 20, 37, 42, 85, 87, 91, 94, 96, 138, 141, 143, 145-146, 149, 154, 156-157, 182, 199; Tsunayoshi, 157, 167, 169, 171; Yoshimune, 149, 179
Tokyo, 79
Tooth-blackening, 84-85, 89, 98, 202
Toyokuni Jinja, 145
Toyotomi Hideyori, 49, 143, 146; Hideyoshi, 20, 27-29, 41-42, 48-50, 61, 88, 116, 134, 142-146, 154, 197-199
Tsuji-giri, 47, 56-57
Tsurezure Gusa, 124, 139-140
Tsurugaoko Hachiman-gū, 26, 44
Tsurugi-watari, 32

Uji, 5-6, 9; ujibumi, 109, 111; ujigami, 5, 46; uji no kami, 5-6
Ukiyo-e, 103-104
Usa Hachiman Jingū, 23-27

Vajra, 30
Valignano, Alessandro, S.J., 147

Wang Yang-ming school of Neo-Confucianism (Ōyōmei-gaku), 156, 158, 164
Willman, Olof Eriksson, 57

Xavier, Francisco, S.J., 146

Yagyū Tajima no Kami Munenori, 69-70
Yahata (Yawata), 24
Yakuza, 101
Yamabushi, 32, 34-35, 102-104, 209
Yamaga Sokō, 105, 155, 160, 162-163, 173, 179, 187-188, 206
Yamato damashii, 76, 107, 189-190
Yamato Takeru, 4, 11, 23, 65, 106-107
Yamazaki Ansai, 163
Yashiki, 95, 169
Yasukuni Jinja, 41, 205
Yayoi, 2
Yōrō Ryō, 7
Yoshida Kaneyoshi (Kenkō), 124
Yoshida Shōin, 187-188
Yudate, 32

Zen school of Buddhism, 21, 68-70, 87, 101-102, 125, 131, 133, 138, 155-156, 178, 194-195, 197, 199